Controlling the Uncontrollable

Controlling the

NORTHERN ILLINOIS UNIVERSITY PRESS ▪ DEKALB ▪ 1989

Uncontrollable

The Fiction of Alice Munro

Ildikó de Papp Carrington

© 1989 by Northern Illinois University Press
Published by the Northern Illinois University Press,
DeKalb, Illinois   60115
Manufactured in the United States of America
Design by Julia Fauci

Library of Congress Cataloging-in-Publication Data

Carrington, Ildikó de Papp, 1929–
        Controlling the uncontrollable : the fiction of Alice Monro /
Ildikó de Papp Carrington.
            p.   cm.
        Bibliography : p.
        Includes index.
        ISBN 0-87580-149-8
        1. Munro, Alice—Criticism and interpretation.   I. Title.
PR9199.3.M8Z58   1989
813'.54—dc20   89-3427
                                        CIP

For George

Contents

Acknowledgments

I wish to thank Professors Robert Lecker and Lorraine M. York of McGill University and Professor Robert Thacker of St. Lawrence University for their help and suggestions.

I also wish to acknowledge with gratitude the assistance of Pam Bentley, Kim Challand, Jane Farmer, and Tobie Miller of the Interlibrary Loan Department of the Northern Illinois University, in obtaining Munro material.

Controlling the Uncontrollable

1

The Medium of Control

The Humiliations of Language

In 1986, shortly before the publication of *The Progress of Love*, her sixth book, Alice Munro defined the relationship between her perception of life and the purpose of her fiction: "I want to write the story that will zero in and give you intense, but not connected, moments of experience. I guess that's the way I see life" (Slopen, 76). Because of her fragmented perception, she classifies herself as a short story writer: "I see everything separate" ("Interview": Hancock, 77). Therefore, although *Lives of Girls and Women* and *Who Do You Think You Are?*, her second and fourth books, can be defined as "open-form" novels, as they both consist of interlocking short stories, Munro protests against the critical assumption that the short stories in her other collections have "to fit into any sort of pattern at all" or to link "up with any other story . . ." She asks, "what on earth is this feeling that somehow things have to connect or . . . have to be part of a larger whole?" (Struthers, "Alice Munro and the American South," 123; "Interview": Hancock, 98).

But in spite of Munro's objections, things do connect and there is a coherent whole. Clearly recognizable patterns unify almost all of her fiction, not only her two open-form novels and her recent novella, "A

Queer Streak," but also her collected and uncollected short stories from 1950 through the present. Four critics, B. Pfaus, Hallvard Dahlie, W. R. Martin, and E. D. Blodgett, have written long studies of Munro, but none of these critics has examined all her work. Pfaus's monograph, *Alice Munro*, was published in 1984, two years before *The Progress of Love*.[1] Dahlie's long essay, "Alice Munro and Her Works," appeared in 1985 in *Canadian Writers and Their Works*, but does not discuss *The Moons of Jupiter*, published "too recently . . . for detailed consideration" (217). Martin's book, *Alice Munro: Paradox and Parallel*, came out in 1987, but he explains in his introduction that *The Progress of Love* "was published after [his] study . . . had gone to press" (xiv). Therefore, although all the stories in *The Progress of Love* had been previously published, his discussion is limited to a very brief analysis of six of its eleven stories; one of the important works he omits is Munro's novella. Blodgett's *Alice Munro*, which appeared in 1988 while this study was in press, devotes a chapter to her most recent collection but does not discuss the uncollected stories published since *The Progress of Love*. Moreover, because Blodgett limits himself to Munro's collected work, he does not include any of her earlier uncollected stories either. Although no study can be completely up-to-date because Munro continues to publish new stories, the purpose of this study is to examine the full span of her published work from 1950 through January 1988 and briefly beyond.

An examination of the nature and development of Munro's work reveals a unity created by the fusion of her most significant major themes with her narrative techniques, her literary, operatic, historical, and biblical allusions, her recurrent metaphors, and her manipulation of point of view. Her recurrent metaphors of splitting—lightning and earthquakes, for example—and her characteristic split point of view are inseparable not only from each other but also from her conception of the artist and her perception of a fragmented and constantly shifting world of disturbing irony, ambiguity, and painfully persistent paradox. Because of the persistence of paradox, the densely detailed surface of her documentary realism connotes neither permanence nor control. Although George Woodcock argues that Munro's use of "documentary methods" makes her a realist who "has never mastered those transformations of form with which major writers handle the great climactic shifts of life," these seismic shifts occur repeatedly in her fiction ("The Plots of Life," 236, 250). The documentary solidity of her surfaces is deceptive, for these surfaces repeatedly split open to reveal uncontrollable forces, both within and without. Many critics—Hallvard Dahlie, Helen Hoy, Lorraine McMullen, W. R. Martin, Lawrence Mathews, Gerald Noonan, Michael Taylor, and Lorraine M. York—have discussed various aspects of Munro's use of paradox in both style and structure.

I am indebted to them all. But the most central and creative paradox of Munro's fiction is its repeated but consciously ambivalent attempt to control what is uncontrollable, to split in half to control a suddenly split world. These internal and external splits produce the "intense . . . moments of experience" that pattern Munro's stories (Slopen, 76). Recognizing and analyzing these patterns may help to suggest some of the many complex reasons that Munro writes as she does.

How does she write? To begin with, although Munro has an ironic sense of humor and can be very funny, her fiction is often intensely uncomfortable to read. The final emotional residue that many of her stories leave behind—paradoxically both because of her humor and in spite of it—is a lingering sense of unresolved ambiguity and dismayed unease. I began this study in a search for possible reasons for such a reaction.

In such a search, the first thing almost immediately apparent is the persistent recurrence of certain words and images in Munro's work. Some of the most frequently used words are *shame, humiliation, watch, back off, power, control, abdicate,* and *abdication.* Shame, humiliation, and the abdication of power are repeatedly combined with graphic images of exposure and helplessness. *Watch, back off, power,* and *control* frequently suggest a voyeur watching the shameful exposure and helplessness of others. The image of the watcher, often a voyeur, is an intrinsic part of Munro's manipulation of point of view. But the second thing that such a search reveals seems to contradict the first, for this contrast between humiliating helplessness and powerful control is pervaded by an ironic, self-reflexive paradox. When the writer watches herself, language, the medium of the writer's control, also becomes a source of shame and humiliation. The purpose of this introductory chapter, therefore, is twofold: to explore the key words in Munro's lexicon as they affect her handling of point of view and as they express her ambivalent attitude toward language as a whole, and to analyze the causal factors of this attitude as they shape her definition of the writer.

The key words *shame* and *humiliation* recur with disquieting frequency in all six of Munro's books. She has described herself as "thin-skinned" (Slopen, 76), and many of her characters, especially her self-consciously ambivalent first-person narrators and her older protagonists, are ashamed and humiliated over and over again. Del Jordan's shattering vision of flesh as humiliation is the most obvious example. Rose in *Who Do You Think You Are?*, the masochistic middle-aged women in *The Moons of Jupiter,* and several characters in *The Progress of Love* are not only humiliated but also ambivalent accomplices in their own humiliation. For example, both parts of "A Queer Streak" (1985, 1986) culminate in the same way: Violet, the heroine, is ashamed.[2]

Along with *shame* and *humiliation,* another word that frequently recurs in this same general pattern is *watch.* The image of the watcher shapes the adroit manipulation of point of view that gives Munro's fiction one of its most characteristic and significant qualities. In *Lives of Girls and Women* (1971) and in the majority of stories in both *Dance of the Happy Shades* (1968) and *Something I've Been Meaning To Tell You* (1974), Munro uses a watching first-person narrator. In *Who Do You Think You Are?* (1978), she switches to a third-person protagonist watched by an omniscient narrator. In *The Moons of Jupiter* (1982), in which half of the stories use the first person and half the third, Munro introduces a multiple point of view in both types of stories. In *The Progress of Love* (1986), she broadens and deepens her use of a multiple point of view. Only three stories have first-person narrators, and originally even one of these, the title story, was a third-person story. The seven other stories and Munro's first novella, "A Queer Streak," are all third-person stories, some of which combine two or even three protagonists' alternating or overlapping perspectives. "A Queer Streak," for example, is written from the double point of view of two protagonists, and "White Dump" (1986), from the overlapping points of view of three characters. In both works, the protagonists are watched by an omniscient narrator. In two of the stories in this collection in which there is only one protagonist, he is an observer who not only watches the action but sometimes explicitly narrates it within the story or comments on how he gathered and interpreted his material. Thus, in both the first-person and third-person stories, the narrator or the protagonist is often a watcher. For example, the narrator of "Miles City, Montana" (1985), a woman writer, defines her method of achieving an "essential composition" in her mind: "It was being a watcher that did it" (PL, 88). She remembers herself as a small child who saw her parents as shamefully sexual beings. Many other Munro watchers are also often the observers of shame and humiliation or of something potentially humiliating. In stories recounted by a first-person narrator or witness, this character not only watches the humiliation or the threatened humiliation of others but also often splits into two selves to watch her own humiliation. In Munro's third-person stories, in which she maintains the intensely immediate perceptions of a first-person narrator, she uses the greater flexibility of the third-person point of view to achieve the same split effect in a variety of ways.

The most important way in which this split effect is created in both points of view is through temporal distance, for a key similarity between the first-person and the third-person stories is that the watcher's point of view is almost always retrospective.[3] In discussing "retrospective techniques" of narration, Dorrit Cohn in *Transparent Minds* points out that "[i]n some respects a first-person narrator's relationship to his past self parallels a narrator's relationship to his protagonist in a third-person [point of view]. The kind and extent of the distance between subject and object, between the narrating and experiencing self, . . . determines [the nature of this relationship]" (143). For example, "the enlightened and knowing [first-person] narrator who elucidates his mental confusions of earlier days" resembles an omniscient author because "[t]he experiencing self in [such] first-person narration . . . is always viewed by a narrator who knows what happened to him next, and who is free to slide up and down the time axis that connects his two selves" (143, 145).

Such sliding "up and down the time axis" is characteristic of Munro's technique in both her first-person and third-person stories. This manipulation of narrative time, especially when it includes epilogues set long after the time frame of the main action, gives many of her short stories the breadth of perspective expected only in novellas and novels. This temporal sliding is also one of the techniques that create the split selves of her characters, women who are often highly ambivalent about language and love, two of the subjects that generate the significantly recurring conflicts and the major themes of her fiction. In her first-person narrators, this temporal sliding produces an internal split between the experiencing participant and the observing, retrospective narrator. This split sometimes generates more dramatic irony than is initially obvious. In her third-person stories, there are often two splits: the same kind of internal split in the protagonist as in the first-person narrator, with one part of the character watching the other part, and also a split between the experiencing protagonist and the omniscient author. The protagonist is watched by an omniscient and frequently ironic narrator whose associative and argumentative observations repeatedly disrupt the narrative chronology. This intrusive narrator not only generalizes in retrospect about the already completed events of the plot but also uses flashforwards to interrupt and interpret the events still being experienced by the protagonist.

In addition to temporal distance, Munro also creates this split effect through psychological distance. The narrating watchers are sometimes not the central characters but witnesses—either first-person witnesses, on the edge of the action as innocent eyes, or third-person observers on the periphery of events narrated from their point of view. When the first-person narrators *are* the central characters, the psychological split occurs in various other ways. The narrator not only watches herself but sometimes also classifies other characters as those who watch themselves or do not. The internal division created by her self-watching is sometimes externally objectified by her observing her mirrored reflection. In later stories, she acquires an imaginary alter ego, and later still, an actual one, a separate character and a second narrator who mirrors her. In one metafictional story this mirroring is not visual but verbal: one part of the writer-narrator keeps a journal while the watcher, the other part, functions like an editor, interrupting and criticizing the journal entries. Like the first-person narrators, the split third-person protagonists sometimes also have alter egos, characters who reflect their situation and whom they watch, as they are all watched by an omniscient narrator. The possibilities of this technique are increased by the multiple point of view in *The Progress of Love*. For example, in "A Queer Streak," in addition to the two protagonists watching each other under the eye of the omniscient narrator, Munro introduces two pairs of alter egos.

Another type of distancing or objectification translates the watching of the split point of view into a photographic or cinematic metaphor. As "The Photographer," the subtitle of the epilogue of *Lives of Girls and Women* illustrates, Munro frequently refers to photographs and photographers. The activity of The Photographer, full of "fluid energy" as he fixes "the big eye" of his camera on the townspeople of Jubilee (LGW, 246), is a metaphorical definition of the activity of the writer, characterized by the "professional photographer's preeminently willful, avid gaze" (Sontag, 77–78).[4] Thus, both first-person narrators and third-person protagonists split in two to watch themselves on film or in photographs. The narrator of the metafictional story concludes her interruptions by watching an imaginary film of herself as a child. Similarly, Colin, the protagonist of "Monsieur les Deux Chapeaux" (1985), imagines his life as a split photograph. Even some of the characters' dreams illustrate this cinematic technique, for they are described as "moviedream[s]" in which the dreamers watch themselves (MJ, 127). Comparable cinematic splits occur in the stories where the narrator zooms into her experiencing character's mind and then pulls sharply away. Thus, all these methods of splitting point of view and manipulating narrative time allow Munro's watching narrators to back off—temporally, psychologically, and spatially—from her participating characters. *Back off*, with its consciously cautious connotations of distance and self-protection, is another frequently repeated phrase.

But what is disquieting and ambiguous about all this avid watching is that in a startling number of stories Munro's watchers are voyeurs, watchers of various forbidden sights, usually, though not always, somehow sexual in nature. For example, although published thirty-one years apart, one of her earliest uncollected stories and one of her 1986 *New Yorker* stories contain a remarkably similar scene. In both stories a preadolescent girl peers through a window to watch an emotionally charged scene between two tense adults. In "At the Other Place," published in *The Canadian Forum* in September 1955, the narrator spies on a highly equivocal scene between her uncle and her ferocious aunt. Although she is upset, she doesn't really understand the subtly sexual nature of what she sees. In "White Dump," Denise watches her father and the wife of her mother's secret lover. When she peeks through a window in the door of the closed room where they are conferring, her brother calls her a "spy" (PL, 286). Although Denise and her brother hear the wife crying, they do not understand what is going on. These watching and listening siblings initially appeared in "Boys and Girls " (1964), a story in Munro's first collection, *Dance of the Happy Shades*. In this story the narrator and her brother secretly watch their father kill a horse. This is not a sexual scene, but they peek through knotholes to watch a specifically forbidden sight.

The forbidden becomes explicitly sexual in *Lives of Girls and Women*, Munro's second book. Although Del Jordan is horrified by her mother's cautionary tale about her retarded cousin, Mary Agnes, stripped by five boys and left lying naked in the mud, she later strips herself and stretches out on a bed to let Jerry Storey, her high-school classmate, look at her body. The hilarious anticlimax of this "Great Comic Scene" is that all he does is look (LGW, 206). Although an earlier scene, in which Del watches Mr. Chamberlain masturbate in front of her, is very different in tone, his self-induced climax is also defined as a "theatrical . . . performance," with Del as the audience (170). This key scene introduces a long list of sexual voyeurs in Munro's work.

Her third book, *Something I've Been Meaning To Tell You*, is defined by a character's comment in "Material" (1973). As some friends spy on a prostitute living in their apartment building, one of them says, "You're all such voyeurs" (34). This comment applies to the stories in this collection, for they include five scenes of actual voyeurism and a sixth imagined one. In the title story, Et sees her sister, Char, and Blaikie Noble just before or just after they have intercourse in the grass. In a very similar scene in "Marrakesh" (1974), Dorothy watches her granddaughter, Jeanette, having intercourse with a neighbor, Blair King. Et and Dorothy are both watching in the dark; both pairs of lovers, however, are illuminated, Jeanette and Blair almost as if on a stage. Another elderly voyeur is Mr. Lougheed in "Walking on Water" (1974), who, when he sees a pair of hippies copulating, recalls paying to watch a brother and sister copulate in the boys' privy of his rural school. In "The Ottawa Valley" (1974), two teenage girls secretly peer through knotholes to watch a young hired hand shed his overalls and urinate. They have staged this coarse little comedy for themselves by sewing his fly shut, then serving him lemonade laced with vinegar to quench his summer thirst. And in "The Spanish Lady" (1974), the narrator imagines not only seeing her husband and her friend naked in bed but also beating their bare bodies with a brush.

In Munro's fourth book, *Who Do You Think You Are?*, the voyeurism continues. The scene of incest recalled by Mr. Lougheed is graphically expanded in "Privilege" (1977), where a privy has "knotholes . . . for spying" (23). In addition to a public *"performance"* of incest, watched and coached by an audience of jostling schoolchildren, there are two other episodes of simultaneous watching and participation in sexual activity (25). In "Wild Swans" (1978), when Rose, unlike Del, participates in masturbation with a man who pretends to be a clergyman, Rose and the omniscient author both watch and comment on Rose's physical and psychological response. The epilogue of "Mischief" (1978) contains another such scene: while Jocelyn watches her husband, Clifford, make love to Rose, the participating Rose analyzes her own reaction to this theatricality. In addition, in "Spelling" (1978), when Rose, an actress, appears bare breasted in a television play, Flo, her stepmother, writes her an angry letter criticizing what she considers her exhibitionistic performance for an audience of voyeurs: "Shame on a bare breast" (186). Although Rose initially ridicules Flo's opinions, reading her letter aloud for its "comic . . . and dramatic effect," she suddenly breaks off because she feels that reducing Flo's objections to comedy is shameful, too. By reading her letter to laughing dinner guests, Rose feels that she is "exposing" Flo's ideas in a "shabby" way (186).

All these scenes share the common element of exposure. They repeatedly imply an equation between voyeurs watching the literal self-exposure of naked, masturbating, or copulating characters and an audience watching the dramatic self-exposure of actors performing a play on stage or on film. This equation connects the voyeurs in the early stories and in *Something I've Been Meaning To Tell You* with the voyeurs and the dramatic metaphors in Munro's two open-form novels.[5] These theatrical metaphors and metaphors of exposure also recur and fuse in a climactic scene in "A Queer Streak." All these scenes of physical and psychological exposure suggest that watching often involves seeing what should be concealed and that watching is therefore a shameful activity.

The shamefulness of watching is also emphasized in a pair of closely related stories in *The Moons of Jupiter* and *The Progress of Love*, in which the images of watching fuse photography with pornography. In both "Bardon Bus" (1982; MJ) and "Lichen" (1985; PL), the heroine struggles against the humiliation of being a metaphorical voyeur. In "Bardon Bus," she watches a permanently playing mental movie of herself just after intercourse. In "Lichen," she is forced to look at her ex-husband's photograph of his young mistress's exposed genitalia. But this aging man is the real voyeur, frantically scrabbling for the power to control his sexual humiliation by his mistress. His behavior illustrates Susan Sontag's definition of "[t]aking photographs" as setting "up a chronic voyeuristic relation to the world": she specifically compares "the act of photographing" with "sexual voyeurism" (11, 12).

Several kinds of sexual voyeurism also characterize five other stories, in *The Progress of Love* and elsewhere. In "Eskimo" (1985; PL), a woman watches another woman making love to a man and is both revolted and aroused. In "Oranges and Apples," an uncollected 1988 *New Yorker* story, a "maliciously observant" husband uses binoculars to watch another man using binoculars (47). In an "obscene, enthralling, unbearable" scene, the second voyeur watches the first voyeur's wife, excitedly posing in a bathing suit (46). In "Meneseteung," another uncollected 1988 *New Yorker* story, the obscenity is much more explicit. A virginal nineteenth-century spinster is awakened by the howls of a woman being beaten by a man. Later, when she hears the "confused . . . grunting" and "pounding" of their violent copulation beside her back fence, she mistakes it for murder (34). The next morning, when she sees the nearly naked woman, still asleep on the ground, the image expands and intensifies Del's description of the naked Mary Agnes. In the voyeur scene in "The Moon in the Orange Street Skating Rink" (1986; PL), copulation never actually occurs, but two clumsy adolescents watch each other's futile attempts with the scrawny little servant in their small-town boardinghouse. In "White Dump" (PL), the voyeurism is once again sexually arousing, but vicarious. When Sophie Vogelsang, an elderly professor, goes swimming in the nude, some young men find her discarded robe on the shore and, by ripping it apart, force her return to her lakeside cottage stark naked. Her son is unmanned by shame at his mother's exposure, but Isabel, her daughter-in-law, imagines taking her place at the lake: she would love to be seen naked by the young men who saw Sophie. Her vicarious excitement soon gives her the perilous power to break out of her protective marriage.

Power is another word that Munro uses with great frequency. Power can be hidden under the deceptive daily surface of life, but only to erupt in the violence that powerful characters inflict upon others and themselves. As suggested by the many examples of voyeurism, self-inflicted violence can be the internal violence of ambivalence, driven by the power of sexual curiosity, sexual desire, and sexual jealousy. But power can also be much stronger than any individual character exerting it, either internally or externally. It can be the annihilating power of death. When this annihilation occurs randomly and accidentally, as it frequently does, it is much more terrifying than natural death. But what is especially significant is that these two kinds of power, the power of sexuality and the power of death, are often paradoxically linked in Munro's fiction. For example, in *Lives of Girls and Women*, she uses the same kinds of splitting metaphors to describe the effects of both kinds of power, which are nearly fused in the climactic river scene of "Baptizing," when Del is almost drowned by her lover. Because she has ceded her power to him, the image of drowning becomes another splitting metaphor: when the drowning person splits the surface of the water and sinks, the water penetrates her body. Similar images and metaphors of drowning also recur in later stories.

The opposite of power is naked helplessness, either literal or symbolic, the inability to shape and control what is happening. Because such helplessness constitutes the deepest kind of humiliation, the frequent, often startling scenes of physical exposure are centrally significant. In the pivotal and paradigmatic scene in "Accident," when Ted Makkavala is about to penetrate Frances, his lover, he hears someone shouting outside that his son has been killed. Unmanned, Ted loses his erection. But characters often try to disguise their helplessness to pretend both to others and themselves that they are maintaining or regaining control. *Control,* therefore, is the most important key word in many stories.

But Munro often sharply limits the amount of controlling power she grants her characters, especially those humiliated by the power of sexuality, unforeseen chance, time, or death. She effects this limitation in various ways. In many stories her female characters, like Del, hand over their powers to men, an act she repeatedly refers to as *abdication.*[6] Many of her characters are also highly ambivalent about what they want. And even when they think they know what they want, Munro shows that what her characters do does not produce the intended effects but, ironically, the opposite. Such irony occurs both when their intentions are good and when they do not foresee any long-term bad effects. Just as the title "Accident" stresses the unforeseen in life, so several stories in *The Progress of Love* develop the results of what was originally intended to create only temporary illusion. In three stories, the characters' crazy jokes or hoaxes produce cruelly real and permanent consequences. In this collection Munro also satirizes various ideologies, such as Marxism and feminism, as rigid forms of control, achieved by oversimplification. But no type of control, Munro insists, can withstand the erosion of time. The human helplessness implied by the title of "Oh, What Avails," a 1987 *New Yorker* story, defines this theme of impermanence and mutability. Thus sometimes her characters' greatest efforts finally become meaningless or superfluous, reduced to the "rubble" of "a useless variety of passing states" (59).

But as the writer creating all these characters and situations, Munro obviously exerts controlling power herself, the power to envision her characters' predicaments and to manipulate language into art. Her attitude toward these artistic powers, however, is deeply and ironically paradoxical. To begin with, she defines the power of her artistic vision as the direct result of her lack of power as a woman. In an interview she has said: "A subject race has a kind of clarity of vision and I feel that women have always had a clarity of vision which men were denied. And, in a way, this is a gift, it goes along with lack of power. And I valued that very much—the value of being able to see clearly" ("Name," 72). But, she emphasizes, this "clear-sightedness stems from not having power" ("Name," 72). Similarly, although Munro has defined her writing as a medium for controlling confusion and humiliation, she is often skeptical about the authenticity or effectiveness of this control. She sees her writing as "a way of getting on top of experience; this is different from one's experience of things in the world, the experience with other people and with oneself, which can be . . . so confusing and humiliating . . . and by dealing with it this way, ... I think it's a way of getting control" ("Alice Munro," 245). But, paradoxically, at the same time she often refers to her writing as a "trick" or "trickery," and admits that psychologically this trick does not always work.[7] Because it is only "control by hindsight," "writing" cannot control the sense of "life rushing in on us. A writer pretends, by writing about it, to have control. Of course a writer actually has no more control than anybody else" ("Alice Munro," 245; "What Is," 15–16). Thus, Munro professes to exercise control over her fiction only to a limited degree.[8]

This self-imposed limitation manifests itself in various ways: in her fondness for ironic or self-reflexive epilogues and in her resistance against neatly conventional plot resolutions, whether old-fashioned or trendily up-to-date; in her fluctuating use of thematic summaries; and in her emphasis upon her inability to understand the insoluble mysteries of life. But when closely examined, all these manifestations turn out to be paradoxical, too. For example, she insists that she does not "see life very much in terms of progress" and therefore does not believe that "people develop and arrive somewhere" ("Interview": Hancock, 102, 89). She believes there is only one very simple resolution: "we finally end up dead" ("Interview": Hancock, 102). However, the title of her latest collection and its title story is *The Progress of Love*, a phrase that suggests not only some kind of resolution but even a positive one. And even though she creates many characters to whom she denies resolution, she of course controls them and what happens to them in her fiction. Confused and helpless characters do *not* mean confused stories or a confused author. The explicit explanations of her omniscient narrators are one illustration of this fact. Such narrators, criticizing and interpreting the characters, are present in stories in her last four books and in later, uncollected stories. For example, in "A Queer Streak," the omniscient narrator not only anticipates the reader's question about Violet's confused behavior—"Why did Violet do this?"—but also answers it. She explains to the reader that Violet does not know and "would never know why" she is behaving in such a self-damaging way, but the narrator knows: "She was sleepless and strung-up and her better judgment had deserted her" (PL, 228). Second, even though Munro has explicitly rejected "the summing up" in the final paragraphs of her early stories in *Dance of the Happy Shades*, some of her later stories in *The Moons of Jupiter* and *The Progress of Love* are just as tightly controlled and thematically defined as these early stories ("Real Material," 9). And although she denies that she has any fictional aesthetic, Munro nevertheless repeatedly articulates such an aesthetic: her conviction that the author cannot really know or control anything completely ("Interview": Hancock, 78). "I don't understand many things," she says (Untitled, 178). Therefore, her stories are about just that: "what we don't understand. What we think is happening and what we understand later on . . ." ("Interview": Hancock, 90). From this confused and delayed understanding, she derives one of the most characteristic patterns in her fiction: the ironic reversal of both the characters' and the readers' expectations. The creation of such a reversal, which Lawrence Mathews accurately labels "the art of disarrangement," is of course, not the result of confusion but the epitome of artistic control (193). Its clearly defined purpose is apparent in her statement: "I know the ending when I start a story" ("Interview": Hancock, 113).

On a fairly superficial level, therefore, some of Munro's professed non-control over ambiguous and ironic occurrences is a traditional literary artifice. But on a deeper level, the paradox persists. There is a close connection in her fiction between theme and technique, between the shame and humiliation that her helpless characters repeatedly experience and the self-reflexive comments about humiliation that she assigns to the authorial personae in her stories. John Moss believes that Munro's work "offers none of the usual puzzles, ambiguities, or clever allusions which the student of literature expects of contemporary writing . . ." (Introduction, 8).[9] But this link between Munro's obsession with controlling humiliation through art and her ambivalence about controlling her art is surely such a puzzle, one that is clearly central to understanding her fiction. Equally central, as I shall show later, are the many ambiguities and literary, operatic, historical, and biblical allusions through which she dramatizes the ambivalence of her characters about love.

Munro's ambivalence about her art, usually assigned to her narrators, appears in her first collection, *Dance of the Happy Shades*. The woman writer in "The Office" (1962) confesses apologetically, "I *try* to write," and adds, "However I put it, the words create . . . the delicate moment of exposure." This deepens into "humiliation" when she finally admits that what she tries to write is fiction (59). At the end of *Lives of Girls and Women*, Del, the narrator, is also trying to write fiction but finally rejects her unwritten novel as an "unreliable structure" (251). In *Something I've Been Meaning To Tell You*, the narrator of "Winter Wind" (1974) is dubious about the truth of her story: "how am I to know what I claim to know?" (201). At the end of "The Ottawa Valley," the narrator criticizes her improper narrative structure. She decides that if she "had been making a proper story . . . , [she] would have ended it" with an earlier scene (SIB, 246). There is no "proper story" at all in "Home" (1974). The metafictional structure of this uncollected story is the result of the narrator's constant self-criticism. Similar self-criticism occurs in *The Moons of Jupiter*. The narrator of "The Turkey Season" (1980) momentarily defines the meaning of her story: "Shame for all of us—that is what I thought then" (74). *Then* refers to the time of the remembered incidents, which occurred when the narrator was fourteen. But in the very next sentence she cautiously revises her interpretation: "Later still, I backed off from this explanation. I got to a stage of backing off from the things I couldn't really know" (74). This characteristic comment fuses one possible definition of the story's theme, "shame for all of us," with the story's reflexive technique, its use of an older, retrospective, self-conscious, first-person narrator who not only interprets what she is doing but once again, as in the five preceding examples, questions whether she can succeed in doing it. This retrospective narrator reappears in *The Progress of Love*. Although the intensity of Munro's ambivalence seems to have decreased with the decrease in the incidence of first-person narrators, in "Miles City, Montana" the writer-narrator is once again concerned with shame. After the narrowly averted death of her small child, she imagines what the child's death would have been like, but then she pulls back to criticize herself and asks: "There's something trashy about this kind of imagining, isn't there?" "Something shameful" seems inherent in exercising her writer's imagination (PL, 103).

These are only a few examples, but, combined with the scenes in which seeing and watching are shameful activities, they suggest a paradoxical possibility. For Munro's watching narrators and protagonists, manipulating and controlling language—the imaginative act of writing itself—somehow becomes a form of shame or humiliation. When the controlling author watches herself, she becomes suspicious of the medium of her control. But why should this be so? Answering this key question must precede any detailed analysis of individual stories, for it has many ramifications. Why does such an accomplished and successful writer, who is published in the *New Yorker*, *The Atlantic Monthly*, and *The Paris Review*, and who now commands an international audience, still seem to feel ambivalent about writing? And why do interviews about her work evoke the same ambivalence, "gratification on the surface," but "underneath . . .almost humiliation. . ." ("Visit," 12)?

Born Alice Laidlaw on 10 July 1931, Munro grew up during the Depression in rural southwestern Ontario. The traditional values of this "closed rural society," in which she places many of her major characters—for example, the heroines of her two open-form novels and of her novella—offer very important clues to understanding the ambivalence of her personae about writing and about closely related intellectual occupations ("Talks," 30). In interviews she has repeatedly emphasized the clear definition of sexual roles in this society. On a farm, "there is a sexual polarity . . . which feels good." The man is responsible for the heavy outside labor; the woman, for the complicated domestic management of the home and the farm. But, Munro adds, "you are a bit out of luck if you don't have the talents for the sexual role that you've been born into." She defines herself as a person lacking these talents. "I'm not good at hooking rugs and making quilts and things like that, so I would have had a very rough time in this life" ("Name," 69). In her memoir about her father, "Working for a Living," she also mentions that he thought of her as "mysteriously incompetent" (36). The importance of surviving in a harsh, still quasi-pioneer environment by being "very good at making things with your hands" is integrally connected to thinking "practically," to not seeing "more than is obviously there . . ." ("Alice Munro," 246). Such limited seeing not only excludes the writer's vision, which penetrates the obvious surface, but also seems to have survived the hard times of the Depression, at least for Munro's characters. She has told an interviewer that, although writing was "the only thing" that she "ever wanted to do," she felt "embarrassment" about "doing something" that she could neither "explain" nor "justify" to her hard-working parents at home ("What Is," 18, 17). This ambivalent attitude is reflected in "Miles City, Montana," where the newly married writer-narrator, helping her farmer-father with his "hard, repetitive, appalling work," admits to herself that she "feel[s] bad about leaving" the farm but does not "want to stay there" (PL, 94). Such ambivalence is also directly reflected in the narrator of "Home," an older writer visiting her farm home in the early 1970s. She has internalized her "upbringing" so completely that, although she insists that she values her work, her inner ear still hears *the hard voice of [her] upbringing telling [her] it is always better to dig potatoes, and feed sheep* than to write (152).

Such a negative attitude toward writing is reflected in several closely related ways in Munro's fiction. The first way is in her creation of a long series of adolescent female characters who are all physically clumsy. Because they lack the manual dexterity required by their sexual role and necessary for their survival in this rural society, they not only feel ashamed of themselves but are also repeatedly humiliated by their impatient and dexterous critics. Evelyn, the fifteen-year-old protagonist of Munro's second published story, "Story for Sunday" (1950), feels "clumsy and homely" (7). The eleven-year-old narrator of "Boys and Girls," being younger than Evelyn, has not internalized this attitude completely. Although she does not feel clumsy, she prefers helping her father on the farm to helping her mother in "the hot dark kitchen." But when she tries to escape from the "endless, dreary and peculiarly depressing" task of home canning, she overhears her frustrated mother complaining to her father, "It's not like I had a girl in the family at all" (DHS, 117). In "Age of Faith" (1971), Del cannot learn to thread a sewing machine in her Household Science class because her "stubby blundering hands" are "slimy with sweat" (LGW, 102). Mrs. Forbes, her teacher, rages at her for imagining that she is "clever" for "memorizing poems fast" (103). Although once again she shows Del what to do, Del is helpless: "her quick hands in front of me astonished and blinded and paralyzed me, with their close flashes of contempt" (103). Humiliated, Del prays not to have to thread the sewing machine again, not to be exposed once more to "public shame" (104). The fourteen-year-old trying to gut turkeys in "The Turkey Season" is another version of the same clumsy girl: "I was clumsy with my hands and had been shamed for it so often that the least show of impatience on the part of the person instructing me could have brought on a dithering paralysis" (MJ, 63). Ashamed of her "ineptness at manual work," she laments: "Work, to everybody I knew, meant doing things I was no good at doing, and work was what people prided themselves on and measured each other by" (MJ, 66). So her exasperated father also complains, "She's got ten thumbs" (MJ, 66).[10] His complaint is shared by Rose's father in an earlier story, "Half a Grapefruit" (1978). Conscious of his irritation and disgust, Rose is "ashamed, just to be in the same room with him" because she is aware of the reasons for his attitude. Her "disgrace [is] that she [is] female but mistakenly so, [will] not turn out to be the right kind of woman." The cause of this potential failure is that "her whole life [is] in her head. She [has] not inherited" her father's "skill with his hands . . . ; in fact she [is] unusually clumsy . . ." (WDY, 45–46). So is Almeda, the amateur poet in "Meneseteung," who writes poetry because her "fingers" are "too clumsy for crochet work" (28).

The length of this list of clumsy characters suggests a deep-seated sense of inferiority. A girl who had a life in her head and who memorized or wrote poems was out of place in this traditional rural society. Such intellectual and verbal talents were considered impractical in either sex, and therefore, as the narrator of "The Turkey Season" explains, "suspect or held in plain contempt" (MJ, 66). The second way in which Munro reflects the attitudes of her rural background is by repeatedly emphasizing this suspicion and contempt. She has told an interviewer, "I always realized that I had a different view of the world, . . . one that would bring me into great trouble and ridicule if it were exposed. I learned very early to disguise everything, and perhaps the escape into making

stories was necessary" ("Alice Munro," 246). In two of her earliest uncollected stories, characters with "a different view of the world" are cruelly
exposed and ridiculed. Both characters have highly developed intellectual and verbal talents and use them to escape into stories of their own
making. In both of these stories, there is also a student who seems to
be Munro in disguise, observing her protagonists from a distance.

In Munro's first published story, "The Dimensions of a Shadow,"
which appeared in *Folio* in April 1950, while she was still an undergraduate at the University of Western Ontario, the third-person protagonist is a thirty-three-year-old unmarried Latin teacher in a small,
rural town. Ironically named Miss Abelhart, she knows that her lonely
heart is able to love, but also that nobody has loved or will ever love
her. She is "so smart" that people laugh at her because they "know"
she isn't "like they are" (7). These cruel words are put in the mouth of
one of her students, but he never actually speaks them. She simply
imagines that he does. Her internal monologue is presented as a spoken
dialogue when, fantasizing that he is in love with her, she has a long,
hallucinatory conversation with the "beautiful" boy on a dark June
street fragrant with the "heavy sweetness of lilacs" (5, 4). He confesses
that he has "a crush" on her but has concealed it: "I hated myself about
it. I was scared to death all the kids would find out. I laughed at you
more than anybody, so they wouldn't . . ." (7). Talking out loud to the
shadow that she has schizophrenically split off from her lonely self,
Miss Abelhart is watched by three pretty young girls from her school.
Horrified to hear their teacher "talking" and to see her "staring and
staring, just like there was a person," they burst into nervously derisive
laughter (10). Their laughter serves the same function as the ironically
omniscient narrator does in Munro's later third-person stories: it makes
the reader back off from the protagonist as she is suddenly revealed
from the outside. The last sentence of the story, which leaves the teacher
"alone in a bottomless silence," figuratively drowned, shows the
frightening fate of such "smart" women (10). Deprived of both love and
language, they split apart and go under.

The protagonist of the second story, "A Basket of Strawberries," published in *Mayfair* in November 1953, is another crazy Latin teacher, but
this time the sexes of the teacher and student are reversed. Unhappily
married to a stupid woman and a failure in his career, the elderly Mr.
Torrance nevertheless struggles to imagine himself as still classically
handsome and heroic in his thankless role as "the last protestor of an
old faith, an ambassador in a distant, alien country, . . . the deaf and
barren little towns of Ontario," where he teaches his ever-dwindling
Latin classes (33). On a warm and fragrant June morning, when Ramona,
one of his remaining five students, brings him a basket of strawberries,

he completely misinterprets the gift and is so touched that he confides his misery to her. As he pours out his unhappiness to this gently sympathetic listener, his name becomes a painful pun on the word *torrents*. Later, however, he realizes that this compulsive self-exposure was a mistake, for he overhears Ramona repeating his confidences to her incredulous friends. "But he must be going bats!" one of them decides, and, although the "troubled" Ramona protests, they all begin "to splutter with delicious irrepressible giggles" (82). In the end, just like the student in the preceding story, Ramona is "laughing too" (82).

The obvious similarities between these two early stories are significant. In both of them the teachers not only teach a dead language but lead a barren existence, symbolically contrasted to the lushly beautiful June setting and to the attractive young people at home in this vernal world. Although Mr. Torrance is married to a student he seduced thirty years ago, the giggling girls refuse to believe the seduction story: "Imagine—Mr. Torrance—seducing anybody!" (82). To them he is as dead as the language that he teaches. Miss Abelhart escapes from her dead life into a schizoid fantasy in which, like a fiction writer, she invents dialogue for herself and the imaginary student. Similarly, excited by the strawberries, Mr. Torrance fantasizes about a classical dream-world, set in "a grove of tall pale-golden trees," where his pretty girl students "innocently" confuse him with Apollo (80). The heavy-handed irony of these two portraits arises from the contrast between the frustrated and fantasizing teachers and the chorus of contemptuously laughing students, a chorus in which the boy and Ramona half-unwillingly participate. But underneath this irony, there is an obvious ambivalence. The two sympathetic but self-protective students are the prototypes of later students, Del and Rose, who have similarly ambivalent attitudes toward language and are even more self-protective. And Munro's own self-protectiveness is suggested by the nature of the imaginary worlds into which Miss Abelhart and Mr. Torrance both escape. These worlds are created by her characters' verbal skills, which are Munro's own talents disguised in two different ways, by her choice of protagonists and by her point of view. By making fun of "A Basket of Strawberries" as one of her very early "stories about old people," she has indirectly admitted the first of these disguises. Ignoring or forgetting the two very similar student characters in "The Dimensions of a Shadow" and "A Basket of Strawberries," Munro admits, "I didn't dare write about young people or anyone at all close to myself for years. Not until I was in my late twenties" ("Interview": Hancock, 80).[11] Thus, by attributing her own talents to two "crazy" older characters, she disguises their nature. And by narrating both stories from the safe distance of a third-person point of view, she can criticize the secret operations of her protagonists' imagination.

Her double disguise is necessary because both students are troubled and confused.

So, although the "shadow" in the first story's title represents the student whom Miss Abelhart imagines, it is also possible to see the two characters' roles reversed. If the nineteen-year-old Munro is the disguised student in this story, she imagines Miss Abelhart as a frightening shadow of what her own life might become. Such an interpretation seems validated by the recurrence of the student's comments about Miss Abelhart's being "so smart." In "Miles City, Montana," the married writer-narrator remembers: "My father, when I was in high school, teased me that I was getting to think I was *so smart* I would never find a boyfriend. He would have forgotten that in a week. I never forgot it" (PL, 97; emphasis added). Although Mr. Torrance did find a wife, he fell in love not with the real girl, but with a shadow created by *his* imagination. He remembers how he fell in love with her name, Goldora, which to his disastrously excited fantasy suggested "Spaniards and the Fountain of Youth, baroque palaces and small white churches in the desert, garish and gilded saints" (32).

Although Munro has made fun of Goldora's name, Mr. Torrance's fantasy about its romantic connotations makes him the first in a long series of major Munro characters who, like their creator, weave similar fantasies about words ("Interview": Hancock, 80). Del's verbal skills in *Lives of Girls and Women* are made vivid in her frequent visualization of words. Long before she tries to write her novel in the "Epilogue," it is abundantly clear that she is a developing writer, for she loves to imagine what words look like and delights in their sounds. These are qualities that she shares with both the child and the adult Rose in *Who Do You Think You Are?* and "Characters." In "Spelling," for instance, when Rose is shocked by a blind and senile patient in the Hanratty nursing home, she optimistically imagines that the old woman enjoys visualizing the words she can still spell for her visitors and nurses. Rose imagines words taking fantastic shapes, like those of animals or "top hats" or "ribbons" (WDY, 184). These fantasies about language are also characteristic of the protagonists of two recent uncollected stories. In "The Ferguson Girls Must Never Marry" (1982), Bonnie, a television scriptwriter and the author of an unfinished adolescent novel very much like Del's, visualizes the word *souls* as "nearly naked travelers, pressed together, as in a medieval painting . . ." (64). Similarly, Joan Fordyce, the poetry-quoting protagonist of "Oh, What Avails," is very much like Mr. Torrance, for she, too, falls in love with a girl's name and imagines *Matilda* as "shining like silver" or "gleam[ing] . . . like a fold of satin" (45).

But the love of language shared by all these characters is an invitation to trouble. As already suggested by the two similar stories about the Latin teachers, verbal skills, like physical clumsiness, can expose their possessors to the danger of ridicule and humiliation and brand them as outsiders. This threat of danger creates an internal conflict of values in Munro's language-loving characters. Michael Taylor has defined Del's and Rose's ambivalent attitudes toward language as "indications of a larger distrust of language and art that makes itself felt throughout Munro's work and may perhaps be held fugitively by Munro herself" (140). But he has not located all the sources of this pervasive ambivalence about language. It is important to do so, however, for Munro's ambivalence about language is the third way in which she reflects not only the general attitudes of her rural background but also her own, intensely personal experience in this setting. To locate these sources, it is necessary to begin by understanding exactly how possession of a skill can evoke the same reaction as the lack of a skill.

There are complicated psychological and social reasons for this paradoxical fact. These reasons are illustrated by the two mothers eventually deprived of language in Munro's fiction, the two women finally condemned, like Miss Abelhart, to the dehumanizing horror of silence. The first of these characters is the painfully inarticulate mother, once a teacher, whose words are now distorted by disease. This character, who is based on Munro's own mother, a victim of Parkinson's disease, haunts a series of painfully autobiographical stories, such as "The Peace of Utrecht" (1960), "The Ottawa Valley," "Winter Wind," and "Home" (all three published in 1974). She also seems to hover in the background of other stories including sick mothers, such as "Memorial" (1974), "Forgiveness in Families" (1974), "Accident" (1977), "Connection" (1978), "A Queer Streak," and "Meneseteung." The second character is the senile and wordless Flo at the end of "Royal Beatings" (1977). But this similarity between these mothers obscures two very important differences. First, the mother in "The Peace of Utrecht" and "Winter Wind" is deprived of intelligible speech long before the end of her life. Second, she and the other educated mothers in Munro's fiction, such as Mrs. Jordan, who appears in stories in *Dance of the Happy Shades* as well as in *Lives of Girls and Women*, are in sharp contrast to Flo.

In "The Peace of Utrecht," the mother's loss of language and its devastating effect upon her two daughters are described in an anguished detail that reveals what seems to be the deepest personal source of Munro's central conviction that there is something shameful about watching someone and something humiliating about the controlled manipulation of language. In this story, these two activities, watching someone and manipulating language, significantly occur *together*. After her mother's death, Helen, the first-person narrator, recalls how she and her sister, Maddy, struggled to conceal their stricken mother from public exposure. Full of the intense self-consciousness of adolescence, they tried "to keep her at home, away from [her] sad notoriety [in the town], not for her sake, but for [their] own," because they "suffered such unnecessary humiliation at the sight of her eyes rolling back in her head . . . , at the sound of her thickened voice, whose embarrassing pronouncements it was [their] job to interpret to outsiders" (DHS, 194–95). Because the daughters acted as her interpreters, their mother's public appearances became painful spectacles in which they were forced to participate while others watched. Both visually and verbally, this spectacle is defined in degrading dramatic metaphors. "So bizarre was the disease . . . in its effects that it made us feel like crying out in apology (though we stayed stiff and white) as if we were accompanying a particularly tasteless sideshow" (195). The mother's "mournful" complaints, "not intelligible or quite human," but addressed to friends and strangers alike, also displayed a "theatricality" that "humiliated" Helen and Maddy "almost to death" (199). By reducing the participants to freaks in a vulgar circus act, these dramatic metaphors make the shamefulness of watching painfully obvious because it is initially experienced as the shamefulness of *being watched*, of being seen, rigid and pale, in the psychological nakedness of personal and social exposure. The necessity that forces the sisters to share the humiliation of being helplessly exposed on a "sideshow" stage makes Helen acutely aware of the audience watching their exposure. When interpreting her mother for this audience, Helen experiences language as an intrinsic part of this humiliation. Her publicly compelled and continued control over the skill her afflicted mother no longer possesses functions in an ironic way: it intensifies the full horror of her mother's involuntary abdication of both physical and verbal control. The story, of course, presents a fictionalized experience. A similar experience in reality would have been damaging to a sensitive adolescent in any society; in the stiffly decorous and rigidly self-controlled society in which Munro was raised, it must have been shatteringly traumatic.

The social contrast between this mother and the other educated mothers, on the one hand, and the uneducated Flo, on the other, suggests yet another very important reason for Munro's frequently ambivalent attitude toward language. This ambivalence was ingrained in childhood: "We always spoke grammatically at home because my father and mother knew how to. But we knew we should speak ungrammatically outside so that people wouldn't be offended, or make fun of us" ("Interview": Hancock, 95–96). This statement suggests that the Laidlaw children instinctively assumed a half-polite, half-self-protective disguise in public. Although Munro has described Mrs. Laidlaw as determined "to show" people "that she was a lady," the Laidlaw children seem to have been determined to do the opposite ("Working for a Living," 27). They seem to have become actors, carefully watching themselves as they performed a part in front of their umbrageous outside audience. This distinction between the two kinds of language, grammatical and ungrammatical, is incorporated into the social differences between the various educated and uneducated mothers in Munro's fiction.

Mrs. Jordan, one of the educated mothers, repeatedly violates the powerful taboo the Laidlaw children observed, the taboo against verbally offending others, and thus exposes her daughter to humiliation. In "Walker Brothers Cowboy" (1968), Mrs. Jordan pronounces the narrator's name in a ladylike "voice so high, proud and ringing, deliberately different from the voice of any other mother on the street," that her daughter feels she loathes her own name (DHS, 5). This reaction is important because the simplest answer to the belligerent question later hurled at both Del and Rose—"Who do you think you are?"—would of course be their own names (LGW, 194; WDY, 13, 196). Thus, for the little girl in "Walker Brothers Cowboy," language has already become a source of humiliation because she senses that there are two kinds of language, both powerful. Because her mother overdresses her when they go shopping, this humiliation is deepened. Her curls and clothes flaunting her mother's status as a lady, the child imagines that "[e]ven the dirty words chalked on the sidewalk are laughing at [them]" (DHS, 5). The sharp conflict between two kinds of language thus ridicules and threatens the child's costumed public identity.

Similarly, in "Princess Ida" (1971), Del sees that her mother's educated skills, publicly manifested in selling encyclopedias, writing letters to the local newspaper, and making speeches, expose her to the ridicule of both her family and her community. When Mrs. Jordan makes a speech at Del's school, Del, sitting miserably in the audience, feels herself "drowning in humiliation" because her "guileless" mother, although exposed on the school stage, is not a self-watcher (LGW, 81). Mrs. Jordan does not know when people are laughing at her, which, according to Del's old aunts, is "the worst thing that could happen in this life" (38). Del, who has thoroughly internalized her aunts' dread of ridicule, is nevertheless painfully conscious of being like her mother. "I myself was not so different from my mother, but concealed it, knowing what dangers there were" (81). Awareness of these dangers makes her dissociate herself from her mother's encyclopedia salespitch. Although Del loves to show off by reciting the facts she has read in the encyclopedia, she does not want to admit her enjoyment: "humiliation prickled my nerve-ends and the lining of my stomach" (67).

This same sense of potential danger and this same confusing internal ambivalence shape the characterization of Rose, but she grows up with a very different kind of mother. On the surface, it may perhaps seem repetitious that Munro has written two open-form novels about a girl growing up in rural Ontario during the Depression. But in spite of some basic similarities between the two characters, Rose's childhood and adolescence are not identical with Del's. After living on the West Coast for twenty years, Munro returned "to live in Huron County," convinced that she had exhausted the possibilities of this Ontario setting in her first novel. She "didn't intend to write anymore about it," but when she "noticed" the difference between the past and present "class system" and "realized how much [the class system had] influenced" her, she saw that she "really hadn't touched" upon its influence in *Lives of Girls and Women* ("Interview": Hancock, 94). Thus, it is very significant that Rose's stepmother belongs to a lower social class than Mrs. Jordan does. The opinions about language held by Flo, Rose's rambunctiously uneducated stepmother, are most clearly contrasted with Mrs. Jordan's opinions in three stories: "Royal Beatings"; "Characters," an uncollected story; and "Half a Grapefruit."

In "Royal Beatings," the "clumsy" Rose is irresistibly fascinated by words that Flo considers filthy but that Rose delights in because they are charged with "the spark and spit of craziness" (WDY, 1, 12). The result of this conflict about language is that Flo insists that Rose is humiliating her and makes Rose's father beat her for this humiliation. Even though he loves words himself and quotes Shakespeare when he thinks that no one is listening, he takes Flo's side against Rose. The formidable Flo thus represents the vindictive triumph of the world that is offended by verbal skills. Although she likes to tell stories herself, her purpose in telling them is often "to see people brought down to earth" (WDY, 23–24). In "Characters," Flo brings a teacher down to earth by humiliating him for the way he talks.

In this story, published in *Ploughshares* in 1978, Rose is a high-school senior in the class of Mr. Cleaver, a wartime substitute teacher who tries in vain to inculcate his class with his love of learning and language. Just like the crazy Miss Abelhart and the crazy Mr. Torrance, the "despised" and "hysterical" teacher is once again an object of ridicule because he is an "intellectual" (72, 76). Although the bored, daydreaming students either do not pay any attention to him or, like the chorus of students in the two earlier stories, giggle uncomprehendingly, Mr. Cleaver talks on, bubbling with "some crazy pleasure" (73). This is a pleasure that Rose secretly shares, but, just like the earlier students—the boy in "The Dimensions of a Shadow," the laughing Ramona in "A Basket of Strawberries," and the dissimulating Del—she carefully pretends not to share it. The insistent repetition of the idea that such pleasure is crazy shows why Rose must pretend. Just like Miss Abelhart and Mr. Torrance, the lonely Mr. Cleaver is also eager for some conversation, but when he tries to talk to Rose in Flo's store, the self-protective adolescent "back[s] off with grunts and monosyllables" (74). Although she, too, loves words like *Pleistocene* and *drumlin*, words that Mr. Cleaver teaches her, she dreads turning into "a character" like him, and this fear forces her to judge "freaks and failure harshly" (76, 73). Munro has used the first of these pejorative words to define her sense of being an outsider, threatened by the community: "In Wingham, Ontario, where I grew up, I very early got the idea that I was pretty freaky. As far as Wingham was concerned, anyway. And that if I didn't hide this I would expose myself to ridicule, . . . the main weapon of such communities" ("Great Dames," 32).

Rose's fear of being a freak is evoked by the possibility of Flo's ridicule, for Flo feels the same way about Mr. Cleaver that Del's schoolmates feel about Mrs. Jordan. Like Del and Rose, Mr. Cleaver is clumsy, "sometimes knocking over a display . . . or a pyramid of . . . boxes" in Flo's store (77). Flo's ridicule is more than private comment. She humiliates Mr. Cleaver by slipping a package of Sen-Sen in with his purchases. He may have a big vocabulary, but he also has a big case of halitosis. What comes out of his mouth, therefore, is doubly offensive. As Flo says, "People don't care for him. . . . He sounds like he thinks he's too good for them" (77). Sounding like that is the cardinal sin.

Rose's fear is also intensified by the contrast between her clumsiness and Flo's manual dexterity. "Characters" opens with a description of Flo's horrifying efficiency in silencing a chicken forever: she "slit the roof of the mouth and . . . . [went] for . . . the back of the throat" and "hit the brain" (72). Such murderous dexterity seems ominously symbolic. But, unlike Mrs. Jordan's speechmaking and letter-writing, it is a useful skill for a rural woman. As Rose notes in "Half a Grapefruit," her father considers the dexterous Flo the epitome of what a "woman ought to be, ...contemptuous of . . . long words and anything in books . . ." (WDY, 45). Flo's "hostility . . . toward all books" is expressed by her deliberate mispronunciation of the titles of Rose's high-school texts (WDY, 44).

And even Rose's high-school English teacher, Miss Hattie Milton, does not really value Rose's verbal gifts. One might expect a teacher to take Rose's side against her uneducated stepmother, but she does not, for, unlike the other three teachers, who are outsiders, Miss Milton in "Who Do You Think You Are?" (1978) is a typical member of the "Scots-Irish community" that Munro has described as "dedicated to slapping down your confidence at every possible point that it emerges" ("Name," 69). This destructive dedication defines Miss Milton's role in the title story. Although Rose quickly memorizes the poem that Miss Milton put on the board, her teacher punishes her for not copying it as she was told. "You can't go on thinking you are better than other people just because you can learn poems," Miss Milton scolds. "Who do you think you are?" (WDY, 196).

The answer to the "put-down" of this repeated question becomes increasingly difficult to formulate as Munro's adult characters move away from their place of origin ("Real Material," 29). Just thinking about the possibility of moving into a new identity is risky. In "Baptizing," Del and Jerry, two bright high-school students anticipating a future beyond the narrow confines of Jubilee, are unable to "get away from the Jubilee belief that there are great, supernatural dangers attached to boasting, or having high hopes of yourself" (LGW, 199). And actually making the change is fraught with guilt. Munro has emphasized that "if you come from a fairly low, a fairly underprivileged class of very limited expectations and then make a big leap into another class, . . . there's some guilt involved in this" ("Interview": Hancock, 95). Thus, the narrator of "The Stone in the Field" (1979), who lives in Vancouver, feels "guilty" whenever she receives a Christmas card from her toil-worn old aunts back on the Ontario farm: "any message from home . . . could let me know I was a traitor" (MJ, 31).

Most significantly, in the process of committing this class treason, Munro's characters discover that their difficulties with the two kinds of language increase and intensify. These difficulties suggest the most important social reason for Munro's ambivalence about language. Moving away from home involves "a betrayal," Munro has told an interviewer, because the "lower class" person deliberately begins to change,

> to talk differently. And I feel very guilty about that. And did for a long time.
> I know I haven't lost my Huron County accent entirely, but believe me, I have lost a great deal of it. I tried to lose it. To me, this seemed a cowardly thing to do. To change oneself. To become more acceptable in this way. ("Interview": Hancock, 95)

Like the clumsiness of the adolescent characters, this sense of betrayal and guilt about speaking "differently" is directly articulated by a long series of Munro characters. It is recognized by the adult narrator of "Home," who, returning on a bus to Huron County, *feel[s] an angry nerve jump* as soon as she *hear[s] . . . the voices* of the local people (142). Similarly, Violet in Part I of "A Queer Streak" returns home after her first semester at normal school in Ottawa and suddenly hears her family's speech with new ears: "She wanted to know if they had always talked this way. What way? With an accent. Weren't they doing it on purpose, to sound funny?" (PL, 214). In contrast to Violet's inability to recognize that she is the one who has changed, the narrator of "Home" is angrily self-conscious about the sound of her "educated" voice and the *"complicated and unresolved"* ambivalence of her *"own attitude"* (150, 142).

This unresolved ambivalence about losing an accent reappears in both "The Beggar Maid" and "Connection." Munro originally intended to include both stories in *Who Do You Think You Are?*, but "Connection" was later collected in *The Moons of Jupiter* instead ("Real Material," 29). However, the two stories were originally published a little more than a year apart, "The Beggar Maid" in the *New Yorker* on 27 June 1977, and "Connection" in *Chatelaine* in November 1978, and the two heroines are very much alike. In "The Beggar Maid," Rose, an undergraduate, is engaged to Patrick, a wealthy graduate student from Vancouver; in "Connection," Janet, the first-person narrator, is married to Richard, an affluent Vancouver lawyer. In both stories, the snobbish man makes the woman feel ashamed of her rural accent, but she is even more ashamed about being ashamed. Initially this confused shame takes the form of self-defensive denial. Soon after Rose and Patrick consummate their relationship, she asks herself what he loves about her, and wryly thinks, "Not her accent, which he was trying hard to alter, though she was often mutinous and unreasonable, declaring in the face of all evidence that she did not have a country accent, everybody talked the way she did." But Patrick is hopeful that "her accent could be eliminated . . ." (WDY, 82). By the time she takes him home to meet her family, she discovers to her surprise and shame that her accent has already changed. "She didn't even have any way that she could talk, and sound natural. With Patrick there, she couldn't slip back into an accent closer to" her family's speech because "[t]hat accent jarred on her ears now . . ." (WDY, 86–87). Janet's accent also jars on her husband's ears in "Connection": "Richard was stern about rural accents, having had so much trouble with [hers]. . . ." His attitude makes her feel "ashamed, as if there was something growing over [her]; mold, something nasty and dreary and inescapable" (MJ, 12). Her resentment that he wants her "amputated from" her "shabby" past is compounded by her uncomfortable aware- ness that part of her—the part that is "vulnerable to Richard"—has elected this self-mutilating surgery (13, 14). This awareness is the under- lying reason for the couple's quarrel after the embarrassing visit of Cousin Iris, one of the relatives from Janet's past. When Richard ridicules the cousin's "grammatical mistakes," pointing out some of the same things that Janet herself has silently noticed, Janet suddenly throws a piece of pie in his face and observes with significant satisfaction that "his speech stopped" (17, 18). These characters' ambivalence about language thus splits all of them in half, one half backing off to listen to and criticize the other half's speech.

The social trauma of these linguistic splits and amputations is suggested in two other stories. In "Mischief" (1978), another story about Rose and Patrick, there is the painfully equivocal friendship in Vancouver between Rose and Jocelyn, the snobbish daughter of two affluent New England physicians. Jocelyn's attitudes clearly resemble both Patrick's and Richard's. From her academic vantage point as a Wellesley alumna, she condescendingly informs Rose that she is "interesting to talk to" because she has "ideas" but is "uneducated." Rose's naive surprise lasts just long enough to let her make the mistake of mentioning "the college she had attended in Western Ontario. Then she saw by an embarrassed withdrawal or regret, a sudden lack of frankness in Jocelyn's face, . . . that that was exactly what Jocelyn had meant" (WDY, 104). This nasty snub makes it painfully clear that Jocelyn finds Rose "interesting" because in some ways she remains an "exotic" outsider in Jocelyn's self-assured world (103). Twenty years later, living again in rural Western Ontario and visiting Jocelyn and her husband, Clifford, who now live in Toronto, Rose still seems to be an outsider. She has become an actress, and perhaps because she got her first role as "a country girl" in "a radio play," she makes another mistake: she tries to amuse her Toronto hosts by the parlor trick of self-parody (131). Reassuming her discarded rural accent, she says, " 'In the Yewnited States they got these special roads what they call turnpikes, and only trucks is allowed to go on them' " (126–27). Clifford's sour comment, "You are getting very weird . . . . [l]iving up there," is a snub that subtly echoes Jocelyn's (127).

In addition to these stories about the transplanted Janet and Rose, there is the indirect suggestion in "Material," an earlier story (1973), that the experience of such trauma may be almost analogous to a transplanted immigrant's compulsion to try to obliterate his past in order to learn a second language, the new language of his new world. Such an analogy becomes especially clear because the traumatic experience includes repeated confrontations with conceited academic "posturing" about language, a kind of linguistic dishonesty that Munro specifically rejects ("Writing's," E1). The narrator of "Material," divorced from Hugo, a writer, and married to Gabe, a Romanian engineer, begins her narration by contrasting her two husbands' relationship to language. But this contrast is shaky from the beginning because she is highly critical of both men. First she bitterly satirizes Hugo's world of "[b]loated, opinionated" academic writers, men whose frequently discarded wives cosset them "for the sake of the words that will come from them" (SIB, 24, 25). In contrast, Gabe, just like Rose and Janet, has been compelled to change the kind of words that come from him. But the narrator questions Gabe's insistence that "[h]e has forgotten how to speak Romanian. How can you forget, how can you forget the language of your childhood?" (25). By indignantly repeating her question, the skeptical narrator stresses that she does not believe Gabe—or anybody—can. Her angry conclusion at the end of the story, that her two husbands "are not really so unalike," shows why her criticism of Hugo and her skepticism about Gabe's second language are both significant (43). The two men are alike because "[b]oth of them have managed something. Both of them have decided what to do about everything they run across in this world, what attitude to take, how to ignore or use things" (43–44). Hugo uses and discards his wives and both disguises and uses his past for writing fiction. Gabe discards the language of his childhood and thus disguises *his* past, too. The cause of the friction between the narrator and her two husbands is, therefore, not just the general difference between a woman's way of seeing the world and a man's, as Bronwen Wallace argues, but also a not quite subliminal tension between one particular woman's two very different ways of using language (61). Although the narrator, a teacher, seems to be writing a story addressed to Hugo (Osachoff, 77), she paradoxically defines herself as a nonwriter, "whose business" as Hugo's wife was to protect him, "to throw [herself] between him and the world . . ." (SIB, 35). For a nonwriter, however, she possesses not only a great many specific opinions on writing but also a keen awareness of the comfortable absence of the writer's split attitude in Gabe: "He does not watch himself" (27). She, like many Munro narrators, obviously does. Perhaps, therefore, these two male characters have to be combined to total what Munro may be distancing here, what she may be ambivalent about in herself. In interviews she modestly insists that she is not an "intellectual," and that, unlike self-consciously theorizing academic writers, she does not "know about using language" or "about traditions of fiction" ("Writing's" E1; "Interview": Hancock, 87). And in the conclusion of "Material," the narrator says that she does not "blame" her husbands, but then, in a characteristic volte-face, she suddenly announces: "I do blame them. I envy and despise" (44). What she both envies and despises—a highly ambivalent combination of emotions—is Hugo's self-assured literary theorizing and both men's ability to separate themselves completely from their earlier selves. In Gabe's case this separation manifests itself in his serenely untroubled use of the second, acceptable language of his new life in a very different world.

Thus, by developing a double set of conflicts between two kinds of language, these stories repeatedly reveal the humiliations of language, which may be some of the possible sources of Munro's self-deprecating ambivalence about exercising the medium of the writer's control. The first conflict is between the uneducated and educated languages of the characters' original community, as illustrated by the uneducated and educated mothers, the latter characters rendered especially painful by their frequent resemblance to Munro's tragically afflicted teacher-mother. The second conflict is between the language acceptable in this narrow community and the language expected in the much wider and very different outside world into which the adult characters move, full of "guilt and alienation for . . . having skipped out" ("Writing's" E1). As shown by the child's loathing of her own name on her mother's ladylike lips, an integrated sense of identity is closely bound up with confidence about language. And as shown by the painfully recurring tension between the adult woman and her lover or husband, the lack of such confidence exposes the woman's identity to internal and external warping. As a result of these double conflicts about language, the answer to the insistent question "Who do you think you are?" must also be a double one. Munro has told an interviewer, "I feel that I am two rather different people, two very different women and so, perhaps, that's where I'm working from. That I would like to get them separate" ("Interview": Hancock, 103).

This conflict about language is only one of the important ways in which Munro seems to be two women. As I shall show later, when she is discussing her characters' ambivalence about love, she also repeatedly defines herself as two women in her own attitude toward love. But in both cases, she separates these two women by writing. For Munro writes not only about her characters but, as already illustrated, about the writing process itself. This reflexive combination is quite natural because many of her characters are writers. Only one narrator in *Dance of the Happy Shades* is a writer, but Del grows up to be one in *Lives of Girls and Women*. In discussing her *Künstlerroman*, Munro hardly discerns a difference between the process of growing up and the process of becoming a writer; for her, the two processes are practically synonymous ("Real Material," 25). Similarly, four of the eight first-person narrators in *Something I've Been Meaning To Tell You* and five of the narrators or protagonists in *The Moons of Jupiter* are writers, as are the heroines of two stories in *The Progress of Love*, "Miles City, Montana" and "Lichen," and of three uncollected stories, "Home," "The Ferguson Girls Must Never Marry," and "Meneseteung." Although Munro insists, "I try not to write about writers because . . . everyone thinks it's autobiography," she has admitted that she "often write[s] about the same heroine," with "a different name and a different occupation," but with the same "psychological make-up" ("Interview": Hancock, 85; "Real Material," 30). This psychological similarity is illustrated by Rose's acting in *Who Do You Think You Are?* Her creation of dramatic characters on film is often a transparent trope for the creation of fictional characters on paper. Criticizing the "peculiar shame" of her acting, she echoes the literary dissatisfaction of Munro's first-person narrators: "The thing she was ashamed of, in acting, was that she might have been paying attention to the wrong things, reporting antics, when there was always something further, a tone, a depth, a light, that she couldn't get and wouldn't get" (205).[12] This similarity of psychological make-up occurs even in those female characters who are not writers, and even in some male characters who are not writers either, but function as oral narrators within the story or as artist-figures. Even if Munro's protagonists do not write or create art in any way, from the very beginning of her work they nevertheless adopt the psychological position of the writer, splitting into two selves, the observer and the participant. The observer can back off from the participant to watch what is happening, not only externally but also internally, within her or his participating self.

Munro's definition of the writer's psychological position occurs in her comment on "An Ounce of Cure," first published in the *Montrealer* in May 1961. This story significantly combines two of her major topics, love and writing. The retrospective first-person narrator, a teenage babysitter in the main time frame of the story, drinks whiskey for the first time in her life to forget her "more or less self-inflicted" suffering after a humiliating rejection by a boy (DHS, 77). Because she drinks the whiskey straight, she soon gets very drunk and very sick. Her friends, including three boys, come to the house where she is babysitting and try to sober her up; they also wash her vomit-stained clothes. When the parents unexpectedly return home, the narrator, still quite drunk, is almost naked; in a room full of boys, she is dressed only in her slip. "I was a self-conscious girl and I suffered a good deal from all this exposure," the narrator later comments. "But the development of events . . . fascinated me; I felt that I had had a glimpse of the shameless, marvellous, shattering absurdity with which the plots of life, though not of fiction, are improvised. I could not take my eyes off it" (87–88). This glimpse finally cures her of her love-sick humiliation by bringing her "back into the world again," a significant phrase that recurs with minor variations in two later stories about women artist-figures split in half by their ambivalence about love (87). Also significant here is the narrator's retrospective emphasis on three key points: her mostly self-created misery, her own physical and psychological exposure, and, most important, her eyes. Separating herself into two people, she backs off to look at herself critically, to watch her own suffering and exposure. The conscious adoption of this split attitude Munro has defined not only as the genesis of a writer but also as a mode of control:

> when the girl's circumstances become hopelessly messy, when nothing is going to go right for her, she gets out of it by looking at the way things happen—by changing from a participant into an observer. This is what I

used to do myself, it is what a writer does; I think it may be one of the things that make a writer in the first place. When I started to write . . . [at] about fifteen, I made the glorious leap from being a victim of my own ineptness and self-conscious miseries to being a godlike arranger of patterns and destinies, even if they were all in my head; I have never leapt back. ("Author's Commentary," 125)

But this "godlike arranger" who "gets out . . . by looking" is often only partially detached from the suffering and exposed self that she is adroitly arranging under her own eyes, and is often incompletely convinced that she has any right to be detached. Although watching can function as a form of control and is therefore of crucial significance to Munro's conception of the woman artist, especially the woman artist in love, nevertheless there is also something shameful in the deliberate exposure involved in the transformation of watching into writing. In discussing people who share Munro's background, a character in "Hard-Luck Stories" (1982) comments, "They dread exposure" (MJ, 191). In discussing her own Scotch-Irish background, Munro has emphasized that "personal revelation" is considered "shameful" and that this attitude still powerfully affects her when she writes ("Alice Munro," 247). Writing is impossible for her, she says, unless she carefully conceals from herself what she is doing, unless she forgets about "being published" and read. "Otherwise," she admits, "the sense of self-exposure or something would be too—I couldn't stand it" ("Alice Munro," 253). Similarly, the first-person narrator of "Material" defines a writer as a person "who work[s] daringly out in the public eye, without the protection of any special discipline . . ." (SIB, 27). This image of the exposed and unprotected writer, abruptly breaking off her own admission, brings us back to the secret and concealed nature of what the observer is watching. But the secret is suddenly revealed by a split in the deceptive surface of reality.

2

The Uncontrollable

The Underground Stream

The basic values of the Scotch-Irish Protestant culture in which Munro grew up provide a key to understanding why the events watched by the detached observers in her fiction are so often secret and concealed. One central value of this culture is dramatized by a brief passage in "A Better Place Than Home" (1979), an uncollected story that served as the basis for "1847," Munro's CBC screenplay about the Irish immigrants of the 1840s.[1] One of its two Catholic protagonists, James Thompson, is a young Irishman emigrating to Canada. During the first storm at sea, James and all the other passengers rush up on deck. Terrified of drowning, the Catholic passengers are crying, vomiting, and praying, frantically calling on "Saint Patrick, Saint Christopher, Saint Michael, and the Mother of God." But the "Protestant family," James observes, "did not weep or pray or vomit, but crouched together and held themselves tight in their Protestant way" (115). This cultural contrast vividly dramatizes the almost superhuman physical and emotional self-control of the "tight" Protestant family.

The descendants of these Canadian Protestant immigrants still define both physical and emotional tightness as desirable. They exhibit what could be termed *claustrophilia*. For example, Munro describes physical tightness as a necessary ingredient of her arrangements for writing. When she writes, she sits facing a "wall" that "slop[es] down in front" of her; thus, she is "very closed in. Very tight." She explains, "I like it that way" ("Interview": Hancock, 110). Elsewhere she suggests, "It's like being inside a warm wooden place" (Slopen, 77). This physically closed setting also suggests emotional tightness, repression valued as a primary virtue. To be unrepressed is to be outside the tightly closed-in community. Thus, it is significant that Harry Brooke, the babbling protagonist of "The Edge of Town" (1955), lives where he does, geographically, as well as emotionally, on the periphery of the community that views him with deep distrust and suspicion because he fails to subscribe to their ethos of silent repression. That Harry once owned a bookstore and is "a great reader of books" about Spiritualism is bad enough (369). But what the town cannot "trust" is his "naked and discomfiting talk" about those books. The adjective "naked" shows that even talk can be a form of shameful exposure. "Among the raw bony faces of the Scotch-Irish, with their unspeaking eyes, the face of Harry was a flickering light, an unsteady blade; his exaggerated flowering talk ran riot amongst barren statements and silences" (371). Such stubborn silences also characterized Munro's Scotch-Presbyterian grandfather, whom she describes in "Working for a Living" as a man who "lived a life of discipline, silence, privacy," a man who almost "never talked" to his son (15, 14). In "Winter Wind" the narrator describes her grandmother in very similar terms, as a woman who "had schooled herself" never to "lose control" (SIB, 206, 204). And in "The Stone in the Field" the narrator's painfully shy maiden aunts lead a life of hard, silent, and unremitting toil and consider any decision contrary to this ethos, even the purchase of labor-saving farm machinery, "a sign of an alarming . . . lack of propriety and self-control" (MJ, 29).

But Munro repeatedly reveals that such rigidly silent repression and self-control have their limits. From time to time, the taut surface is shattered by violent emotional outbursts.[2] "[T]hese people are very controlled . . . on the surface, very *very* careful. Life is very circumscribed and then occasionally something—well, Gothic—will happen." When it does, "there will be an incident that is a kind of outbreak. . . ." This incident "will be perhaps a murder, a fire[,] . . . something very black, very horrible" (Untitled, 171, 170, 171). In a later interview she has defined these Gothic incidents as "big bustings-out and grotesque crime. . . . There's always this sort of boiling life going on" ("Interview": Hancock, 93). One clue to the nature of this "boiling life" is the "junkyard" in "The Edge of Town," "where the wrecked cars lie overturned" (368). Similarly, in *Lives of Girls and Women* the local young men bust out by drinking "like fish" and driving "like fools" (195); gory accidents are the inevitable results. The narrator of "Home," as she returns to the family farm in southwestern Ontario where she grew up, also notes these appalling accidents: "drunks on Saturday nights manage regularly to disembowel and decapitate themselves . . ." (134). Musing on the reasons for their suicidal speeding, she refers to *"[a]n underground stream that surfaces in the murderous driving . . ."* (142). This image of a subterranean force suddenly splitting the earth and bursting forth in an uncontrolled and destructive fury is a metaphor for the violently "boiling life" that resists repression. The relative infrequency of these outbursts makes them all the more terrifyingly shameful when they do occur. Such an eruption first appears in one of Munro's early uncollected stories, "At the Other Place." A detailed analysis of this revealing story illuminates the techniques and themes developed in many later major stories.

Published in September 1955 under her maiden name, Alice Laidlaw, "At the Other Place" is narrated by a retrospective first-person narrator who is a preadolescent girl in the time frame of the story. During a Sunday picnic with her family "at the other place," the poor sheep farm where her father and his brother, Uncle Bert, grew up, the girl hears a conversation between her parents that reminds her of an earlier episode involving the uncle and his wife, Aunt Thelma. The flashback to the earlier episode is preceded by a description of the narrator's parents, which not only contrasts them to Bert and Thelma but also introduces their arrival. The uncle and aunt disrupt the pleasant picnic in a climactic scene of horrible quarreling.

At the beginning of the story, the girl describes the elaborate food her mother has prepared for the picnic and her mother's appearance in a rose dress and pink makeup. In contrast, her father looks stiff and uncomfortable in his Sunday best, but "in the fields . . . he was sure and powerful, a little more than life-size" (131). This difference between the narrator's parents emphasizes the clearly defined "sexual polarity" that Munro says "feels good" ("Name," 69): the conventional social role of the feminine, food-preparing, pink mother and the masculine self-confidence and power of the farmer-father in his working element, the fields. But in the marriage of Uncle Bert and Aunt Thelma, this conventional sexual difference is significantly reversed. He, too, is a farmer, but his "hungry, watchful, distempered" wife runs the show when he threshes, when he taps maple trees, and even when he is "dealing with his oldest neighbor," whom she forces him to cheat. Uncle Bert "did not go against her in anything." The narrator's description of red-faced, weather-beaten Aunt Thelma, wearing "a man's leather jacket" and always carrying a phallic stick, suggests that she has figuratively castrated her "miserable" husband. Not only powerfully male but also ferociously sadistic, she beats her children regularly, "with a leather belt or a halter strap" ("At the Other Place," 132).

In their picnic conversation the parents tell an anecdote about Uncle Bert watching Aunt Thelma thrash a dog with a horsewhip. Bert and Thelma apparently were not yet married, for this episode is identified as occurring the "first time" that Uncle Bert brought Thelma to the farm; the family dog, who "didn't like strangers round the barn," had nipped her on the ankle. As the narrator's father recalls his brother's behavior, he is very puzzled: "Bert just stood and watched her. That was a queer thing to see" (132). What is "queer," of course, is that Bert is not at all repelled by this violence in his future wife. His silence makes him Thelma's accomplice in her sadism. This revealing anecdote reminds the narrator of another significant episode in which she, too, watched her aunt in blindly brutal action.

The point of view from which this memory is narrated, the powerful emotional connotations of what the narrator sees and describes, the interpretive comments that the retrospective, older narrator makes about her experience, and the connection between this remembered experience and the reason behind the quarrel at the story's climax—all these significant elements in this story are either repeated or developed with variations in many later, major stories. In his discussion of Munro's earlier stories, Robert Thacker has pointed out that "'At the Other Place' is the first story in which the narrator's voice reveals two personae," a child's and a "more mature" person's (4).[3] In the remembered scene, however, the child's physical position gives the story's simple title an additional meaning that defines the narrator's point of view not as that of a protagonist but as that of a witness. She is in "the other place" of a first-person narrator, the position of a peripheral character quite literally on the edge of the action, looking in at and watching the frightening adult characters. "I was with Marjory, my oldest cousin, and we were looking in the window of the back kitchen, watching Aunt Thelma punish . . . Alma . . ." (132). What happens then is narrated in a way that allows the reader to comprehend far more than the young Peeping Tom, peering in through a split in a concealing surface, can understand. Her innocent eye sees, but she records without fully articulated comprehension. Aunt Thelma

> was excited, and sucked her breath in . . . ; she rocked on her feet to the rhythm of the blows, and her face was dark and glowing with the blood underneath. Uncle Bert came in; she was out of breath and let Alma run away. She and Uncle Bert stood looking at each other; her face looked blind, and seemed to throb with blood coming up in it; his was ashamed and desperate, but it reflected the look in hers—and in the moment of

this look they seemed to me so alien and frightful that I did not need to have Marjory drag me away from the window. (132)

Both the narrator's frightened reaction to the adults' exchanged and naked "look" and Marjory's dragging her away emphasize the subliminal sexual connotations of Thelma's orgasmic rocking and throbbing and Bert's instinctive but unwilling complicity in her sadistic excitement. Seeing Marjory's "sly pale face," the narrator "angrily" asks her cousin why she is laughing. Marjory's evasive reply, "I'm older than you are," prompts the retrospective narrator, older than both of them, to interject a very important insight: "[F]rom that time on I knew there was something here I could not understand, a secret, an ugly bondage" (132). But the precise meaning of the obviously sexual "bondage" in this scene is left undefined, and is deeply confused, both by Alma's role and by her mother's masculinity.

After this flashback Aunt Thelma, ravaged by terminal cancer, suddenly arrives at the picnic with Uncle Bert and their children. The narrator remarks that she and her siblings "did not know Death to see it but were afraid of her in a different way than ever before" (132). This somewhat heavy-handed personification of death in Thelma's terrifying figure, her face "the dirty yellowish color of an old bruise" and her skin hanging "slack from the bones," begins a series of such symbolic characters in Munro's early fiction (132). These symbolic figures are "Old Bram," the scissors-man in "The Time of Death" (1956); the mysterious hypnotist in "A Trip to the Coast" (1961); and Joe Phippen, the paranoid old hermit in "Images" (1968) (Ross, 118). More significant, this description also juxtaposes the image of shameful sexual excitement with the frightening image of death: the narrator's two memories of Aunt Thelma's blind, throbbing face and of her dying face, drained of its excitedly glowing blood, are recalled one after the other.

The climax of this story is a second terrible scene between the uncle and the aunt, once again witnessed by the narrator and once again not completely comprehended. It is introduced by Marjory telling the narrator that she has to nurse her mother. Humiliated by her helplessness in the face of impending death, Aunt Thelma is now weak enough for her husband to humiliate *her*, for usurping his masculine role throughout their marriage and holding him in lifelong bondage. Although she still has her symbolic stick, she holds it up "shakily"; she has become powerless. In a quarrel about how many of the sheep on the farm belong to his wife, Uncle Bert yells at her in a voice "full of rage and loathing," a "terrible, hating, vengeful voice," mocking her and laughing "straight into her face" (133). Horrified by this eruption, the narrator's parents drag their children away from the scene, just as Marjory dragged the watching narrator away from the window. The shameful revelations of this second drama are clearly the explosive consequence of the first one, typical of Bert and Thelma's marriage. The children are bursting with bewildered questions, but their parents refuse to answer. Hastily piling their family into the truck, they drive home "in the sunlight, the golden air of July," an ironic contrast to the dark scene of sadistic humiliation, revenge, and impending death that they have left behind them (133).

This slightly clumsy, but immensely powerful, early story can be seen as the prototype of many major Munro stories, for it contains many of the characteristic elements that recur in her later work. These include a watcher, a sense of something secret, a sudden revelation of the secret, and a struggle to control the threatening results of this revelation. The watcher is either a character—a retrospective first-person narrator or a third-person observer—or the omniscient author. The secret is something either shameful or frightening or both, temporarily concealed from the watching character. The most typical secret is often a combination of death and sex, the impending death of a family member or the character's apprehension of her or his own mortality or sexuality. A sudden split in the concealing surface reveals this secret through an unexpected event or experience that threatens the character's control. Struggling to maintain or regain control, the character may attempt to control the threatening external or internal forces, to dominate a relationship with another character, or often to do both.

For the purposes of this study, I have divided Munro's stories into four large and occasionally overlapping groups. They overlap mainly because, as already indicated, the inevitability of death hovers over much of Munro's fiction.[4] Haunted by her mother's death, Munro believes that it imbued her with "a great sense of fatality" and evoked a "tremendous guilt" ("What Is," 18; "Name," 70).[5] This sense of fatality, however, produces her compulsion to watch life: "[T]he thing I most want to do," she says, "is *look* at things, and see the way everything is. And I only have a few years to do that. The collection of molecules that is me isn't going to be here very long" ("Name," 71). But often what she makes her characters look at is ghosts. She peoples her fiction not only with the ghosts of dead mothers, as many critics have pointed out, but also with those of accidentally killed children and young people. Unlike Del in "Baptizing," who fights against drowning, six of her characters actually drown, and the literal or metaphorical image of a drowned corpse reappears in story after story, from *Lives of Girls and Women* to *The Progress of Love*, and "Meneseteung." Thus, even when these deaths do not constitute the major plot elements, they create a backdrop that intensifies the struggles of the living characters in the foreground. For thirty years—from "The Time of Death" (1956), through

"Heirs of the Living Body" (1971), "Memorial" (1974), and "Accident" (1977), and right on to her most recent stories, "The Ferguson Girls Must Never Marry" (1982), "Miles City, Montana" (1985), and "Circle of Prayer" (1986)—Munro's fiction has been full of funerals. For her, death is one of those "intense . . . moments of experience" in which she can "zero in" on life (Slopen, 76).

But death is by no means the only recurrent topic in her fiction. In discussing the fiction of other writers, Munro has made an important observation that characterizes her own work, too:

> I disagree with this picture of writing that you progress from one book to the next and that you do different things, you open up new areas of your consciousness and for your readers, and that it's supposed to be a kind of step-ladder. . . . It may be that you . . . have to go back over and over again and mine the same material and look at it in different ways, or in the same way, and sometimes you get to it and sometimes you don't. ("Real Material," 12)

As the list of characteristic elements in her stories suggests, Munro recognizes that she returns to "the same material": "I've been writing the same kind of stories all along" (Adachi, D3). She repeatedly returns to her sudden revelations of the submerged but rock-hard realities of life, certain sets of situations that threaten her characters' sense of control over their lives. Because her emphasis upon controlling these essentially uncontrollable realities is the central, paradoxical theme of her work, I have classified her stories into four groups according to the specific source of the external or internal power that threatens her narrators' or protagonists' sense of control. By comparing her techniques in these stories, I will show that, although the basic material of her stories remains much the same, she changes and develops her methods, especially those methods that connect her retrospective split point of view with her recurrent splitting metaphors.

In the first group is a series of stories about different characters—major male protagonists as well as female ones—presented from both the first-person and the third-person points of view. These characters observe, and sometimes participate in, external violence—not only beatings and murders but also accidents that end the lives of children. In this group of stories, the common element is the eruption of either deliberate or accidental violence that, like an underground stream that splits the earth, suddenly bursts through the seemly surface of everyday behavior. These frightening eruptions make the characters lose control of themselves or of the events in their lives, but then they struggle to regain it somehow. This pattern of eruptions, which can be traced through the thirty-nine years of Munro's fiction, climaxes in two of the stories in *The Progress of Love*, "Fits" and "Miles City, Montana." This is the group of stories I will discuss in this chapter.

In the second, and chronologically earlier group, to be discussed in chapter 3, is a series of stories told by the same first-person narrator, the unnamed little girl who appears in three stories in *Dance of the Happy Shades* and who reappears as Del Jordan, the retrospective narrator of *Lives of Girls and Women*. Like the watching narrator in "At the Other Place," who not only senses the power of both sexuality and natural death but also apprehends them in a particularly frightening synergistic combination, Del repeatedly sees these two centrally defining human experiences as closely related forces. Although both are, of course, internal forces, she sees them as terrifying powers loose in the world, powers that she must try to understand and, through understanding, somehow to control. Thus the fear of losing control and the importance of trying to maintain or regain it constitute a thematic similarity that these stories share with the first group. The two groups also have an important metaphorical similarity. "Images" (1968), one of the three stories narrated by Ben Jordan's daughter in *Dance of the Happy Shades*, and the interrelated stories of the novel narrated by Del Jordan are linked by a repeated metaphorical pattern, which reappears in the later stories of the first group. The function of this pattern, which equates the power of both sexuality and death with electric power or lightning, is analogous to the function of the pattern of eruptions that Munro repeatedly uses in the stories about violence. They both split open surfaces to reveal what is hidden inside or underneath. This analogous function is an important key to comprehending what Munro repeatedly demonstrates about sexuality, a dangerous power that threatens her characters' control.

But there are also major differences between these two groups of stories. In the first group, Munro uses different characters and also manipulates point of view in steadily more complicated and ironic ways than in the earlier Del stories. The second group, the Del stories, is also linked both thematically and metaphorically to the third and fourth groups of stories, both of which extend from Munro's first collection to her most recent collected and uncollected stories. To analyze and emphasize these important thematic and metaphorical links, I will discuss the Del stories out of chronological order. Because Del is a writer-figure ironically ambivalent both about sexuality and her relationship to her mother, Del is Munro's most significant character. This double ambivalence and the deep internal struggles it creates in Del as a woman and as a writer link her thematically with the narrators and protagonists in both earlier and later stories.

Because Munro is much more interested in the psychological

paradoxes of internal violence than in the final simplicity of external force, the third group of stories is by far the largest group. It consists mainly, though not completely, of stories about ambivalent characters struggling for power, primarily the power to control sexual encounters, love affairs, and marriages. But the situations that expose these characters' internal vulnerability sometimes also include aging or the ultimate humiliation of approaching death, especially as it affects sexuality. The vulnerability of these characters is revealed by their exposure either to sexual scenes or to scenes in which others are trying or failing to achieve control. The metaphorical link between some of these stories and *Lives of Girls and Women* is that the loss of control or the failure to achieve control is repeatedly equated with drowning, as in the climactic river scene of the novel. Thus, in this group of stories the question of control is often the humiliating question of *being* controlled by the power of sexual desire and the sexual partner. Most of the characters thus humiliated are deeply ambivalent female narrators or protagonists who abdicate their power. Like Del, they are ambivalent because a part of them wants to be controlled by the man but at the same time another part struggles for self-assertion against such control. At the conclusion of several of these stories, however, the question of which sex is in control is shown to be "beside the point" (SIB, 190). As at the end of "At the Other Place," death is in control. However, in Munro's most recent collection, *The Progress of Love*, the question sometimes has a new answer, for, although she continues to create deeply ambivalent female characters, there are also humiliated male characters and some controlling female ones. But the concept of control is shown to be ironically illusory in "White Dump" and in her satiric novella, "A Queer Streak." This third group of stories will be discussed in chapter 4.

The final group of stories is about parents and daughters, mainly mothers and daughters. These stories also examine the humiliations caused by the loss of control, but these losses repeatedly involve a daughter's failure to achieve emotional distance from her obsessive relationship with her mother. It is only in some of her most recent stories, the title stories in *The Moons of Jupiter* and *The Progress of Love*, that Munro grants these daughter-characters the emotional freedom that they seek. In these stories the daughters have become middle-aged mothers with adult daughters of their own. This last group of stories will be discussed in chapter 5.

In discussing these four major groups of stories, I will take the same freedom to slide up and down the time axis that Munro gives her retrospective narrators and protagonists. As already indicated, my basis of classification is, therefore, not primarily chronological but thematic and metaphorical. So I will not discuss the stories in Munro's six books in strict chronological order; neither will I discuss every story in every book. But within the four groups of stories that I have defined, I will generally discuss the works in chronological order, though sometimes I will also range back and forth within closely related thematic clusters in a given group to illuminate significant relationships between them. One such cluster, for example, consists of three stories in three different collections: "Lives of Girls and Women" (LGW), "Wild Swans" (WDY), and "Jesse and Meribeth" (PL) are all about adolescent sexual curiosity. Occasionally I will also discuss key stories more than once to illustrate different sets of relationships between them.

In adopting this type of organization, I will be following Munro's practice in yet another way, spatially as well as temporally. She has a uniquely nonlinear method of reading other writers' stories: "I can start reading them anywhere; from beginning to end, from end to beginning, from any point in between in either direction." The result of this non-linear reading is that she goes "into" a story "and move[s] back and forth . . . and stay[s] in it for a while," as if the story were "like a house," a "structure" that "encloses space and makes connections between one enclosed space and another . . ." ("What Is Real," 5). I will demonstrate the unity of Munro's fiction by making such connections myself, not only between the spaces or rooms in her carefully constructed story-houses but also between the structures of those she has built in similar architectural styles.

The shameful pattern of watching beatings and murderous humiliations that is introduced in "At the Other Place" recurs briefly in "The Ottawa Valley" (1974), and much more significantly in "Royal Beatings" (1977), "Executioners" (1974), and "Fits" (1986). Although both *Lives of Girls and Women* and *Who Do You Think You Are?* begin with a story in which a child is beaten—"The Flats Road" and "Royal Beatings," respectively—there is a significant difference: the beating episodes in "The Flats Road" are not watched by Del, the narrator. She only hears Uncle Benny's "stories" of how Madeleine, his teenage mail-order wife, beats Diane, her daughter (LGW, 22). Even though Diane has visible "bruises on her legs," at the end of the story Del's mother suggests, "Uncle Benny could have made up the beatings" (18, 26–27). This ambiguity about what happened disappears in "The Ottawa Valley," where, as in "At the Other Place," the first-person narrator actually watches her aunt beat her children. Aunt Lena's name is very similar to both Aunt Thelma's and Madeleine's, and Aunt Lena's physique and personality also resemble Thelma's. Lena has "arms . . . as long and strong as a man's," dominates her husband, and beats her children (SIB, 232). Like both Uncle

Bert and Uncle Benny, Uncle James, Lena's husband, "never held [the children] back from being beaten, never protested" (233). Sometimes Aunt Lena dwindles to "an unthreatening dark shape," holding a child on her lap, but when the visiting first-person narrator watches her beat her howling children, the scene repeats the earlier one in "At the Other Place" in two key ways: in the presence of the watching observer and in the humiliation evoked (238). The narrator comments that, although her cousins soon forgot Aunt Lena's beatings, "[w]ith me, such a humili-ation could last for weeks, or forever" (232). Although the word *humili-ation* has many meanings in this story, as I will show in chapter 5, the phrase "such a humiliation" restricts the meaning in this sentence to the humiliation of being beaten. It is this meaning that recurs in "Royal Beatings," the opening story in *Who Do You Think You Are?*, first pub-lished on 14 March 1977, in the *New Yorker.*

If the watching narrator in "The Ottawa Valley" is one of Munro's personae, the eternal duration of the humiliation with which the narrator identifies is confirmed by the second reappearance of the character that she watches, the beaten child. But in "Royal Beatings," which Munro has defined as "a *big* breakthrough story, a kind of story that [she] didn't intend to write at all," the narrative method she uses to describe the child's beatings changes in several significant ways ("Real Material," 21). First, in contrast to "At the Other Place" and "The Ottawa Valley," where she describes the beatings in the past tense, in "Royal Beatings" she uses the present tense, with present progressive verbs narrating the actual action: "her father is . . . cracking the belt at her . . ." (WDY, 17). The psychological effect created by this use of the "dramatic Present" is defined by Otto Jespersen in *Essentials of English Grammar:* "the speaker . . . forgets all about time and recalls what he is recounting as vividly as if it were now present before his eyes" (238, 239). The signifi-cance of Jespersen's reference to the speaker's eyes is emphasized by Munro's revealing comment on the beating scene: "I just wanted to look at it and think about it and it was a drama in my mind" ("Interview": Hancock, 101). Thus, the point of view has also changed, for the author herself is the watching narrator here. In contrast to the first-person narrators Munro uses in the two earlier stories, in "Royal Beatings" she uses a split third-person point of view. The speaker, therefore, is not Rose, the child being beaten, but the narrating author who is watching her as the drama of the relived memory of the beating is synchronized with its narration. The dreamlike nature of this memory is suggested by Munro's reference to "Royal Beatings" as "the story about the child being beaten" ("Interview": Hancock, 101); this phrase echoes the title of Freud's essay about beating fantasies, "A Child Is Being Beaten." That Munro consciously conceived of the memory of the beating as Rose's repeatedly relived fantasy is indicated not only by her description of the beating scene as a mental drama but also by her use of the present tense and the third person for its narration.

The third and most important difference between this story and the two earlier ones is that Rose, the child being beaten, is no longer a minor character but the protagonist. In significant correlation with this difference, the parents' roles have also been reversed. Although Flo, Rose's stepmother, instigates the beating because she wants Rose punished for verbally humiliating her, it is Rose's father who beats her while Flo watches. This double change, however, does not alter one basic similarity between the reactions of the two sets of parents in this story and in "At the Other Place." Both stories suggest that the adults' behavior reveals something shameful about them. At the beginning of "Royal Beatings," Rose thinks, "she could not stand to know anymore, about her father, or about Flo; she pushed any discovery aside with embarrassment and dread" (3). But because of the shift in point of view, the shameful revelations in this story include a significant addition to the adults' behavior: Rose's pleasurable complicity in her own beating.

In his essay "A Child Is Being Beaten," Freud discusses the genesis of such masochism in the "high degree of pleasure and . . . pleasurable, auto-erotic gratification" associated with girls' beating fantasies (173). In the first stage of these fantasies, as in "At the Other Place" and "The Ottawa Valley," a girl watches another child being beaten by an adult. In later stages, as in "Royal Beatings," she watches *herself* being beaten by her father. The change in the identity of the beating adult clarifies the secret significance of both Aunt Thelma's and Aunt Lena's powerful masculinity: they are fathers in disguise. The second stage of the beating fantasies, "the most important and the most momentous" (179), Freud defines as "a meeting-place between the sense of guilt and sexual love. *It is not only the punishment for the forbidden genital relation, but also the regressive substitute for it*, and from this latter source it derives the libidinal excitation which is from this time attached to it, and which finds its outlet in onanistic acts. Here for the first time we have the essence of masochism" (184). The similarities and differences between "At the Other Place" and "Royal Beatings" illustrate these two stages vividly.

In both stories the beating is administered in almost exactly the same way, with sexual overtones of almost orgasmic release. When Aunt Thelma beat Alma, her daughter, "[s]he was swinging the belt and it flew out of her hand, so she used the flat of her hands against the sides of Alma's head" (132). When Rose's father beats her, he too begins with his belt, then switches to his hands: "Her father is . . . cracking the belt at her when he can, then abandoning it and using his hands. Bang over the ear, then bang over the other ear" (WDY, 17). Just as the narrator in

"At the Other Place" observes Aunt Thelma's sadistic pleasure, so Rose observes the same feeling building up in her father as she watches his reaction to Flo's accusations against her. She sees the appalling revelations in his face: "It fills with hatred and pleasure. Rose sees that and knows it. Is that just a description of anger, should she see his eyes filling up with anger? No. Hatred is right. Pleasure is right. His face loosens and changes and grows younger . . ." as he "starts to loosen his belt" (16). The combination of these two loosening actions is highly suggestive.

The other two participants also experience a release charged with guilt because it is felt and defined in sexually suggestive terms. After instigating and watching the sickening family charade, Flo becomes very solicitous. The cold cream she brings Rose, the tempting snack that she prepares and takes to Rose in her bedroom, and the acrobatic tricks that she later performs to amuse the family all reveal her guilt about the pleasure that she has derived from Rose's beating.

But Rose's masochistic pleasure is the most significant because it is the new element in this story and because it is both psychological and physical. During the beating she splits in half to become observer and observed, listening to her own "willing sound of humiliation and defeat," and watching herself playing her father's "victim with a self-indulgence that arouses, and maybe hopes to arouse, his final, sickened contempt" (17). The key word here, *self-indulgence*, with its autoerotic connotations, also suggests the true nature of Rose's intensely sensual enjoyment of her sweet snack. At first she tries to resist the miserable temptation to eat the sandwiches, chocolate cookies, and chocolate milk, but soon she is "roused and troubled . . . by the smell of salmon, the anticipation of crisp chocolate. . . ." Finally, "in helpless corruption," with chocolate syrup smeared on her fingers, she eats everything, "though she sniffles with shame" (19). The highly ambiguous connotations of *roused, corruption,* and *shame* do not suggest a simple, childish appetite. And Rose succumbs to its pleasurable gratification much as her father, seduced by Flo, succumbs to the pleasure of beating his daughter.

After the beating and its aftermath are both over, the family members "feel a queer lassitude, a convalescent indolence, not far off satisfaction," that, as their mutual embarrassment evaporates, gradually mellows into "a feeling of permission, relaxation, even a current of happiness . . ." (19, 20). These distinctly postcoital interpretations by the ironic, omniscient narrator, who, along with Rose, has watched the royal beating, are further intensified by the story's narrative structure. The story begins with Flo's threat to Rose, "You are going to get one Royal Beating," but she does not carry out her threat of punishment immediately (1). Instead, Flo's conversation with a visitor to her store introduces the story of Becky Tyde, a dwarf deformed by polio, and Becky's late father, the prosperous English butcher who once owned a large brick house, a slaughterhouse, and an orchard. The much discussed parallels between this story and the story of Rose's beating, which it interrupts, are derived from two subtly intertwined sets of similarities.[6]

The first set of similarities connects Flo's steaming resentment of her stepdaughter's verbal skills and the community's envy and resentment of the well-to-do outsider. After Becky contracted polio and became deformed, Tyde kept her out of school: "He didn't want people gloating" (7). The second set of similarities emerges from the rumors that the ignorant community manufactures when its itch to gloat is frustrated. The community's malicious fantasies about Tyde and his daughter explicitly emphasize the elements only subliminally suggested by Rose's sensually self-indulgent complicity in her beating. These rumors include tales not only of beatings but also of incest, pregnancy, and infanticide to explain why Becky was deformed and why she never left the house. Telling these "lurid" tales about Becky and Tyde, Flo "regretfully" admits, "It was all lies in all probability" (7). The adverb suggests that Flo would dearly love the stories to be true, for Tyde, with his prosperity and his position, has the same effect on the community as Rose has on Flo. Before calling in Rose's father to beat her *for* her, Flo angrily asks, "Who do you think you are?" (13). Symbolically, the community asked Tyde exactly the same angry question when it, too, decided to call in somebody to beat him on its behalf, powerful surrogates to cut him and his pretensions of superiority down to size. "Three useless young men" were "got together, by more influential" members of the community to give Tyde "a horsewhipping in the interests of public morality" (7). Flo uses an analogous moral argument when she accuses Rose of teaching Brian, her brother, dirty words. Both arguments are transparently trumped-up rationalizations to justify persecution, for Rose silently protests that Flo has been "telling the grossest sort of lies, twisting everything to suit herself," just as the townspeople told lies about Tyde, distorting everything to suit themselves about him (15). When he later died as a result of the vicious beating that symbolically reduced him to the source of his resented wealth, bloody *"Butcher's meat,"* the three young men received prison sentences; but these sentences were merely more pretense, for the men were soon released and even given jobs (8).

In an essay entitled "What Is Real?" Munro has identified the story of Tyde's beating as "a big chunk of reality," a true "story out of an old newspaper," that shows "the dark side of human nature, the beast let loose, the evil we can run up against in communities and families" (36). But she characteristically rejects a didactic purpose in inserting this chunk of terrible reality into her story. "I don't do it to show anything," she protests. "I put this story at the heart of my story because I need it there and it belongs there. It is the black room at the centre of the house," the "structure which encloses the soul of my story," and all the other rooms lead "to and away from" this evil black room (36). This metaphor of the house with the central black room shows why Munro uses the Tyde story to interrupt the scene of Rose's beating: to emphasize both the psychological and the perversely theatrical parallels between them. Like the theatrical beating of Rose by her father, the trial and the abbreviated punishment of the three horsewhippers constitute a "farce" (WDY, 9). Both of these episodes are farcical performances in which every participant plays a preassigned role. So in the case of Rose's beating, these roles are not the "savage and splendid" ones that Rose imagines at the beginning of the story, when she childishly fantasizes about a royal beating, witnessed by "a crowd of formal spectators" (1). Freud comments on the "artistic superstructure of day-dreams, . . . of great significance for the life of the person concerned, [which] had grown up over the masochistic beating-phantasy. The function of this superstructure was to make possible a feeling of gratified excitation . . ." (185). But in Rose's case this gratified excitation is soon replaced by a shameful reality devoid of all "dignity" (WDY, 1).

Rose thinks of her father as "king of the royal beatings," but this fantasy image is ironically exploded when she overhears him quote from *The Tempest* (1). Gassed in World War I, he constantly coughs and mutters to himself in the shed where he works. Here she overhears him speak Prospero's lines, "The cloud-capped towers, the gorgeous palaces" (4). Although Rose does not recognize the passage, the allusion to Prospero deepens Munro's irony by emphasizing the difference between *The Tempest* and the sordid farce in which Rose's father performs. Prospero is the rightful Duke of Milan, so when he uses his magic powers to punish his wicked enemies, his revenge *is* a royal beating that the usurpers richly deserve. This subtle contrast between a powerful, aristocratic magician and a chronically ill man manipulated by his wife emphasizes Munro's ironic point that a similar release of tension in "real life" swiftly degenerates from a "gorgeous" fantasy into something shabby and shameful, into *farce noire*, a vengeful triumph of the underground id (1).

This emphasis on the shameful release from analogous tensions hidden under the surface of family and community life also characterizes the aftermath of the beating, the story's epilogue, and Munro's further comments on her story. After the beating, Flo and Rose's father discuss the old men who sit in front of Flo's store. To explain the presence of the planet Venus in the evening sky, the old men make up their own fantasies: they say it is an American airship. The ignorant old men have "never heard of the planet Venus," and, Rose knows, neither has Flo (20). Just as the old men do not recognize what they are looking at, neither do the members of Rose's family recognize what they are doing. Venus is the goddess of sexual love, and there is a shameful and secretly sexual component in the sadomasochistic family farce in which all three participate. Although my references to Freud's analysis of masochistic fantasies are not meant to suggest that Munro had Freud consciously in mind, this final allusion to Venus, combined with the genesis of the tense family situation in "a dream . . . go[ing] back and back into other dreams, . . . maddeningly dim . . . and familiar and elusive," reinforces a sexual interpretation of the dark underground of family relationships (WDY, 11).

In the epilogue, set in the present, Hat Nettleton, one of the horse-whippers egged on to get Tyde, and Flo, who egged on Rose's father and originally told her Tyde's story, are both residents in the county home for the aged. Like the formidable Aunt Thelma in "At the Other Place," the two ferocious characters have both been diminished by old age. When Rose hears Nettleton interviewed on the radio, she thinks that if she could tell Flo about the interview, Flo would have "her worst suspicions gorgeously confirmed" (22). But the completely senile Flo no longer talks or listens to anyone, although she occasionally bites her nurse, and Nettleton, although cackling with belligerent obscenity, does not say anything at all about the long-ago Tyde affair. Thus, because both characters are confined and reduced, the parallels between them continue.

Munro's further comments on the story make it clear that her psychological purpose in writing it is to control *her* worst suspicions about the shameful, hidden secrets of human nature by turning their confirmation into art: "Who told me to write [Tyde's] story? Who feels any need of it before it's written? I do. I do, so that I might grab off this piece of horrid reality and install it where I see fit, even if Hat Nettleton and his friends are still around to make me sorry" ("What Is Real?," 36).

Munro's comment implies that the desire for revenge is always burning in "the beast let loose," and this beast breaks out even more violently in a story published three years earlier, "Executioners" ("What Is Real?," 36). Here again, the watching narrator's primary emotion begins as humiliation; here again, as Sandra Djwa has pointed out, the narrative structure of the story develops a thematic parallel between two situations (186); here again, the metaphors emphasize the sudden bursting out of what was rigidly repressed; and here again, the final irony is generated by allusions to literary concepts of dignity.

Helena, the retrospective first-person narrator of "Executioners," is humiliated by her classmates' taunts about her clothes; like the narrator of "Walker Brothers Cowboy," she is overdressed by her ladylike mother. Helena puts herself into an even more humiliating situation, however, by condescending to a bootlegger's son, Howard Troy, a retarded classmate so unteachable that both teachers and students simply ignore him. By giving him a piece of paper and a pencil, Helena brings herself to his attention.

She soon regrets her deed. Howard begins to waylay her and to torment her with sexual taunts: *"You want to fuck"* (SIB, 142). This obscenity is the spoken equivalent of the dirty words on the sidewalk in "Walker Brothers Cowboy." In the story's epilogue, Helena, now an elderly widow, tries to explain how deeply the word *fuck* humiliated her in the past:

> It used to be a word that could be thrown against you, that could bring you to an absolute stop. Humiliation was promised, but was perhaps already there, was contained in the hearing, the being stopped, having to acknowledge. Shame could choke you. . . . quantities of greasy shame, . . . indigestible bad secrets. The vulnerability which is in itself a shame. We are shamefully made. (142–43)

Convinced that only she is vulnerable to such torment, Helena never tells anyone what is happening. But of course her silence and rigid repression do not work: "it had to be concealed and blotted out, stamped out, quick, quick, but I could never get it all, the knowledge, the memory, it was running underground and spurting out at another place in my mind" (143). Like the *"underground stream that surfaces in the murderous driving"* of the drunken rural drivers in "Home" (a story published in 1974, the same year as "Executioners"), this subterranean urge surfaces in murderous thoughts (142): Helena imagines horribly sadistic punishments for Howard.

Her sadistic fantasies are closely connected to her description of her relationship with the family of Robina, her mother's sinister maid. There is a deeply rankling enmity between Stump Troy, Howard's legless father, crippled in a mill accident, and Jimmy and Duval, Robina's brothers. Stump and the brothers are "rivals, or fallen-out accomplices, in the bootlegging business" (148). After Robina tells Helena how much her brothers hate Stump Troy, Helena thinks of how much she hates Howard. Helena's relationship with Jimmy and Duval suggests the hidden reason for her violent reaction to Howard's sexual taunts: he knows what she wants. When Jimmy and Duval tickle her "to make [her] break into screams of jittery pleasure," call her their "girl friend," and "play-[fight] over [her]," each of them grabbing [her] from the other and trapping

[her] in a hard hug," her reaction to these mock battles for her possession is obviously sexual (147). That reaction is the unacknowledged reason for her fantasy about stabbing Howard: then "all kinds of pus, venomous substances, would spurt and flow, everything would leak away" (149). Her fantasy of revenge combines an image of Howard's suffering with an act of denial through projection, in which his tortured body becomes her tortured mind. What she is really describing is the foul purging of her own ambivalent hatred, her guilty lust not only for vengeance but for denial.

In the very next sentence after this fantasy, in a sudden associative leap forward in time, the two parts of the plot are fused (Djwa, 185–86). Helena narrates: "The fire filled the house the way blood fills a boil. It seemed every minute ready to burst, but the skin still held" (SIB, 149). Robina, who knows that her brothers have committed arson to transform *their* fantasies of revenge into reality, watches the Troys' burning house "in a great state of excitement. She trembled and crackled, she was like a burning beam herself" (150). This scarlet simile links Robina not only with the burning house but also with the blood-filled boil of hate that is Helena's mind. Like Helena fantasizing about Howard's horrible punishment, Robina, who has only one arm herself, licks her chops with sadistic relish over the legless Stump trapped in the blazing house: "He's not going to walk out of there, is he?" (151). This gloating question echoes Helena's earlier description of how she walked past Howard when he called "fuck" after her: "I walked past him with . . . my breath drawn, just like somebody walking through a wall of flame" (142). As the burning house collapses, this simile leaps into reality. Howard, whose initial attempt to rescue his father has been prevented, has been watching the fire helplessly, but suddenly he rushes into the collapsing house and dies with his father.

As the epilogue transfers the reader to the present, Helena's sense of complicity in the bootleggers' revenge is still festering in her mind. Although she tries to drown her memory in whiskey, to her Calvinistic conscience the fire still seems an eruption of her own secret desire: she wished and she watched. Like the constantly replayed beating in "Royal Beatings," the fire will continue burning in her mind as long as she or anybody else "who could have remembered it" is alive (155). Confession, therefore, is not catharsis.

The Homeric allusions in the names of Helena and Troy and in the burning of the house also function in much the same ironic way as the allusions to *The Tempest* and the theatrical metaphors do in "Royal Beatings." Helena is not a beautiful queen fought over by the Greeks and Trojans but an overdressed and sexually confused schoolgirl "play-fought" over by two bootleggers (147). The burning of the Troys' house is not the fabled destruction of the topless towers of Ilium, but an act of arson committed against a legless man and his retarded son. Howard's rush into the burning house is "far too late to save anybody," although those onlookers who interpret his action as a second desperate attempt to rescue his father see him as "heroic" (152). This adjective ironically links Howard with the semidivine hero Aeneas, who carried his crippled old father, Anchises, out of the burning ruins of Troy. Anchises was crippled by a lightning bolt for boasting of the love of Venus, Aeneas's mother. It is almost as if Munro were rewriting "A Basket of Strawberries," once again to reject Mr. Torrance's far-fetched fantasies about a classical dreamworld. Howard does not found a new empire, no one composes a classical epic about him, and no one has any definitive "explanations" of what he has done (152). But the pathetic difference between Vergil's hero and the retarded, but crazily courageous, Howard subtly shifts the reader's final sympathies from Helena to Howard. And through this completely unexpected shift, these allusions emphasize the same shameful irony that the fantasizing theatricality of "Royal Beatings" does. In both stories, the final result is murder.

Munro has defined the genesis of her stories as her desire to get "*at* some kind of emotional core that [she] want[s] to investigate" or to approach "something that is mysterious and important" ("What Is," 17; Untitled, 178). These three stories—"At the Other Place," "Royal Beatings," and "Executioners"—all get at the same violent and mysterious emotional core, and although "Royal Beatings," unlike the other two, is written in the third person, the role of the watching observer is clear both in the repeated splits in Rose's perception and in the author's comments. As already illustrated, Rose not only watches herself performing at the time but, from the retrospective vantage point of a later time, she or the narrating author also comments on what has happened earlier. At the critical moment, for instance, just before Rose's father begins beating her, the narration is interrupted to describe Rose's thoughts in the future: "She has since wondered about murders, and murderers. Does the thing have to be carried through . . . to prove . . . that such a thing can happen, that there is nothing that can't happen . . . ?" (WDY, 16). When the interrupted beating scene is resumed, Rose is seeking "rescue" by staring down at the kitchen linoleum instead of at her father's shamefully excited face as he removes his belt. But she sees that "the patterns of linoleum can leer up at you, treachery is the other side of dailiness" (16). The startling personification in this interpretive hindsight emphasizes the scene's sexual significance: not the mother but the *father* beats the daughter. The displacement of the leer from the father's far too naked face to a much safer, disguised location—the linoleum—seems to be an observation from the point of view of the generalizing narrator rather than of Rose. The distance of this narrator from Rose suggests a frightening answer to Rose's question about murders: when the rigid dailiness is shattered, anything *can* happen, including murder.[7]

Murder also shatters the decent daily surface in a story in Munro's latest collection, *The Progress of Love*. In "Fits" (1986), as in "Royal Beatings" and "Executioners," the narrative structure develops a thematic parallel between several situations, and here again Munro's images and metaphors dramatize a violent emotional eruption. But the manipulation of point of view is something definitely different from both the retrospective first-person point of view in "Executioners" and the third-person point of view in "Royal Beatings." The third-person male protagonist of "Fits," Robert Kuiper, does not observe the violence. Instead, Peg, his wife, delivering some eggs to their neighbors, Walter and Nora Weebles, discovers their corpses. Walter has murdered his wife and then shot himself. But instead of being narrated directly, Peg's experience is related indirectly from Robert's point of view.

Robert's role as an observer is defined in the beginning of the story: he is described as an outsider in Gilmore, the rural community on Lake Huron where the action is set. Although his father used to own stores in Gilmore, Robert does not settle there until his father dies and he himself is over forty. After Peg's discovery, he gradually reconstructs her experience from several direct and indirect sources. "He picture[s] what happened" from what he is told by her; by the constable to whom she initially reports her discovery; by Karen, Peg's co-worker; and by various other characters, including Clayton, one of Peg's teenage sons from her first marriage (PL, 111). Thus, the "many abominable details" of what Peg must have seen in the Weebles' bedroom are *doubly* distanced by being filtered through the point of view of an outsider and a second-hand observer, a witness who observes not the murder scene itself but only the bloodstained observer returned from that scene (130).

Robert first hears what has happened from the constable who has already investigated the Weebles' house. Then rushing to the store where Peg works, Robert sees that her coat is smeared with blood. Karen, Peg's co-worker, tells him that Peg also left bloody footprints when she entered the store. Later, at home, he observes his wife: "Robert was watching her, from time to time. He would have said that he was watching to see . . . if she seemed numb, or strange, or showed a quiver. . . . But in fact he was watching her just because there was no sign of such difficulty and because he knew there wouldn't be (124). The repetition of the word *watching* emphasizes Robert's role as a third-person observer. He is not surprised by his wife's behavior because he has always considered her calm and "self-contained" (109). His limited knowledge of the Weebles also underscores their seemly self-control; he knew them only as a good-looking, well-dressed, fairly affluent retired couple who lived in an immaculate house.

The other characters with whom Robert discusses the Weebles all speculate about various possible reasons for the catastrophe, such as imminent financial ruin or terminal illness, but all these speculations prove false. Although there seems to be no explanation, Clayton, Peg's son, insists that his mother was not "surprised" that the Weebles "could do it" (125). When she insists that she *was* surprised, Clayton suddenly reminds her of the terrible quarrels that she used to have with his father, from whom she is divorced. During these quarrels Clayton "used to lie in bed and think" that one of his parents "was going to come and kill [him] with a knife" (126).

At this point Munro has the listening Robert interject a metaphorical comment that suggests his function as not only an observer but also a narrator. His comment explains the title of the story, "Fits," and defines the parallel between the Weebles' marriage and Peg's marriage to Dave, her first husband. Robert tells Clayton, "[I]t's like an earthquake or a volcano. It's that kind of happening. It's a kind of fit. People can take a fit like the earth takes a fit. But it only happens once in a long while. It's a freak occurrence" (126). This metaphor of an earthquake splitting the earth or a volcano erupting is like the "underground stream" in "Home," the leering linoleum in "Royal Beatings," and the bursting boil in "Executioners."[8] But Clayton rejects the freakishness of earthquakes and volcanoes and insists, "If you want to call that a fit, you'd have to call it a periodic fit. Such as people have, married people have" (126). Although this remark could also describe the fits of two earlier married couples, Aunt Thelma and Uncle Bert in "At the Other Place," and Rose's father and stepmother in "Royal Beatings," a comparison of these two couples and the Weebles shows that the reasons for their "fits" become more mysterious. In "At the Other Place," at least one reason is perfectly clear; in "Royal Beatings," the reason is only subliminally suggested; in "Fits" it not only remains mysterious but mirrors the mysteriousness of the two other relationships.

After his conversation with Peg and Clayton, Robert goes for a long walk, during which he recalls his relationship with Lee, his lover before his marriage to Peg. Just as violence erupted through the deceptively ordinary surface of the Weebles' marriage and of Peg and Dave's, so an earthquake "split open" Lee and Robert's relationship. "[T]hey found themselves saying the cruellest things to each other that they could imagine," and they said these things with "loathing," the same noun Munro used to describe Uncle Bert's hatred of his dying wife (127). And just as the face of Rose's father "fills with hatred and pleasure" as he prepares to inflict pain upon her (WDY, 16), so Robert and Lee "trembled with murderous pleasure, . . . they exulted in wounds inflicted but also in wounds received . . ." (PL, 128). Here the separation between verbal and specifically sexual sadism quickly dissolves, for Robert remembers that their volcanic quarrel culminated in making love "with a self-conscious brutality," after which "they were enormously and finally sick of each other . . ." (128).[9] Extrapolating from his own experience, therefore, he imagines that something similar must have occurred between Peg and Dave, who abandoned his family to work in the Arctic.

But during these reminiscences on his walk, Robert is still worrying about what Peg told him that she saw outside the Weebles' bedroom. She said that she saw Walter's "leg stretched out into the hall," and then she entered the room (125). Having heard the constable's description of the murder scene before he heard Peg's, Robert knows that she has lied to him on this point. But to increase the suspense of her narration, Munro delays until the very end of her story Robert's memory of the constable's description of the bedroom scene.

Worrying about Peg's false story, Robert slowly approaches what he eventually recognizes as an auto junkyard full of wrecked cars almost completely buried in deep drifts of frozen snow. These "[t]wisted" and "gutted" cars, piled crazily on top of each other, recall the junkyard full of wrecked cars in "The Edge of Town" and the drunken accidents in "Home" (131). Here Munro develops the buried cars into a complex symbol. Robert's doubly distanced point of view, combined with his slow, puzzled approach to the junkyard, emphasizes the many layers of mystery concealing the true nature not only of the Weebles but also of his "preternaturally reserved" wife (Duchêne, 109).

When he began his walk, Robert noticed curious townspeople driving by the Weebles' house. These drivers "seemed joined to their cars, making some new kind of monster that came poking around in a brutally curious way" (PL, 126). Now in the deep snow covering the auto junkyard, he sees "a new kind of glitter under the trees" (130). Through the repetition of the phrase "new kind," Munro suggests the metaphorical function of the junkyard. The "congestion of shapes, with black holes in them, and unmatched arms or petals reaching up to the lower branches of the trees" seem monstrous (130). As Robert approaches, he at first cannot identify these vaguely human shapes: "They did not look like anything, except perhaps a bit like armed giants half collapsed, frozen in combat. . . . He kept waiting for an explanation, and not getting one, until he got very close. He was so close he could almost have touched one of these monstrosities before he saw that they were just old cars" (130–31). His puzzled curiosity about the "new kind of glitter" finally satisfied, he then remembers what the constable told him: Walter Weebles blew off his head. "What was left of it was laying out in the hall" (131). This description links Walter's mangled corpse with the anthropomorphic car wrecks buried in the snow, a fusion foreshadowed by the earlier link between the "brutally curious" neighbors and their cars. But the murderous Walter and his neighbors are not the only monsters loose in the story.

Going home to his wife, Robert suddenly realizes that she has seen Walter's shattered skull, *not* his leg. "That was not what anybody turning at the top of the stairs would see and would have to step over, step through, . . . to go into the bedroom to look at the rest of what was there" (131). This realization forces the reader to reinterpret Robert's picture of Peg. He has seen her as "reserved" and "self-contained," with "a scrubbed, youthful look," created not only by her schoolgirlish wardrobe but also by her earnest participation in cultural courses at the local high school (108, 109). He has read her neat notes on Prince Henry the Navigator, whose *"importance . . . was in the inspiration and encouragement of other explorers for Portugal, even though he did not go on voyages himself"* (109). But ironically, this description applies to Walter and Peg as well as to Prince Henry and the Portuguese explorers, for Walter inspired Peg's exploration of his bedroom. All the townspeople expect Peg to be "absolutely shattered" by her experience, but, on the contrary, she was so fascinated by what Walter had done that she wanted to see more of it (120). So, instead of screaming and running away, she stepped through whatever remained of Walter's exploded head and entered the bedroom to look at Nora's corpse. That is how her feet and coat got bloodstained. Although incapable of Walter's physical violence, Peg was thus exhibiting a much more violent form of the same brutal curiosity that her neighbors exhibited later on. Along with Robert, the reader is forced to figure this all out like a detective, for, like Walter's mysteriously hidden motives and like the anthropomorphic monsters in the snow, Peg's real nature is buried and frozen, rigid and deeply repressed. Only when Clayton reminds her of her quarrels with his father does the watching Robert see her expression of "steady, helpless, unapologetic pain" (126). This expression is as close as she comes to revealing to Robert the eruptions in her past life, the emotional upheavals that occurred when she, like Walter, suddenly lost control. This superbly crafted story, in which the peripheral point of view is reinforced by the central symbol, is the climax of Munro's collected stories about murderous violence.

Although Walter's suicide and the anthropomorphic wrecked cars in "Fits" suggest the psychological ambiguity of any distinction between deliberate and accidental violence, the second type of story about external violence is the accident story. In a significant group of seven stories—"The Time of Death" (1956), "Memorial" (1974), "Accident" (1977), "Wood" (1980), "Circle of Prayer" (1986), "Monsieur les Deux Chapeaux"

(1985), and "Miles City, Montana" (1985)—accidents symbolize the sudden, violent eruption of a different world into the controlled daily one. Only in "Circle of Prayer" is the accident not the main pivot of the plot. Although not all the accidents are fatal, the characters who die are all children; thus the shock is intensified. In different ways the surviving characters in all these stories try to reestablish their shattered sense of control.

Munro's technique in "Time of Death" resembles, although in a limited way, the subtly indirect method just discussed in "Fits." Originally published in the *Canadian Forum*, this story is not narrated directly but pieced together nonchronologically by an omniscient author. Like the Weebles murder-suicide, the pivotal event of the story, the fatal scalding of retarded Benny Parry, happens before the story begins and is never actually described. Instead, Munro gives the reader three reactions to the child's death—by Leona, his mother; Patricia, his sister; and a neighbor, Allie McGee—and a concluding description of the frozen small-town setting by the omniscient author. At the beginning of the story, Allie briefly and ironically observes Leona's reaction to her son's death. Allie's perspective, similar to Robert's internal and peripheral angle in "Fits," defines Allie as the watcher in this story, noting Leona's self-defensive lies and evasions but saying nothing, just as Robert says nothing to his wife about her lies.

It is nine-year-old Patricia's reaction, delayed until the story's climax, that dramatizes the terrible price of self-control. Unlike her mother, who has hysterics almost immediately and therefore bounces back to normality, Patricia, who feels responsible for Benny's death because she was boiling the water that scalded him, exerts formidable self-control and succeeds in repressing her guilt until the visit of Brandon, the scissorsman. Because Benny was fond of the old man, Patricia associates the two of them. When she hears Brandon coming down the road with "his unintelligible chant, mournful and shrill, and so strange that you would think . . . that there was a madman loose in the world," she begins "to scream . . . " (DHS, 98). Because she has tried very hard to act "the way a grown-up does," and to be the careful mother to her siblings that the slovenly Leona is not, her terror of something completely uncontrolled in the world shatters her: she turns into "a wretched little animal insane with rage or fear" (92, 99). The sharp contrast between Leona's and Patricia's reactions makes this early story about self-control memorable, although Munro has criticized it as "a kind of imitation Southern story" and has noted both its lack of complexity and the lack of "compassion" for Leona ("Real Material," 23; Untitled, 181).

"Memorial," published eighteen years later in 1974, handles the same subject of accidental death in an infinitely more complicated and sophisticated fashion. Set in an affluent, suburban Vancouver home in the 1960s, this satirical story is narrated mainly, but not completely, from the point of view of Eileen, the aunt of seventeen-year-old Douglas, who has just been killed in a freakish car crash. Like Robert in "Fits" and Allie in "The Time of Death," Eileen is a third-person observer, on the periphery of the main action, watching her trendy sister, June, and her wealthy brother-in-law, Ewart, on the day of their son's funeral or "memorial." Like Allie, silently critical of Leona, Eileen is inwardly disapproving of the psychological jargon June uses in her determined efforts to demonstrate self-control despite her son's death. In the past, the two sisters have quarreled about June's compulsion to control everything, and Eileen has tried "to turn June's own language against her" by insisting, "Order is an anal perversion" (SIB, 210). Now, however, she expects June's body to "have loosened, in her grief, . . . her voice" to "have grown uncertain, or been silenced" (208).

But on the morning of her son's funeral, June chats on the telephone in "a cheerful buoyant matter-of-fact voice" in which Eileen disapprovingly discerns "some lively insistence on control" (209). She suspects that both her sister, still confidently mouthing the clichés of pop psychology she acquired in college, and Ewart, her earnest husband, see the funeral as "[a]n occasion to display . . . [their] values" (214), and Eileen recognizes that their "earnestness was no joke. Here was a system of digestion which found everything to its purposes," including the terror of "accidental death," which it "accepted, chewed and altered, assimilated, destroyed" (216). Eileen admits that "[w]ithout religion" it is impossible to face "the fact of . . . death," and even with it, "it [can]not be done" (215). Nevertheless, she is "offended" when a passage from *The Prophet* is read at Douglas's memorial service (221). She rejects this "modern equivalent of piety" as a fraudulent attempt to conceal and control the harsh facts of accidental death, which she compares to being struck by "lightning" (221, 215). "People die; they suffer, they die. . . . Illness and accidents. They ought to be respected, not explained. Words are all shameful. They ought to crumble in shame" (221). In this critical mood, she rejects all words, even though she was a literature major in college. She decides that "[s]ilence" is "the only possible thing" because, listening to her sister's determined psychobabble, she feels that speaking any words at all is pretending to have control and therefore perpetrating some kind of verbal and emotional "fraud" (221).

If this story ended here, the contrast between the two sisters' attitudes would be clearly defined. But in her insistence on complexity, clear definition is exactly what Munro wishes to avoid. Therefore, the story continues to a very ironic conclusion in which the contrast between the two sisters, unlike the contrast between Leona and Patricia Parry, is deliberately blurred by the sudden and repeatedly dissonant intrusion of another point of view, that of an omniscient narrator who evokes the reader's criticism of the highly critical Eileen.[10] Munro has commented that "there's a kind of smugness" about Eileen's "point of view" in this story ("Real Material," 24). This smugness is what she wants her reader to recognize when she introduces an ironically observing narrator. This narrator temporarily becomes the second watcher in the story when, on the night of the funeral, Eileen permits the drunk and grieving Ewart to make love to her in his car.

During the love scene, Eileen notices that Ewart keeps repeating her name, but her question, "What did Ewart mean by that name, what was Eileen to him?," is not immediately answered (SIB, 224). Instead, an omniscient narrator intrudes with a series of generalizations in the plural and in the present tense: "Women have to wonder. Pinned down not too comfortably on a car seat . . . they will still look for clues, and store things up in a hurry to be considered later. They have to believe that more is going on than seems to be going on; that is part of the trouble" (224). In discussing such interruptions of narration from a character's point of view, Cohn points out in *Transparent Minds* that "the most emphatic of all marks of narratorial disparity" is "a gnomic generalization" (150).[11] Here the disparity is between what Eileen has been telling herself about how totally different she is from June and what the author now tells the reader. This disparity effectively throws into confusion not only everything that Eileen has already made the reader believe, but also her answer to the question about what she means to her brother-in-law when he makes loves to her: "What Eileen meant to Ewart, she would tell herself later, was confusion. The opposite of June, wasn't that what she was? . . . . Eileen . . . comes out of the same part of the world accidents come from. He lies in her to acknowledge, to yield—but temporarily, safely—to whatever has got his son, whatever cannot be spoken of in his house" (SIB, 224).

Eileen's subjective point of view returns in this narrated monologue, but immediately afterwards the omniscient narrator intrudes again. Cohn explains that "narrated monologues . . . tend to commit the narrator to attitudes of sympathy or irony. Precisely because they cast the language of a subjective mind into the grammar of objective narration, they amplify emotional notes, but also throw into ironic relief all false notes struck by a figural mind" (117). These false notes are "most clearly in evidence when narrated monologues show up in a pronouncedly authorial milieu, framed by explicit commentary" (118). That is precisely what happens here as the narrator critically examines Eileen's future thoughts: "So Eileen, with her fruitful background of reading, her nimble habit of analysis (material and direction different from June's, but the habit not so different, after all), can later explain and arrange it for herself. Not knowing, never knowing, if that is not all literary, fanciful" (SIB, 224). Eileen has been contrasting her study of literature to her sister's psychology major, but now the deflating narrator describes their resulting mental habits as "not so different, after all." Then the narrator increases the disparity between herself and Eileen even farther by emphasizing Eileen's fatuous mistake in investing Ewart's words with meaning. This error, the narrator's generalization points out, once again in the present tense, is one commonly committed by women who would naturally love to believe that their own "woman's body" is uniquely significant (224). But it is not: "Before and during the act [men] seem to invest this body with certain individual powers, they will say its name in a way that indicates something particular, something unique, that is sought for. Afterwards it appears that they have changed their minds, they wish it understood that such bodies are interchangeable. Women's bodies" (224–25).

Eileen is unaware of her mistaken attempt at self-definition because it lies in the future. Thus her delusion is a piece of information shared only by the subtly mocking narrator and the sadly nodding reader. But when Eileen tries to apologize to June the next morning, Eileen becomes aware of the terrible unreliability of her own verbal attempt to control her present situation. When Eileen says, "I haven't helped you the way I meant to," she cringes at the unintentional irony of her words. "No sooner was that sentence out than it flung itself inside out and grinned at her. This was a day when there was nothing she could say that would work" (225). And glimpsing her face in the mirror, she is guiltily surprised by the discrepancy between her inner thoughts and her outward, "wonderfully appropriate look of tactfulness and concern" as she listens to her sister describe her son's freakish death (226).

Through these double splits in point of view—shifting from Eileen in the present to the ironically omniscient narrator in the future, and then splitting Eileen in half by having her look at her false reflection in the mirror—Munro suggests that the compulsive drive to define, explain, and thus control the uncontrollable, the terrifying "part of the world accidents come from," is not limited just to June and to her obvious misuse of language (224). The situation is more complicated than that. Eileen also uses language spuriously, to inflate herself and her sexual favors with false and smugly fanciful significance by concealing the true nature of what happens between herself and her sister's husband. Thus, she has no real moral right to criticize because, without fully realizing it, she is just as confused about herself as her sister is.

"Accident," a story originally published three years after "Memorial," is similar to "Memorial" in two ways: a son is accidentally killed, as if suddenly struck by lightning, and an ironically omniscient narrator comments on the characters' reactions to this eruption of confusion and violence into their lives. But in "Accident" there are two central characters instead of one. Frances Wright, a high-school music teacher in Hanratty, and Ted Makkavala, a married colleague, are carrying on an adulterous love affair. They both believe it is a well-concealed secret, but the omniscient narrator gleefully informs the reader that it is not a secret at all. In this story there are thus really three clearly defined points of view, Frances's, Ted's, and that of the omniscient author, who is the watcher.

In discussing her own fiction, Margaret Atwood has defined the advantages of using such a triple point of view. Two characters, she says,

> can . . . think for themselves, and what they think won't always be what [another character] thinks of *them*. If I like, I can add in yet another point of view, that of the omniscient author, . . . yet another voice within the [story]. The omniscient author can claim to know things about the characters that even they don't know, thus letting the reader know these things as well. (426)

In "Accident" Munro introduces such a fully developed, alternating, multiple point of view and thus creates exactly the kind of situation that Atwood defines. The omniscient author watches Frances and Ted and keeps interrupting their internal comments with her own ironic reflections. Her purpose is to show how mistaken they are in what they believe about the townspeople of Hanratty, about each other, and—most significantly—about themselves. This narrator functions throughout the story, rather than just at the conclusion, as in "Memorial." By interjecting these ironic revelations, she emphasizes the uncontrolled repercussions of the fatal accident that permanently alters the lives of Frances and Ted.

In the opening scene, narrated from Frances's third-person point of view, Frances "shamefully" eavesdrops outside Ted's science classroom. Although she hears only a normal schoolroom pattern of "order and acquiescence," Frances feels "a familiar pressure, of longing or foreboding, that strange lump of something you can feel sometimes in music or a landscape, barely withheld, promising to burst and reveal itself, but it doesn't, it dissolves and goes away" (MJ, 79). However, this time the lump does burst, in an accident that kills two children, and this foreshadowing metaphor of bursting and revelation clearly links this story with the ones already discussed.

The reasons motivating the lovers' belief that their relationship is a secret constitute another link between this story and the later "Fits." Like Robert, Frances and Ted are outsiders, although in Frances's case this role is merely the result of her four years of study at an out-of-town out-of-town conservatory. "It is in imagining her affair to be a secret," the omniscient author explains, "that Frances shows, most clearly, a lack of small-town instincts, a trust and recklessness she is unaware of; this is what people mean when they say of her that it sure shows that she has been away" (80). It shows in "the outsider's innocent way of supposing herself unobserved as she dashes from one place to another around town . . ." (81). Ted actually is an outsider, not only from a "frontier settlement" in Northern Ontario but also from an intellectual Finnish family "banished from Finland" for their political activities (96, 98). During the main time frame of the narrative, 1943, Ted is "considered an enemy alien" in Canada, and he is "proud of it" (98). By characterizing both protagonists in this way, Munro sharpens the irony of her narrator's comment that the high-school secretary, "[l]ike almost everybody else in town, . . . had known about [Frances and Ted] for some time" (86).

This secretary interrupts their excited preparations for intercourse in a school storeroom. While undressing, Frances has been remembering their previous encounters in the same place, associating them with "lightning, a crazy and shattering, painful kind of lust," and admiring Ted's "ruddy cheerful penis, upright and workmanlike" (85, 86). But when the secretary yells through the door, "Mr. Makkavala! . . . Your son's been killed!," Frances sees him unmanned, "that workman . . . losing color [and] . . .drooping . . . " (87). This sudden physiological change symbolizes a more shattering and painful kind of lightning, Bobby's sudden death and Ted's consequent loss of control over his life.

The following scene is narrated from Ted's third-person point of view. When Bobby Makkavala and another boy tied their sleds to the back of a car, they were accidentally run over. The other boy has died, but Bobby is still alive, although obviously dying. As Ted and Greta, his wife, wait helplessly in the hospital, Ted thinks, "Everything was changed" (87). Struggling to exercise some control over this unbelievably changed world in which his only son can die, he suddenly thinks of bargaining with God to let Bobby live. He will give up Frances in exchange for his son: "by not even thinking about her, by willing her to stop existing in his life, he could increase Bobby's chances, hold off his death" (88). The terrible irony of Ted's desperate maneuvering for control is that he is an atheist. After his son's death, he himself realizes this irony: he tells Frances "his thoughts of bargains" to illustrate "the way the most rational mind can relapse and grovel" (89).

In the next scene, narrated once again from Frances's point of view, she callously rages against Bobby because she believes that the accident will end her relationship with Ted. "She felt fury at that child, at his stupidity, at his stupid risk, . . . his breaking through into other people's lives, into her life" (94). This metaphor of "breaking through" connects

Frances's present reaction with her initial apprehension of something ready to "burst and reveal itself" (79). Almost as if she intuited Ted's attempt to bargain with God, she believes that Greta and Ted will be reunited by their shared grief and that she will not see him anymore. But she is mistaken, for exactly the opposite happens. This plot structure embodies Munro's main point about the effect of Bobby's death on Ted, his sense of losing control of his life.

After Bobby's funeral, Ted boasts to Frances of how he imposed his will upon Greta's huge, bossy, devoutly Lutheran family, who descended en masse from Northern Ontario. Although the clan insisted on bringing a Finnish Lutheran pastor to the funeral, Ted proudly tells Frances that at the grave he outshouted the family, wailing in Finnish, to read the "few memorial paragraphs" that he had written (101). He did not allow "that pack of maniacs" any hymns or prayers (102). But by narrating this scene from Frances's point of view, Munro reveals that Ted's conscious motives in confessing his temporary irrationality in the hospital are not his real motives. He confesses to emphasize his swiftly restored rationality and his decisiveness. "I knew I couldn't show a moment's hesitation" (102). But underneath his confession and boasting, Frances clearly observes his selfish and frightened egotism: "He did it all for himself, Frances was thinking. He wasn't thinking of Greta for a moment. Or of Bobby. He was thinking of himself and his beliefs and not giving in to his enemies. That was what mattered to him. She could not help seeing this and she did not like it" (103). Immediately after his boasting, Ted insists on making love, even though Frances is "not ready"; he is "too intent to notice" how she feels, for, like Ewart in "Memorial," he sees the act as another way to reassert his control (103).

In the next scene, the omniscient author adds her own ironic comments on Ted's motives in an interview with his principal. When the principal tries to elicit some pro forma promise from Ted to terminate his affair, Ted furiously announces that he is going to divorce Greta and marry Frances: "My mind was made up long ago." The narrator wryly observes, "He believed that was true" (104). And Frances feels the same skepticism when he later insists that he would have married her in any case, accident or no accident: "But it didn't seem so to Frances, and she wondered if he said it just because he could not bear the thought of anything being set in motion outside his control—and so wastefully, so cruelly . . ." (106). In an interview, Munro has defined "Accident" as a story about "love . . . suddenly catapulted into having to be real . . ." ("Visit," 13). Because the accident is the cruel catapult, Frances's part in Ted's frantic decision remains "ambiguous" (MJ, 106).

But in an epilogue "nearly thirty years later," when Frances returns to Hanratty for another funeral, she meets the man who accidentally ran over Bobby (107). She is forced to admit that Bobby's death gave her Ted and their marriage, but she pushes this admission out of her mind as "too ugly" and "monstrous" (109). Even a generation after the event, the eruption of accidental violence into life's routine orderliness is so intensely frightening that it cannot be faced. The dark parentheses of the two funerals, the alternating points of view, and the intruding, ironic narrator all emphasize Ted's self-deluding attempts to convince himself and Frances that, after only a momentary loss, he has regained full control of his life.[12]

Munro's comments on "Wood," another story in which an accident is the pivotal plot element, emphasize the same loss of control. Describing Roy Fowler, the main character in this uncollected *New Yorker* story, she has said: "The man's accident when he's alone in the woods brings him out of that ordinary world of control and inquisitiveness and into a completely different world" ("Interview": Hancock, 90). Like Robert in "Fits" and Ted in "Accident," Roy is an outsider, not so much in Logan, Ontario, where he lives, as in the huge and "closeknit clan" into which he has married but to which he has not contributed any children. "As a rule," he notes, "they don't take much notice of people who aren't like themselves" ("Wood,"46). He is a woodcutter who classifies and catalogues the trees in every bush or forest because he wants to exert control. "Roy's thoughts about wood are covetous and nearly obsessive. . . . He would like to map every bush he sees, get it in his mind, know what is there" (48). His inquisitiveness, like Munro's documentary urge, constitutes part of his desire for control. Very proud of his experienced knowledge of the bush, he "thinks that there is very little danger in going tree cutting alone if you know what you are doing" (47). Knowing that includes the self-vigilance of constant awareness: "In the bush it isn't good to let your mind wander or your worries intrude" (48).

But, ironically, that is exactly what Roy does when old Percy Marshall, a local character, tells him a confused rumor that another, unidentified man has secured a lucrative contract for cutting the same trees that Roy has received the owner's verbal permission to cut. Initially Roy considers the "possibility" that Percy may "have got [the story] badly twisted," but in his eagerness to cut some of the promised trees, he forgets this suspicion (50). Even though it has begun to snow, he hurries out into the bush alone to begin cutting.

As a result of these psychological and physical conditions, Roy has an accident. Hurrying over the rough, snow-covered, hummocky ground, he slips, falls, and breaks his ankle. Unable to walk, he has "to abandon his axe and his chain saw and get down on his hands and knees and crawl" (53). Munro has emphasized that what is "important to [her] in the story is what his experience is like when he is crawling back trying to get to the truck" ("Interview": Hancock, 90). He has quite literally split the concealing surface in his fall, his "feet . . . plung[ing] through a cover of snowy brush to the ground, . . . farther down than he expected" (52). Then, as he slowly and painfully crawls over "rotten leaves and dirt," hatless and gloveless in the steadily falling snow, he is gradually forced to accept the reality of his situation, to stop "believing in an order of things in which [his accident] couldn't happen" (53). Beginning "to feel almost light-headed," he becomes increasingly detached from his worries: "Nobody knows what anybody else is thinking about or how anybody else is feeling. . . . Nobody knows how others see themselves" (54). This generalization introduces a significant split in his self-perception. He backs off to look at himself and at how this absurd accident has occurred. As he sees a hawk or a buzzard circling above him, "its eye on him" in his exposed and potentially vulnerable situation, he suddenly realizes how his generalization about other people applies to him (54). Because he momentarily sees himself as the watching bird sees him, he also sees what the rumormongers have been thinking about him.

Percy's rumor about the unidentified woodcutter with the contract is about "Roy himself" (54). Percy has simply distorted the story of Roy's agreement with the owner of the bush because "[e]verything that involves money, in this county, gets talked up, distorted, . . . turned into a story" (54). By not recognizing himself in Percy's "big fable," Roy has ironically and very painfully lost control of himself in the very setting in which he has been the most confident of both his mental and physical control (54). It is almost a case of hubris, but there is no tragedy.

The concluding paragraph of the story pulls sharply away from Roy to emphasize this thematic irony. An omnisicent author, distancing herself from her protagonist, observes:

> Roy's mind operates very economically at this moment—perhaps more selectively than ever before. It manages to turn everything to good account. It no longer dwells on the foolishness of the accident but triumphs in the long, successful crawl and the approach to the truck. (He is on his way again.) It cancels out any embarrassment at his having been so mistaken; it pushes out any troubling detection of waste and calamity; it ushers in a decent sense of victory. Safe. (54)

This ironic conclusion, with its emphasis on Roy's rejection of "waste and calamity" and on his triumphant reassertion of control, leaves him in a state of mind very similar to Ted's when he deluded himself about his motives for marrying Frances: "he could not bear the thought of anything being set in motion outside his control—and so wastefully . . ." (MJ, 106). In both stories, published three years apart ("Accident" appeared in *Toronto Life* in November 1977; "Wood," in the *New Yorker* on 24 November 1980), the ironic distance of the omniscient narrator from her protagonists emphasizes their loss of control as something so terrifying that they unconsciously deny it.[13]

Accidents occur in the background of other stories. For instance, Sandy Desmond drowns in "Something I've Been Meaning to Tell You," and Frank McArter drowns in "Walking on Water." But in Munro's first three non-interrelated collections—*Dance of the Happy Shades, Something I've Been Meaning To Tell You,* and *The Moons of Jupiter*—there is only one major accident story apiece. In contrast, *The Progress of Love* includes three such stories: "Circle of Prayer," "Monsieur les Deux Chapeaux," and "Miles City, Montana." Interviewed upon the publication of this collection, Munro commented that her "way of thinking . . . embraces randomness pretty well" (Kolson, 4C). The increased number of accidents suggests her intensified concentration on life's frightening fragility. The randomness of accidents represents the most frightening fact of life, its uncontrollability.[14]

In "Circle of Prayer," originally published in the *Paris Review,* the fatal accident is not the central plot element, for the story describes the disintegration of a marriage two years before the accident. But, although Trudy, the central character, initially manages to come to terms with the loss of Dan, her husband, the accident later forces her to confront the finality of this loss as something almost like a death. To unify her story, Munro establishes the parallels between these two losses in several subtle ways. When Dan leaves Trudy for a woman whom he meets by chance and who exploits him, he destroys his marriage in what he himself initially recognizes as "a middle-aged fit" (PL, 265). Similarly, when their daughter's drunk or stoned friend, fifteen-year-old Tracy Lee, accidentally drives a truck into a tree, she, too, is "self-destructive" and "stupid" (259). After Dan's defection Trudy keeps three objects in a jug, her engagement and wedding rings and a valuable jet necklace Dan's mother has willed to Robin, their daughter. In the opening scene of the story, when Trudy discovers that this necklace is missing, she immediately suspects what Robin has done with it, and, in a fit of destructive rage, throws the heavy jug across Robin's room. Robin says that her mother "could have killed" her, and eventually Trudy admits the truth of this accusation (255). By starting her story with this jug-throwing scene, Munro shows that Trudy, like Dan and Tracy Lee, is capable of fits of uncontrolled and potentially dangerous behavior. When the necklace is buried with Tracy Lee, its loss becomes a symbolic burial of Dan and Trudy's dead marriage.

The circumstances under which the necklace ends up in the dead girl's coffin not only emphasize the parallel between the two types of deaths but also demonstrate, once again, the crucial importance of trying to assert control in an uncontrollable world. The "crying" and "shivering" teenage girls who attend Tracy Lee's funeral-home visitation file past her open coffin. As they do, they sing what they believe to be "an old hymn" (263). Although it is actually a song from a movie, the carpe diem theme of its lyrics explains their naive mistake. When they reach the coffin, they strip off their jewelry—rings, bracelets, earrings, necklaces, and chains—and drop them all in, "flashing and sparkling down on the dead girl. . . ." With unconscious irony, they all behave as if this were "a religious ceremony," and the bereaved family gratefully agrees: "It was like church" (263). Like Eileen in "Memorial," the girls, including Robin, find it impossible to face death without any religious faith. Trying to fill the frightening emptiness created by the sudden and accidental death of one of their own peers, they rediscover a ritual reminiscent of many pre-Christian burial practices. Thus they form the first circle of prayer around the coffin.

This circle's adult counterpart is the "Circle of Prayer" that Trudy's friend, Janet, tells her about on the morning of the funeral. Janet suggests that Judy join the women in this circle to pray for the return of the necklace and Dan, her husband. To this suggestion, Trudy replies: "I'll just go down on my knees right now and pray. . . . that I get the necklace back and I get Dan back, and why do I have to stop there? I can pray that Tracy Lee never died. I can pray that she comes back to life. Why didn't her mother ever think of that?" (269–70). Although later Trudy not only apologizes for this outburst but even asks another character whether *he* prays, her sarcastic rejection of prayer completes the many parallels between Tracy Lee's death and the death of Trudy and Dan's marriage. In different ways, both losses are the results of random accidents, beyond anything but symbolic control.

In "Monsieur les Deux Chapeaux" this compulsion to control the frightening uncontrollability of life becomes the lifelong obsession of Colin, the protagonist, after a fatal accident, or rather what momentarily appears to be one. In the climactic flashback that concludes the story, Colin believes that he has accidentally killed Ross, his younger brother. Although he soon finds out that Ross was only pretending to be dead, this childhood trauma of imagining himself a murderer shapes his adult life. He becomes what Cain, the first fratricide, protests to God he cannot be: Colin—the name is symbolically similar to Cain—becomes his brother's keeper.

In the opening scene, the principal of the school where Colin teaches and Ross does occasional yard work asks Colin, "Is that your brother out there?" (PL, 56). This question echoes the one God asked the guilty Cain: "Where is Abel, thy brother?" The principal's query is prompted by the fact that Ross, while clipping the school grass, is wearing two hats, one on top of the other. A French teacher also notices the two hats and dubs Ross "Monsieur les Deux Chapeaux," but when she later mentions seeing him, Ross denies what he was doing. "You're seeing things. You got double vision" (69). In a symbolical sense, however, it is Colin, not Ross, who wears two hats; it is also Colin, not the French teacher, who has double vision because he is constantly watching his brother, the "secret weight on" his life (66).

Initially Ross's weird behavior and his proneness to car accidents seem to be the only reasons for Colin's hovering protectiveness. But gradually Munro builds up to the revelation of something "horrible" that occurred in the past and "could've been tragic" (74). These suspenseful allusions to the past are embedded in a discussion of something dangerous that Ross is doing in the present, installing an engine in a car not big enough for it. The French teacher warns Colin that the powerful engine "will simply break the drive shaft" and "literally flip [the car] over" (70). Colin is anxious not only to prevent Ross from doing this but also to avoid hurting his feelings by criticizing him.

The climactic flashback at the end of the story reveals that Colin's protectiveness is not only the result but, paradoxically, also the cause of the traumatic event that shaped his life. When the two brothers and several young boys find a rifle and start playing with it, Colin grabs it to prevent Ross from doing something dangerous. Somehow the gun goes off, there are screams and shouts, and in the confusion Colin sees "Ross lying on the ground, on his back, with his arms flung out, a dark stain spilled out from the top of his head" (77). This description also echoes Abel's death, whose "blood crieth unto [God] from the ground." But what Colin imagines to be blood is actually a puddle of water, for Ross is only feigning death: "The bullet hadn't come near him" (77).

In the final scene of the flashback, Colin is sitting on a bridge girder. From this perch above nothingness, he sees "all the jumble of his life, and other people's lives . . . , rolled back, just like a photograph split and rolled back, so it shows what was underneath all along. Nothing" (81–82). Like so many other Munro characters at the moment of crisis, Colin feels not only completely dissociated from himself but also suddenly separated from the safe world, whose surface he has broken through. "How silly it was that he should have a name and it should be Colin. . . . His life had split open, and nothing had to be figured out anymore" (82). But then a crowd of people arrives, with the living and laughing Ross in tow, shouting, "I ain't dead, Colin!" and calling him to come down (82). As Colin obeys, "sick with the force of things coming back to life," and trying not to think about what has nearly happened, he knows "that to watch out for something like that happening—to Ross, and to himself—[is] going to be his job in life from then on" (83). Thus he becomes one of Munro's watchers, but in an almost saintly sense: he stays permanently split, permanently double. The final irony is that the new identity shaped by his brother's unintentionally cruel hoax is the exact opposite of Cain's, but marks him nonetheless.

The dramatic culmination of these stories about accidents is "Miles City, Montana," the only accident story with a first-person narrator who is not only the mother of a small child threatened by a fatal accident but also a writer. In this tightly unified story, the retrospective narrator—who seems to be speaking in the actual present—tells the stories of two accidents occurring twenty years apart. The later story, which she dates in the summer of 1961, is framed within her confused childhood memory of the other event, a boy's accidental drowning. The two stories are associatively linked by a third memory: the narrator remembers helping her farmer father rescue stranded turkeys who "had managed to crowd to higher ground and avoid drowning" in a rainstorm that flooded the fields (PL, 94). In the first accident, Steve Gauley fell into a flooded gravel pit; his father did not watch him, and even his "fatherhood seemed accidental . . . " (85). In the later accident, the narrator's little girl, Meg, falls into the deep end of a public pool in Miles City when nobody is watching her, but she comes up swimming and is swiftly rescued by Andrew, her father. These two accidents are focused in parallel images of a father carrying a child. The story opens with this ominous sentence: "My father came across the field carrying the body of the boy who had been drowned" (84). When Andrew rescues Meg, he also carries her. But the narrator's role in these two incidents is radically different. In the first story she is a six-year-old child who has partially seen and partially imagined a dark and indelible image of death: the corpse of another child, a motherless little boy, whose "hair and clothes were mud-colored," whose nostrils and ears "were plugged up with greenish mud" (84). In the second story she is the mother of a three-year-old child who has escaped drowning. The associative link, however, is not merely the common theme of drowning but the painful paradox of parents as the begetters of death, a paradox that the narrator discovers as a result of the change in her role from watching child to writing parent.

In the first drowning story, the six-year-old child attends the drowned boy's funeral. Holding "a white narcissus" and wearing innocent white stockings, she stands "removed from" her hymn-singing parents. "[W]atching" them, she feels "a furious and sickening disgust" (86). Thirty years separate this narrator from the narrator of "At the Other Place," removed from the adults and watching them, but she, too, remembers seeing them as grossly sexual beings. Although her parents are decorously dressed for the formal occasion, she is disgusted by their "bloated power" and by what she insists on imagining under their dark clothes: their "lumpy shapes," their "coarseness, . . . hairiness, [and] . . . horrid secretions," all of which fill her with "a thin, familiar misgiving" (86).

After Meg's rescue from the swimming pool, the narrator suddenly understands what this dimly perceived "misgiving" really meant. As a child she had suspected that her parents were not her protection from death but some kind of threat. Now she and her husband, Andrew, have become a threat to their own children. Trying to imagine what Meg's death and its aftermath would have been like, "a blind sinking and shifting," she tells herself that it is "shameful" to place her "finger on the wire to get the safe shock, feeling a bit of what it's like, then pulling back" (103). These metaphors dramatically combine three forms of splitting: "sinking" suggests drowning, "shifting" suggests an earthquake, and "the wire" suggests electricity, lightning in its safely controlled form. That is why the narrator tells herself that her imagination is shameful: to do what the writer does, "changing from a participant into an observer," is to play with lightning, to arrange "patterns and destinies" like God ("Author's Commentary," 125). It is shameful for another reason, too. This deliberate exercise of the writer's controlling imagination reveals an appalling fact: just as Andrew has always suspected, his wife, the narrator, "really" is "a secret monster of egotism" because she can contemplate the death of her own child (PL, 91). Recognizing this fact makes her remember her parents at the funeral once again, and now she feels that her parents consented to her own death simply by the act of begetting her: "Their big, stiff, dressed-up bodies did not stand between me and sudden death, or any kind of death. They gave consent. So it seemed. They gave consent to the death of children and to my death . . . by the very fact that they had made children—they had made me" (103). Their hypocritical hymn-singing at the funeral only made things worse because it denied or attempted to conceal the frightening facts.

The narrator thus sees the treacherous world of sudden and accidental death, where children can drown in "clear blue water," as a world into which parents thrust their children simply by begetting them and exposing them to inevitable mortality (102). In retrospect, the scene in "Accident" in which Ted loses his erection as he hears the premature announcement of his son's death becomes a paradigm of the paradox explicitly developed here: sexual desire sows the seeds not only of new life but also of death. Children are forced to trust their parents, but their parents have thrust them into a trap.

Thus, even though baby Meg blithely observes, "I didn't drown," and even though her parents exult in their luck, "Miles City, Montana" seems the most deeply pessimistic of this group of stories in which accidents are the pivotal plot elements (102). The dimly persistent image of the drowned boy haunting the background of the two earlier stories already mentioned—the memory of little Sandy Desmond in "Something I've Been Meaning to Tell You," and of young Frank McArter in "Walking on Water"—now comes into focus as the central image (SIB, 7, 90). Meg's escape from tragedy on a sunny summer day does *not* mean that life is not a tragedy. Although the narrator longs for the right of children to be "free, to live a new, superior kind of life," she knows that they are "caught in the snares of vanquished grownups, with their sex and funerals" (PL, 104).

These close links between the shocking power of death and the literal shock of electric power and between sex and funerals constitute a recurrent thematic pattern in Munro's work. As already shown, she describes sexual excitement and impending death on the same page in both "At the Other Place" and "Accident" and sex and a funeral on the very same day in "Memorial." The electric metaphor first occurs in "Images," where the shocking power of death is perceived as electric power, and both this metaphor and the close link between death significantly recur in *Lives of Girls and Women,* at the climax of which Del, the narrator, is nearly drowned immediately after intercourse.

3

The Uncontrollable

A Power Loose in the World

Just as the emotional core of the group of stories discussed in chapter 2 is defined by the common element of uncontrollability shared by the key metaphors in these stories—the surfacing subterranean stream, the bursting boil, the earth-splitting quake, the erupting volcano, and the sudden irruptive violence of often fatal accidents—a second set of somewhat similar metaphors defines the emotional core of earlier stories. These metaphors associate sexuality and death with each other as a terrifying power loose in the world. This association occurs through the metaphorical definition of this power as fire or electricity.

These metaphorical patterns first appear in "Images," one of Munro's three early stories about Del Jordan, the same character who later narrates *Lives of Girls and Women*. In "Walker Brothers Cowboy," "Images," "Boys and Girls," and the novel, Del, first as a little girl and then as an adolescent, is always the first-person narrator. The little girl in the first two of these stories, although she remains nameless, is identified as Ben Jordan's daughter, so the reader sees her as younger versions of the same Del Jordan who reappears as a fourth-grader at the beginning of the novel and graduates from high school at its end. The close connection between the novel and "Walker Brothers Cowboy" and "Images" is also established by the date of their composition. Although these two stories are the first and third stories in *Dance of the Happy Shades*, Munro's first collection, they were actually the last stories that she wrote for this collection. They were written in 1967, just four years before the novel was published in 1971 ("Real Material," 20).

The developing narrator in these stories and in the novel is concerned with coming to know the world, especially the same dark world of sexuality and death that the first-person narrator confronts in "At the Other Place." In "Walker Brothers Cowboy," the little girl is getting ready to go to school; in "Images" she is so young that she can still remember trying to fall asleep in a crib. In both of these stories, she is a first-person narrator who functions both as the protagonist in the center of what she sees as her story and as the older narrator remembering her younger self.

But in these two stories, even more than in "At the Other Place," the remembered child's innocence and ignorance push her to the periphery of the story's main action, which is what the adults are doing. This effect is less marked in "Walker Brothers Cowboy" than in "Images." The child in the first story is proud of being older and therefore more observant than her little brother, who "does not notice enough" (DHS, 18). But in "Images" she herself does not grasp the central fact of the story, that her mysteriously altered mother is about to give birth. In spite of this difference, however, the two stories have a basic similarity in their manipulation of point of view: they use not only a dual point of view but what is sometimes actually a triple one to emphasize the child's peripheral position, her innocent eye's incomprehension of the most powerful facts of life. In both stories these are the sexual facts; in the second story, the "images" also include images of death, as in "At the Other Place," and these images become metaphors of terrifying electric power.

In "Walker Brothers Cowboy" the main episode is Ben Jordan's visit to the Cronin farm, but in the introductory section his explanation of how the Great Lakes were formed leaves his little daughter appalled by "[t]he tiny share we have of time" (3). Although muted and indirect, this initial allusion to death is the somber background against which she then describes the emotional reactions of Nora Cronin to the totally unexpected visit of her former suitor, Ben Jordan, a Walker Brothers salesman. The narrator reports the outward details of how Nora speaks and acts but shows no real comprehension of the complicated reasons for Nora's behavior. Although the child intuitively senses that the visit to the farm should be kept secret from her stay-at-home mother, at the end she identifies as "things not to be mentioned" only that her father, supposedly a teetotaler, drank whiskey and that Nora tried to teach her to dance (18). In spite of the explicit thematic summary at the end of the story, the child's sense of darkness and mystery in her father's life does not include any emotional comprehension of Nora's life. Naturally the child concentrates on her sudden sense of strangeness in a very familiar figure, her own kind father, but the reader is made to see more.

Through this additional, implied dimension to the situation, Munro emphasizes the peripheral position of the child reporting the action. The child narrator reports that Nora speaks "harshly" and as if her stomach "hurt" when Jordan and his two children arrive at the Cronin farm (10). But the narrator does not attempt to explain why Nora, after this obviously painful initial reaction, is suddenly galvanized into action. She changes into a sheer, flowered dress, applies cologne, drinks whiskey, puts a record on the gramophone, and begins to laugh and dance with "strange gaiety" (16). However, when the father refuses Nora's breathlessly hopeful invitation to dance with her—a temptation to which he must not yield, in spite of, or perhaps because of, the implied sexual tension between him and his sickly, over-refined wife—Nora, still sweaty with exertion and excitement, takes the record off. By the time her visitors leave, her almost hysterical excitement has turned into bitterness. The reader sees the complicated reasons for Nora's painfully confused arousal, but the young narrator in the time frame of the story does not state them. She senses that Nora's Catholicism, indicated by a picture of the Virgin in the Cronin house, was the obstacle preventing her father's marriage to Nora. But she is too young to grasp Nora's feelings of betrayal, physical loneliness, and loss, as she struggles to support herself and her blind mother on a farm during the Depression. As in "At the Other Place," the adults' sexual emotions are left unstated, but what the child at the edge of the action cannot grasp Munro lets her readers recognize and define for themselves.

In "Images" the child's position at the outer edge of the central action shapes the entire story. It is a story of death, birth, and copulation, all from a young child's point of view. Although she never actually sees any of these things happen, she is intensely apprehensive that there are hidden things to *be* seen. The initial piece of action hidden from her is the slow dying of her grandfather in a hot, darkened room presided over by her cousin, Mary McQuade, a practical nurse.[1] This situation recalls Munro's reference to a metaphorical "black room at the centre of the house with all other rooms leading to and away from it" ("What Is Real?," 36). While the grandfather lies on his deathbed, the first-person narrator lies in her crib "across the hall," listening to the adults' voices and feeling "without knowing what it was, just what everybody else in the house must have felt—*under* the sweating heat the fact of death . . ." (DHS, 31; emphasis added). Her inarticulate awareness of this concealed fact focuses on Mary, sitting with the grandfather and looking as "big and gloomy as an iceberg. . . . I held her responsible" (31).

The word *under* is a link to the second piece of adult action hidden from the child, her mother's advancing pregnancy. When Mary comes to the child's home for reasons not explained to her, she feels threatened by the association between Mary and the power of death. "She came, . . . and let her power loose in the house. If she had never come my mother would never have taken to her bed" (32–33).[2] This childish misinterpretation of what is happening to her mother is confirmed by the innocent eye's view of the physical alteration in her mother's appearance, of her heavy body *"under* the covers . . . changed into some large, fragile and mysterious object, difficult to move" (33; emphasis added). The repetition of *under* draws a parallel between the images of the two figures in the two beds, the grandfather about to die and the mother about to give birth, and emphasizes, once again, the child's sense of something somehow sexual under a concealing surface. She does not understand Mary's coarsely cheerful allusion to her mother's impending labor: "[Y]ou'll be worse before you're better!" (33). As Munro has told an interviewer, Mary, "though she's loud and jolly," functions as "the embodiment . . . of terror, to the child" ("Interview": Hancock, 111). This terror is increased by the child's guilt whenever her strangely altered mother warns her to be careful not to "hurt Mother." "Every time she said Mother I felt chilled, and a kind of wretchedness and shame spread through me as it did at the name of Jesus. This *Mother* that my own real, warm-necked, irascible and comforting human mother set up between us was an everlasting wounded phantom, sorrowing like Him over all the wickedness I did not yet know I would commit" (33). Although this analogy between Mother and a typically Protestant, guilt-producing Jesus is, of course, the comment of the retrospective adult narrator, the child's miserable sense of guilty bewilderment is the emotion of the innocent "I," not at the center of the action but quivering at the edge of it.

Her innocent ignorance of copulation is shown by her inability to see the concealed connection between her mother's impending delivery and her father's teasing Mary about not having a husband. In a highly charged atmosphere of mutual horseplay, Mary plays practical jokes on the father while he, anticipating the successful outcome of his own mating, offers the laughing, red-faced Mary all kinds of men to consider for "preposterous imagined matings" (34). The nature of these jokes is indicated by the retrospective narrator's comment that her mother would have criticized them as "cruel and indecent" (35). Thus, the bewildered child watches the shadows of these coarsely joking adults, "gigantic shadows" created by an oil lamp in the evening—the farmhouse does not have electricity—and tries "to understand the danger, to read the signs of invasion" (35). Munro has emphasized the child's exaggeration of what is going on, which is "[n]othing very awful . . . but [she] keeps feeling a threat and a horror because her grandfather had died" and because of her "mother's pregnancy . . ." ("Interview": Hancock, 111). The child obviously understands neither death nor sex and its conse-quences, but once again, as in "At the Other Place," the two frightening experiences are conflated in the narrator's imagination as she watches the adults.

In this highly apprehensive mood, in which she fears Mary's "power loose in the house," the child encounters old Joe Phippen, a hermit, on the riverbank with her father (32–33). Munro has explained the genesis of this symbolic character in her imagination:

[The story] started with the picture in my mind of the man met in the woods, coming obliquely down the riverbank, carrying the hatchet, and the child watching him. . . . Of course the character did not spring from nowhere. His ancestors were a few old men, half hermits, half madmen, often paranoid, occasionally dangerous, living around the country where I grew up. . . . I had always heard stories about them; they were estab-lished early as semi-legendary figures in my mind. ("The Colonel's Hash Resettled," 182)

The significant point here is the image of the child watching the hatchet-bearing man, the innocent eye watching death. In the child's paralyzed recognition of the man as the embodiment of her worst fears, two factors are operating. The first factor is the link that the child imagines between old Joe and death coming to her grandfather: "All my life I had known there was a man like this and he was behind doors, around the corner at the dark end of a hall" (DHS, 38). The precise location of this death-fig-ure is derived from the child's recent memory of her grandfather dying in the dark room across the hall. The second factor is the link between her resentment of Mary and her reaction to old Joe. She believes that Mary has "let her power loose in the house," an especially vivid metaphor in a farmhouse without electric power (32–33); then she uses an extended electrical metaphor to unify her description of her terror upon seeing the hermit.

People say they have been paralyzed by fear, but I was transfixed, as if struck by lightning, and what hit me did not feel like fear so much as recognition. I was not surprised. This is the sight that does not surprise you, the thing you have always known was there that comes so naturally, moving delicately and contentedly and in no hurry, as if it was made, in the first place, from a wish of yours, a hope of something final, terrifying. All my life I had known there was a man like this. . . . So now I saw him and just waited, like a child in an old negative, electrified against the dark noon sky, with blazing hair and burned-out Orphan Annie eyes. (38)

The child fully expects Joe to kill her father with his hatchet. Although Joe turns out to be more dangerous to himself than to anyone else, the fact that he burned down his own house underscores his association in her mind with a dangerous power loose in the atmosphere, blazing like lightning.

This mad old man, who imagines that enemies burned down his house and who now lives in what is left—a low-roofed, earth-floored cellar—is similar to old Brandon, "a madman loose in the world," in "The Time of Death" (DHS, 98). Although neither is dangerous, they both embody the child protagonist's terror of something sinister, powerful, and completely uncontrolled. Munro's description of evil in "What Is Real?" as "the beast let loose" is echoed by these descriptions of death as a "power loose in the house," "lightning," and "a madman loose in the world" (36). The word *loose* crackles with frightening connotations because it is the opposite of rigidly holding yourself "tight" in the "Protestant way" ("A Better Place Than Home," 115). Anything uncontrolled is therefore potentially terrifying.

When the narrator in "Images" returns home, reassured by her father about old Joe and this time sworn to secrecy about their adventure, there is another explicit thematic summary, as in "Walker Brothers Cowboy." The retrospective narrator compares her state of mind, after her visit to old Joe's house, to that of "the children in fairy stories who have seen their parents make pacts with terrifying strangers, [and] who have discovered that our fears are based on nothing but the truth . . ." (43). The two "terrifying strangers" are jolly Mary and crazy old Joe, and although the child's experience with Joe dispels her fear of Mary, the conclusion is ironic. The goggle-eyed little girl feels "dazed and powerful with secrets," and "never" says "a word," as she has promised her father (43). But the real secret, the sexual invasion of the mother's body, that has already taken place without the narrator's knowledge, and the impending birth that has occasioned Mary's invasion of the house—all this is a powerful secret about which the *adults* have never said a word to the child. That is why she remains an innocent eye, observing both sexuality and death from the edge of the adult action. The threatening images are in the center, and the "I" watches.

The child watching death recurs in another story in this first collection, "Boys and Girls." The eleven-year-old first-person narrator and her younger brother, Laird, seem to be the same children as in "Walker Brothers Cowboy." Their father has forbidden them to watch him shoot a horse, but the girl decides that if they hide in the barn they can watch in secret: "It was not something I wanted to see; just the same, if a thing really happened, it was better to see it, and know" (DHS, 121). Like the girl secretly looking in through the window at Uncle Bert and Aunt Thelma in "At the Other Place," the girl here looks out through a knothole in the hayloft wall and watches the forbidden sight, her father shooting the horse, which falls, kicks, quivers, and dies. Although she is a farm child accustomed to the death of animals, this experience leaves her shaky, "ashamed," and guilty, but also suddenly wary of her father, whom she has definitely preferred to her mother until now (124). More significant, however, is the girl's motive in forcing herself to watch this forbidden sight: she wants to know what happens. This desire to control something unpleasant by looking at it from a detached point of observation is very different from the reactions of the earlier characters, the girl in "At the Other Place," who lets herself be dragged away from the window where she has been spying on the adults, and the paralyzed child in "Images," who watches what she believes to be death approaching her father.

This difference is emphasized by the fact that when the father in "Boys and Girls" prepares to shoot another horse, the narrator lets the horse escape. "Instead of shutting the gate, I opened it as wide as I could" (125). The horse is caught and shot anyway, but when the narrator, accused by Laird, admits that she tried to save the horse from its fate, her father does not scold her because "[s]he's only a girl" (127). In analyzing the father's attitude here, Munro has explained that his comment grants her freedom to protest against the brutality of what she has seen, but that this freedom is paradoxically a product of her powerlessness: "if she's a girl, she's allowed to protest. . . . But . . . her protest doesn't count; because she is only a girl, she has no power. And it's the lack of power that gives her the freedom to speak" and gives her "a clarity of vision" ("Name," 71, 72).

Like the narrator at the beginning of "Boys and Girls," Del Jordan, the first-person narrator of *Lives of Girls and Women*, is at first a controlling figure with clear vision because she is only watching, not participating. In the opening story, "The Flats Road," she is still a little girl, ready to begin the fourth grade. When she is attacked by a teenage "madwoman," the mail-order wife of her father's hired hand, Uncle Benny, Del is not frightened by the stove-lid lifter that Madeleine is brandishing (LGW, 27). On the contrary, she is "fascinated." When Madeleine accuses her of "spyin'," in a way she is right, for Del not only wants "to stay and watch it, as if [Madeleine's violent threats] were a show," but she is also intuitively aware of complications of her own attitude in Madeleine. She senses that Madeleine's "calculated, theatrical" violence means that "[s]he was watching herself" (17). Thus, a spying watcher, Del watches a self-watcher, Madeleine, which—as already shown in chapter 2—is the point of view that Munro later uses in "Royal Beatings."

But in "Heirs of the Living Body," the second story, Del's ability to control by clear-eyed watching becomes much more difficult to maintain, for what she watches are revelations of sexuality and death, the powerfully disturbing combination already seen in the two key scenes watched by the child narrator in "At the Other Place" and sensed by the apprehensive child in "Images." Now Del finds herself very ambivalent about what she encounters because seeing is confused and colored by its psychological opposite, *being seen*. As already illustrated by the sideshow metaphor in "The Peace of Utrecht," the sensation of being watched by an audience is intensely disturbing. In "Heirs of the Living Body" Del's self-conscious dread of being watched, of being seen naked and ashamed, shows that she is no longer a child: "Having to be naked . . . , the thought of being naked, stabbed me with shame in the pit of my stomach. Every time I thought of the doctor pulling down my pants and jabbing the needle in my buttocks, . . . I felt outraged, frantic, unbearably, almost exquisitely humiliated" (42). The startlingly unexpected combination of these two adverbs, "unbearably" and "exquisitely," dramatically reveals the sexual fear and the sexual desire roiling together under the concealing surface of Del's ferocious modesty.

Her ambivalence about seeing involves the same confusion. The long story is full of Del's conflicting statements: "I did not want to hear anymore" (39); "I wanted to know" (46); "I was alarmed. . . . I was afraid they would go on and show me something . . ." (49). Del is afraid of learning more secrets about sexuality and death than her young mind can cope with all at once. Her fear finally bursts out at her uncle's funeral when her retarded cousin, Mary Agnes, insists, "You come and—*see*—Uncle Craig" (55). Frantically resisting Mary Agnes's efforts to drag her out of her hiding place and up to the open coffin for the ritual of the "Last Look," Del bites her cousin's arm. By this regressive action, she hopes to avoid seeing what she fears: "nobody would dare ask me to look at a dead man, or anything else, again" (55).

What is "anything else"? It includes not only the corpse of a cow, which Del encounters earlier in the story and which foreshadows the corpse of her uncle, but also what David Stouck labels a comic episode, the description of Aunt Moira's delayed delivery of Mary Agnes and of Aunt Moira's "gynecological odour" (266–67; LGW, 40). The "anything else" that Del does not want to see but cannot avoid seeing goes beyond a vision of death to include a vision of female sexuality from the point of view of a young and nervous adolescent girl. It includes her apprehensiveness about Aunt Moira and her long list of sordid female afflictions, which the older, retrospective narrator "now" rather grimly recognizes as the badges of the "wrecked survivors of the female life" (40). The specific nature of these afflictions is concealed from young Del's conscious knowledge. But just like the earlier narrator in "Images," aware of her mother's pregnant body concealed under the covers, and just like the later narrator in "Miles City, Montana," aware of her parents' horrid secretions concealed under their clothes, Del smells the gloomy "gynecological odour" that exudes from the "dark" layers of Aunt Moira's clothing (40). Because Del can smell the threatening facts she does not know about, she is as apprehensive as an alert young animal, scenting hidden danger. Thus, the comment of her older self here emphasizes her younger self's scared ignorance. And this younger self is already apprehensive about the hidden bloodiness of the birth canal, which her mother has described to her, and which Del then imagines all too vividly for herself, not because she is artistic but simply because she is frightened by her mother's talk about Aunt Moira's hemorrhage during childbirth. Del thinks, "I did not want to hear anymore" (39). She is simply not ready to face all the possible future threats to the integrity of her own body. She contrasts Aunt Moira to her two unmarried aunts, still active, still slender, and still smelling "fresh and healthy," and on the basis of this contrast she wryly concludes, "Not much could be said for marriage really . . ." (40).[3]

And Mrs. Jordan does not limit herself to gory stories about Mary Agnes's birth. She also warns Del about the dangers of sex by telling her the story of how Mary Agnes was stripped naked by five boys and left lying in the mud. Identifying with her in her humiliation, Del imagines "Mary Agnes's body lying exposed . . . , her prickly cold buttocks sticking out—that seemed to me the most shameful, helpless looking part of anybody's body," and concludes, "if it had happened to me, to be seen like that, I could not live afterwards" (42).

The dead cow that Del and Mary Agnes see together and Del's later reaction to Uncle Craig's death introduce the second part of what Del does not want to see, death. These two episodes, seeing the cow and attending the funeral, are closely linked by Munro's repetition of her key metaphor for death in "Images" and in "The Time of Death": the idea of a frightening power loose in the world, a power imagined as fire or electricity. Del looks at the dead cow and feels that "[b]eing dead, it invited desecration. . . . But still it had power . . ." (44). Later, when her mother tells her that her uncle has died, Del bombards her with questions because she seeks some control over her fear of what has happened. Like the narrator of "Boys and Girls," Del says, "I wanted to know. There is no protection, unless it is in knowing. I wanted death pinned down and isolated behind a wall of particular facts and circumstances, not floating around loose, ignored but powerful, waiting to get in anywhere" (46). This dangerously loose power and fire are metaphorically connected when Del visualizes her uncle's fatal heart attack as "an explosion, like fireworks going off, shooting sticks of light in all directions . . ." (46). But later, when her mother tells her that she must attend the funeral, Del has already changed her mind about wanting to know: "I did not want to hear anything more about Uncle Craig, or about death" (46). When her mother insists that she will "have to learn to face things sometime," Del's reluctance to know deepens into a suspicion of her mother, who seems to be rushing her sadistically toward some kind of "pain or obscenity . . ." (47). After Mrs. Jordan optimistically suggests that organ transplants will eventually eliminate the idea of death, Mr. Jordan warns her against expounding her medical predictions at the funeral. Deflated, Mrs. Jordan lets her husband embrace her, and their embrace is something else that Del does not want to see. "I was alarmed. . . . I was afraid that they would go on and show me something I no more wanted to see than I wanted to see Uncle Craig dead" (49). In contrast to the grossly sexual parents at the funeral in "Miles City, Montana," what alarms Del here is not a sexual scene. Her parents sadly clinging together in the face of death, "bewildered" and "grieving," reveal the same adult powerlessness, however, and it is that impotence against death that disturbs their already apprehensively watching daughter (49).

The powerfully synergistic combination of all these emotions makes the word *see* sinister and terrifying to Del when her cousin insists at the funeral, "You come and—*see*—Uncle Craig" (55). Later, forgiven for biting her cousin and excused from seeing her uncle, she is left alone in his office. It is here that the most shattering passage in Munro's fiction occurs, Del's obscene vision of flesh as humiliation.[4] Listening to the hymn-singing in the front room, "full of people pressed together, melted together like blunt old crayons," she feels that she is "in the middle of them, in spite of being shut up . . . by [herself]," but nevertheless she imagines the faithful defining her as "a *borderline case*" (57). In contrast to the teenage girls in the later story, "Circle of Prayer," who are completely outside any traditionally defined Christian circle, Del is on its perimeter. Her temporary mental position on this border makes it possible for her to see her vision, the terrible reality that Christian faith both confronts and denies. In her vision, her sexual dread of being seen naked and of losing physical control—of being excited, perhaps almost to the point of orgasm—is combined with her deep dread of seeing the dangerous power of death:

> Being forgiven creates a peculiar shame. . . . This shame was physical,
> but went far beyond sexual shame, my former shame of nakedness; now
> it was as if not the naked body but all the organs inside it . . . were laid
> bare and helpless. The nearest thing to this that I had ever known before
> was the feeling I got when I was tickled beyond endurance—horrible,
> voluptuous feeling of exposure, of impotence, self-betrayal. And shame
> went spreading out from me all through the house, covered everybody,
> even Mary Agnes, even Uncle Craig in his present disposable, vacated
> condition. To be made of flesh was humiliation. I was caught in a vision
> . . . of confusion and obscenity—of helplessness, . . . the most obscene
> thing there could be. (57–58)

The combination of these two kind of helplessness, sexual helplessness and the complete helplessness of death, is the same combination
that horrifies the more innocent narrator in "At the Other Place." Here
the repetition of the words *helpless* and *helplessness* imbues them with
multiple connotations. First, they emphasize Del's fear of the "horrible,
voluptuous feeling of exposure" and "impotence" that she associates
so far only with being "tickled beyond endurance." Although she refers
to the "sexual shame" of nakedness, she does not consciously recognize
these feelings of helpless "self-betrayal" as specifically sexual, but they
clearly suggest looseness, not in the moral sense, but in the sense of
being the opposite of tight self-control. The connotations of helplessness
also include Aunt Moira's heaving female flesh, hemorrhaging in
childbirth; the naked Mary Agnes and the dead cow, both lying exposed
in the mud; the grieving Jordans; and the ultimate helplessness of Uncle
Craig lying silently in his coffin, exposed to everyone's gaze. After her
terrible vision, when Del finally forces herself to look at him, she is
once again acutely aware of the loose electric power that she has imagined before. Touching his corpse, she feels, would be like touching "a
live wire. Uncle Craig . . . was the terrible, silent, indifferent conductor
of forces that could flare up, in an instant, and burn through this room,
all reality, leave us dark. I turned away with humming in my ears . . . ."
(59). This is the same wire that the adult narrator in "Miles City, Montana" touches for a moment in her guilty imagination.

Munro's image of death as electric power flaring through the darkness
and humming in the terrified observer's ears links this Del not only
with the child Del in "Images," "electrified against the dark noon sky,"
but also with the slightly older Del stubbornly searching for knowledge
of God in "Age of Faith" (DHS, 38). Against her mother's wishes, Del
starts to attend church to try to discover God, and thus to belong to a
group made safe and cohesive by its faith. Here again, therefore, her
motive is to know and, through knowing, to achieve some kind of

control over this frighteningly loose power. "If God could be discovered," she thinks, "everything would be safe." The "world could be borne . . . if all those atoms, galaxies of atoms, were safe all the time, whirling away in God's mind," instead of "floating loose on that howling hopeless dark" (LGW, 100, 101). But instead of finding some safe anchor for this frightening looseness, at the end of this story she wonders, in something close to terror, if God could be *alien and unacceptable as death? Could there be God amazing, indifferent, beyond faith?"* (115).

Although there is no answer to Del's frightened question in the novel, Munro has explicitly linked her character's sense of flesh as humiliation to the purpose of her own writing. Interviewing Munro, Graeme Gibson carefully distinguished between Munro's "desire to write and what motivates" Del, her character, but he then suggested that perhaps Del's "need to do something remarkable has something to do with [Del's] sense of humiliation" ("Alice Munro," 243). Munro blurred Gibson's distinction by agreeing that her own writing "has something to do with the fight against death, the feeling that we lose everything every day, and writing is a way of convincing yourself perhaps that you're doing something about this. You're not really, because the writing itself does not last much longer than you do; but I would say it's partly the feeling that I can't stand to have things go" ("Alice Munro," 243). This feeling is directly reflected in the lists that Del makes in the Epilogue of her novel—lists of buildings, families, names, streets, physical sensations, "every last thing," in her "crazy, heartbreaking" greediness to try to make everything "everlasting" (LGW, 253). Munro's reply to Gibson's perceptive question and Del's list both show how closely Del's struggle to control a frighteningly loose power embodies one of Munro's own purposes in writing.[5]

The metaphors of fire and electric power associated with the fleshly humiliation of death in the stories discussed thus far in this chapter are also repeatedly associated with sexual experience in "Lives of Girls and Women," the title story of the novel, and in "Baptizing," its climax. But in these two later stories, Del's attitude toward nakedness and sexuality paradoxically changes from one of dreading humiliation to its diametrical opposite. Her initial ambivalence resolves itself in a powerful desire to see nakedness and to be seen naked, to "know" and be known in the biblical sense. But the satisfying fulfillment of this desire unexpectedly leads to a second and even more disturbing ambivalence about the frightening power of sexuality, something that Del sensed only dimly in her vision of helpless humiliation at the funeral. These changing feelings are clarified in the stages of Del's relationships with three male characters: Mr. Chamberlain in "Lives of Girls and Women," and Jerry Storey and Garnet French in "Baptizing." In the climactic scene in "Baptizing," sexuality and death are finally almost fused in the symbolic threat of drowning.

In "Lives of Girls and Women," Del's adolescent sexual fantasies about Art Chamberlain, the handsome but already gray-haired and middle-aged radio announcer in Jubilee, can be fully understood only if they are linked with her key experiences in "Heirs of the Living Body." One of these experiences is with the dead cow. First, when Del starts poking at its corpse with a stick, she simultaneously wants to destroy it and understand it, for it represents a powerful fact with which she has to come to terms. Resisting her impulse "to punish it, to show what contempt [she] had for its being dead," she begins to dig "the stick in, trying to make a definite line" around a spot on the cow's hide, and paying "attention to its shape as [she] would sometimes pay attention to the shape of . . . continents or islands on . . . maps, as if the shape itself were a revelation beyond words, and [she] would be able to make sense of it, if [she] tried hard enough, and had time" (44, 45). When Mary Agnes calmly lays her hand over the cow's fly-infested eye, Del is both frightened and astonished by her totally unexpected discovery of the real Mary Agnes that other people are unaware of, people who speak of the retarded girl "as if she had no secrets . . . of her own . . ." (45). Mary Agnes's secret here is her ability to touch the cow's eye and through her touch to comprehend its shape, the key to its "revelation beyond words" (45).

Fascinated by words, Del is a great reader, but Munro also stresses the significance of shape as a key to *nonverbal*, tactile comprehension. She does this by developing Del's obsession with the hidden shape of the male genitalia. In describing a "Laocoön inkwell," Del is disappointed by "the serpent so cunningly draped around the three male figures that" it is impossible to "discover whether there were or were not marble genitals underneath" (93). Later, poring over a sex manual with Naomi, her friend and foil, Del reads about the erect size of "the male organ" (148); the two girls then invent a game of using wet chewing gum to shape what they imagine, a game that becomes especially exciting when, with coy prurience, they play it in Mr. Chamberlain's unsuspecting presence. But when Mrs. Jordan shows him a photograph of Michelangelo's David—Mr. Chamberlain has been in Florence as a soldier and Mrs. Jordan is envious—Del feels condescendingly superior to her mother. "A naked man. His marble thing hanging on him for everybody to look at; like a drooping lily petal. Who but my mother . . . would show a man, would show us all, a picture like that?" (151–52). With deft dramatic irony, Munro shows that it never occurs to Del that the statue might have something else worth looking at besides the focal point of her own feverishly obsessed attention.

When Del's imagination is further inflamed by Mr. Chamberlain's reminiscences about the Italian girls who were offered to the conquering soldiers in World War II, Munro conveys her narrator's erotic excitement through the same electric metaphors that described the power of death at Uncle Craig's funeral, the second key experience in "Heirs of the Living Body." Fantasizing about Mr. Chamberlain seeing her naked, Del imagines "[t]he moment" as "a stab of light," and Mr. Chamberlain as "powerful, humming away electrically like a blue fluorescent light" (155). To solidify this exciting fantasy, she encourages the all-too-willing Mr. Chamberlain to make passes at her. These, too, are charged with electricity: "He went straight for the breasts, the buttocks, the upper thighs, brutal as lightning. And this was what I expected sexual communication to be—a flash of insanity, a dreamlike, ruthless, contemptuous breakthrough in a world of decent appearances" (162). She expects "one stroke of lightning" to be succeeded "by the next stroke of lightning" (162–63).

In this state of electrified anticipation, very similar to the terrified anticipation of the child in "Images," "electrified . . . with blazing hair" and "hop[ing] for . . . the worst," Del accepts her first ride in Mr. Chamberlain's car (DHS, 30). So excited and so terrified that she can "hardly speak," she, too, avidly hopes for the worst. "Was this what desire was? Wish to know, fear to know, amounting to anguish?" (LGW, 163). This explicitly defined ambivalence is the same confusing mixture of violent anxiety as in "Heirs of the Living Body," but now it is focused upon knowing about sex. This first ride is a disappointment, however, for Mr. Chamberlain merely asks Del to search the room of Fern, her mother's boarder, for incriminating letters from him. In her search Del finds and reads pornographic verses, and in her reaction to this material, the metaphor of dangerous electricity recurs: "the words themselves . . . gave off flashes of power, particularly *fuck*, which I had never been able to really look at, on fences or sidewalks" (167).

At the end of her second ride with Mr. Chamberlain, Del is partially disappointed again, but for a different reason. Instead of making love to her, he masturbates in front of her. In this scene both Mr. Chamberlain and Del become voyeurs of a sexual act metaphorically equated with the performance of a play. Mr. Chamberlain is not only the actor in this perverted drama but also one member of the audience, watching the other member, Del, watch him. Like Madeleine brandishing the stove-lid lifter, he is acutely aware of his double role as both participant and observer. His first role, as the participating actor, is defined by the way he doubly exposes himself. He reaches into his unzipped pants "to part some inner curtains" and thrust forward his erect organ; then he "thrust[s] out" his excited face, "wobbling like a mask on a stick" (169,

170). Much of his excitement, however, derives from his second role, as the observer of Del's reaction to his "theatrical . . . performance" (170). He displays his penis with a "tightly watching look," and then, "[s]till watching" her, begins to masturbate. In his escalating excitement, "his eyes" are "still fixed on" her (169–70). As his audience, watching him watching her, Del is not excited, but she is not completely disappointed either. Now she knows one aspect of what she has been eager to know, the shape of the male organ.

Her coldly clinical description of Mr. Chamberlain's penis defines its shape in a series of pejorative visual similes:

> Not at all like marble David's, it was sticking straight out in front of him. . . . It had a sort of head on it, like a mushroom. . . . It looked blunt and stupid, compared, say, to fingers and toes with their intelligent expressiveness. . . . Raw and blunt, ugly-coloured as a wound, it looked . . . like some strong snouted animal. . . .. It did not bring back any of my excitement, though. It did not seem to have anything to do with me. (169–70)

Not a work of art like David's, but a vegetable, a wound, and an animal, Mr. Chamberlain's penis has nothing to do with Del because his onanism limits her to the touchless watching of a voyeur. Therefore, the expected lightning has not struck.

But her attempt to control this visual experience is significantly incomplete until she can verbalize it, not only for herself but for somebody else. Naomi has become so self-absorbed that she is no longer interested in Mr. Chamberlain. "So," Del remarks, "I had not the relief of making what Mr. Chamberlain had done into a funny, though horrifying, story. I did not know what to do with it" (173–74). But in "Baptizing," when Naomi and Del are once again exchanging intimate confidences, Del tells her about the masturbation episode.[6] "I was rewarded with her pounding the bed with her fist, laughing and saying, 'Jesus, I never yet saw anybody do that!'" (235). The contrast between Del's two remarks is the difference between frustration and relief, but the relief comes not primarily from the reward of Naomi's laughter but, much more importantly, from Del's achievement of verbal control. Although Naomi's response does not cancel out Del's disappointing discovery that in Mr. Chamberlain's case "flesh . . . has to be thumped into ecstasy," it does help her "to do" something with "the stubborn puzzle and dark turns" that his perversity has exposed to her (174). She does what Munro herself has done: she makes a story out of it to control both her own confusion and Mr. Chamberlain's "powerful" electric "humming," just as the story of Uncle Craig's death controls the "humming" in Del's ears as she turns away from the power of his open casket (155, 59).

In "Baptizing," Del's interest shifts from voyeurism, from seeing naked men, to actually being seen naked herself, not just fantasizing about it. She has already confided, "I liked looking . . . at myself naked in the glass" (185). So when Jerry Storey, her curious classmate, suggests that it would be "educational" for him to see "a real live naked woman," she strips with alacrity. "The words 'naked woman' were secretly pleasing to me, making me feel opulent, a dispenser of treasure. Also, I thought my body handsomer than my face, and handsomer naked than clothed; I had often wished to show it off to somebody" (203). In her physical self-confidence, Del is like the first-person narrator of Munro's later story, "How I Met My Husband," a teenage girl who innocently admits, "I . . . admired myself naked . . ." (SIB, 49). These two images of girls watching their naked bodies in mirrors foreshadow later scenes in Munro's fiction in which much older characters imagine seeing photographic images of themselves naked in bed with a man.

Stretched out on Jerry's bed, Del feels "absurd and dazzling," but this episode fizzles out in a comic anticlimax when Jerry's mother unexpectedly returns home (LGW, 204). His inexperience and his mother's arrival limit Jerry to the role of voyeur that Del plays with Mr. Chamberlain. But, as when Del tells Naomi about the masturbation scene, Del and Jerry escape humiliation through humor. Although Jerry is embarrassed and Del is furious when he locks her naked in the cellar to avoid meeting Mrs. Storey, by the next day the two of them can convert their mutual humiliation into a funny play: "after school we transformed the night before into a Great Comic Scene, something jerky and insane from a silent movie," complete with dialogue in a fake English accent (206). Though "humiliated by the disguise of high-school sweethearts" forced upon them by their contemptuous classmates, Del recalls, "we found that the way to survive the situation was to make fun of it. Parody, self-mockery were our salvation" (197). By defusing this second situation in the same way, their self-deprecatory clowning controls their humiliation.

But when Del meets Garnet French, the salvation of control through humor is no longer available to her because, in acquiring the exciting new revelation of touch, "the revelation beyond words," she loses the power of words (45). In this climactic section of "Baptizing," Del completely loses control for a while, although she naively imagines that she is doing just the opposite. When she finally regains control, she does so only at a great cost to part of herself, a cost that once again clearly shows the close connection between the double humiliations of the flesh, sexuality and death. The cost that Del pays shows how using the language and maintaining the attitude of the writer are a way of achieving—or trying to achieve—emotional control. This key thematic pattern of struggling for control recurs in many later stories of women ambivalent about love.

A full understanding of Del's loss of control in "Baptizing" depends upon recognizing Munro's repeated association of the Del-Garnet love story with the love story in *Carmen*. Just as the title story of her first collection, "Dance of the Happy Shades," alludes to Gluck's opera *Orpheus and Eurydice*, so "Baptizing" alludes to Bizet's *Carmen*. In "Lives of Girls and Women," Del refers to her mother's habit of listening to Saturday-afternoon Metropolitan Opera broadcasts on the radio. In "Baptizing" she describes her own reactions to hearing *Carmen:* "I loved most of all *Carmen*, at the end. *Et laissez-moi passer!* I hissed it between my teeth; I was shaken, imagining the other surrender, more tempting, more gorgeous even than the surrender to sex . . . Carmen's surrender to the final importance of gesture, image, self-created self" (184). That Carmen dies to maintain that proudly independent self foreshadows the climax of "Baptizing," when Del, struggling with Garnet underwater, says, "I thought that I was fighting for my life" (239).

At the end of "Lives," Del's mother predicts "a change coming . . . in the lives of girls and women," but she warns Del not to be "distracted" by a man and to maintain her "self-respect" (176). In describing her fascination with Carmen's proud adamance, Del once again speaks with dramatic irony, for she is unaware that she is echoing her mother's advice about self-respect. But there is a complicated, *double* irony at work here: neither Del nor her mother knows what she is talking about and for essentially the same reason. Full of "virginal brusqueness" and "innocence," her mother ignores the power of sex by rejecting it (181). Del, as her older, retrospective self recognizes at the end of "Lives of Girls and Women," is also quite ignorant. She is very naive about her own sexuality, but like all adolescent girls defiantly determined to disagree with her mother. "I was set up to resist . . . . anything she told me with such earnestness, such stubborn hopefulness" (177). Her resulting determination to behave like a man, "to go out and take on all kinds of experiences and shuck off what [she doesn't] want and come back proud," cannot be taken at face value (177); rather, it is a prime example of Munro's definition of her fiction as dealing with "[w]hat we think is happening and what we understand later on . . ." ("Interview": Hancock, 90). In the next sentence the retrospective narrator warns that her younger self's determination to behave like a man is to be read as dramatic irony: "Without even thinking about it, I had decided to do the same" (LGW, 177). Del's lack of thought is not proof of how right she is but proof of her naive ignorance. She can't think about it because she does not know anything about it. Mr. Chamberlain and Jerry have not introduced her to passion. Her affair with Garnet therefore serves to dramatize her ironically stubborn adolescent resistance to her mother's advice and significantly reverses the sexual roles in *Carmen*. This reversal continues until the climactic river scene and emphasizes the power of passionate sex as Del comes to experience it. The narrating adult Del is fully aware of this power, but her younger self at this point is virginal both in body and, much more importantly, in mind.

In the opera, Carmen, the fiery and beautiful gypsy, initiates Don José into sexual passion. But in Munro's story, Garnet is the dark and erotic gypsy who initiates Del into the sexual mysteries of shape and touch. The two gypsy characters' names have similar connotations: Carmen suggests carmine, a vivid crimson or scarlet; the most common variety of garnet is a dark red stone. These hot colors connote the sexual desire that Del has already experienced as that "heat and dancing itch between [her] legs" (169). The identification of Garnet as the gypsy and the link between him and the opera occur when Del first sees Garnet at a revival meeting. Instantly certain that he will come to stand beside her, she mockingly compares her certainty to "a recognition in an opera" (211). Then the congregation sings a hymn about *"a gypsy boy,"* a description that fits Garnet's "dark-skinned" appearance and "grave, unconsciously arrogant expression" (211). Before they exchange a single word, they touch. His arm grazes her shoulder "like fire," and when he takes her hand, she feels "angelic with gratitude" and immediately elevated to "another level of existence" (211, 213). In spite of her initial self-mockery, Del thus falls into the same mental pattern that the retrospective narrator has already called to the reader's attention at the beginning of the story. After reading an article about how a woman projects her *"own experience"* into *"works of art,"* Del was indignant, but this indignation becomes dramatic irony when she later identifies with Carmen and hisses her words (181). The older narrator comments, "It never occurred to me that I was doing what the article said women did, with works of art" (184).[7]

Del falls in love with the "dark side, the strange side" of Garnet, with "the life of his instincts," just as Don José falls in love with the dark and instinctual Carmen (220, 221). Although Garnet, like Carmen, has been arrested and jailed for fighting, Del, like José, falls in love against her better judgment, overcome by the feverishly intense delights of physical pleasure. To dramatize these, Munro once again uses the same metaphors of fire and power. Learning love with Garnet, Del feels that she possesses "unlimited power" and redefines the word *pleasure* as "explosive, . . . spurting up like fireworks . . ." (218). Like José, who deserts from the army to live with Carmen, Del soon deserts her duty of studying for the examinations that she hopes will win her a university scholarship. Initially she recognizes Garnet's hate-filled hostility to the "big words" and ideas that have given her the power to control the experiences of her life (220). But gradually his attitude becomes contagious.

Just as Don José moves up into the mountains to live with the gypsy smugglers, so Del moves into Garnet's world, where she soon finds herself unable to study, to "put one word after another," or even to read billboards (221). She follows him into a world of the body where "words" are their "enemies," an animal "world without names" (221). When he takes her home to meet his huge, backwoods family, he introduces her to nobody, and "they never [call her] by [her] name at all" (222). After their lovemaking is finally consummated, Del finds herself unable to concentrate on writing her examinations. An English literature question seems "nonsensical, oblique, baleful as some sentence [in] a dream" (228). Overcome by "a radiant sense of importance, physical grandeur," she languidly floats in her own wordless dream, in which her lover's power transforms even the streets that he travels into "bright wires" (228, 229). Lightning finally strikes when, thoroughly acquainted with her body through masturbation, she reaches orgasm with Garnet. But, although she is "amazed" by their shared "seizures"—a word suggestive of electrocution—they "never" speak "a word, to each other, about any of this" (229, 230).

The complete wordlessness of the sensual world into which Garnet pulls Del underscores the dramatic irony of her belief that she now possesses unlimited power. In fact she is losing the power to control her life, because, as her experiences with both Mr. Chamberlain and Jerry have shown, her power depends upon her ability to manipulate language as a detached observer. Her loss of this power is so complete that, when her mother reads course descriptions to her from a university catalogue, Del, "frightened" by the "damp" sexual smell of her body, cannot comprehend the words. First reading, then writing, and finally even hearing words become impossible in this escalating aphasia of sexual love. "Such words," Del thinks, "would not stay in my head. I had to think, instead, of the dark . . . hairs on Garnet's forearms . . ." (231). In a brief passage in which Del describes herself in the third person, she continues to focus on her intensely physical sensations: semen running down her legs and enormous sexual lassitude at noon. In this sensual excitement Del has lost her detachment. She never describes Garnet's sex organ at all, and certainly not in the detached way in which she described Mr. Chamberlain's. Instead, she describes her lover's powerful sexual effect on her, and this obsessed sensuality renders impossible the writer-observer's separation from experience. As every woman reader recognizes, if Del were monitoring her own responses, she could not be orgasmic. She is not looking at Garnet's body or at her own because she is totally inside her body and immersed in its fusion with her lover's. Shape and touch, therefore, have become everything.

But then two closely related events rupture her complete absorption in her physical experience. First, Del learns that Naomi has to get married because she is pregnant. Munro has defined Naomi's function as a "tough" foil character representing the "adjustment made by the female in these communities, the female who can't get out, who doesn't have whatever Del's [advantage] is, and who will live in that community all her life . . ." (Untitled, 180). In contrast, Del does intend to get out: under pressure from her mother, Del has angrily admitted that she does not want to live in Jubilee all her life. But, although she envisions a broader future for herself, she pays no more attention to her mother's sensible advice than Don José does to his mother's.

The second rupturing event reveals not only the significant difference between Garnet's sexual experience and Del's but also the basic difference between the male and female biological roles. Noting how swiftly Garnet recovers his strength after orgasm, Del thinks, "How quickly he came back, after crying out the way he did, and turning his eyes up and throbbing all over and sinking into me like a shot gull!" (LGW, 236). The two have gone for a postcoital swim, and Del, unlike her resilient lover, still feels "weak from making love, . . . warm and lazy, like a big cabbage spreading, . . . big cabbage leaves loosening and spreading on the ground" (236–37). Because she has been thinking about Naomi's pregnancy, she answers, "Yes," when Garnet asks her whether she would like to have a baby (236). Immediately afterwards, however, she thinks, "Where would such a lie come from? It was not a lie" (237). To emphasize the mounting tension between Del's conflicting impulses, Munro thus combines Del's thoughts about Naomi's pregnancy, her sudden awareness of Garnet's swift recovery after sex, and her confusion about whether she, too, wants to be pregnant.

Munro has also discussed the reasons for Del's intense ambivalence in this scene. She has pointed out the paradox that Del is "responding to" Garnet and her own instinctively powerful sexual desires but, at the same time, struggling to escape from them. Although Munro defines herself as "intellectually a great supporter of the women's movement," she emphasizes that intellectual support is one thing and "the thing of responding to men is something else . . . something else is going on . . . ." Thus, although Del "in the baptizing scene . . . . works against the promptings of her body and gets out, . . . it's very difficult for women to make this choice" ("Name," 43). The reason for this difficulty is inherent in Del's definition of sexual intercourse as "all surrender—not the woman's to the man but the person's to the body . . . " (LGW, 218). This distinction emphasizes that Del's struggle is not only against Garnet but also against *herself;* part of her prompts her to "knuckle under" to him in his "struggle . . . to dominate" her ("Name," 43). Until the baptizing scene, until she realizes what surrendering to her body would actually mean, she floats, "like somebody suspended in clear and warm and irresistibly moving water . . ." (LGW, 219). But when she does realize it, the deliciously languid "floating" metaphor suddenly changes (218). In the climactic scene of the story, she is threatened by drowning.

At this crucial turning point in the action, the sexual roles in "Baptizing" become what they are in *Carmen:* Garnet is now Don José and Del, Carmen. When Garnet tries to persuade Del to be baptized in his church and she keeps refusing, they are replaying the last scene of her favorite opera. Garnet is like Don José pleading with the faithless Carmen to return to him. Just as Don José becomes increasingly desperate and furious, Garnet's verbal attempts at persuasion escalate into physical force as he repeatedly pushes Del underwater. And just as Carmen proudly resists Don José's attempts to force her to return to him, Del resists Garnet. Like Carmen, she will buy her freedom at any price. Like Don José, Garnet is "broken by rage, a helpless sense of insult" (238). In his rage the proud Spaniard finally murders Carmen, and Del is convinced that, like Carmen, she, too, is "fighting for" her "life," not only in the literal physical sense but also in the sense of her "self-created self" (239, 184).

During her symbolic underwater struggle with Garnet, Del compares their love affair to a dreamlike "game that required you to be buried alive. I fought underwater exactly as you would fight in such a dream, with a feeling of desperation . . . that had to work upward through layers of incredulity" (239). What Del finds incredible is Garnet's mistaken conviction that he possesses power over her: "it seemed to me impossible that he should not understand that all the powers I granted him were in play . . ." (238). Although Del *has* been projecting her life into a play, the plot of *Carmen,* at the same time she feels that the opera has almost turned into her life.

Through the desperate intensity of Del's struggle in this scene, Munro dramatizes what some readers—along with Del's mother—are reluctant to recognize, the enormous power of passionate sexuality.[8] In an interview, Munro has defined Addie Jordan as "an old-fashioned feminist" and has insisted on the naive limitations of her inexperienced attitude:

> You know that line "there's a change coming in the lives of girls and women." I meant that to be ironic because the changes I think Addie [Jordan] sees as possible and the whole situation as she sees it is touchingly

oversimplified. . . . For instance, she totally disregards sexual passion. It's just something you forget about and it will go away. . . . She thinks the whole dark side of nature can be easily dealt with. *I meant that language that people have taken so seriously to be sort of sad and funny.*

I didn't mean to make fun of her. But I meant her vision to be quite inadequate. ("Interview": Hancock, 103; emphasis added)

Although Munro very realistically deglamorizes Del's first act of complete intercourse, by no means does she debunk the dark power of passionate sexuality.[9] If she did, she would not bring Del's love affair to a climax by using the same metaphors of fire and electricity to represent both the power of sexuality and of death. If she did, she would not develop this climax through dramatic allusions to *Carmen*, where the two powers of sex and death are symbolically fused when Don José, with a phallic dagger, murders Carmen to possess her. If she did, there would be no ambivalence, conflict, or loss for Munro's struggling Carmen. And, most importantly, this pattern of suffering loss and struggling for controlling power would not keep recurring in Munro's many stories of highly ambivalent and often masochistic women in love affairs and marriages. When Del says, "I thought that he might drown me," she is describing much more than the underwater fight (239). She is also describing her total immersion in the world of shape and touch, her drowning in a wordless sea of sexuality. Such symbolic drowning is echoed in Munro's metaphorical definition of "[s]ex and obsessive love" as "a kind of throwing yourself into something larger" ("Writing's," E1).

In the Epilogue to the novel, in a number of Munro's later stories, and in her novella, this symbolic idea of drowning significantly reappears. Some of the characters in these later works recognize what the retrospective narrator of "Baptizing" knows the two angry young lovers fail to see—that reality, unlike opera, rarely possesses "absolute seriousness and finality," especially when it comes to lovers' quarrels (LGW, 240). But because anxious adult women, unlike adolescent girls or operatic heroines, hang on to justify their behavior, their confusing humiliations in many later stories, especially in *The Moons of Jupiter*, are often much more self-destructively protracted than Del's. Munro ascribes her fascination with these women to "fear" of how easy it is to succumb to such "awful" self-destruction ("Writing's," E1).

But, as the living Carmen, Del triumphantly rediscovers her "old devious, ironic, isolated self" (LGW, 240). Though still suffering from the painful loss of her lover, she reenters the world "uncoloured by love" in which she can control her emotions and try to plan her future. Just like the narrator of Munro's earlier story, "An Ounce of Cure," she announces, "I repossessed the world" (240). By using words to do so, she is once again able to split herself in two to distance herself from her experience. This split is visually objectified by the reflection of her crying face in a mirror: "I observed myself; I was amazed to think that the person suffering was me, for it was not me at all; I was watching. I was watching, I was suffering" (241). But this split into subject and object, introduced and emphasized by Del's recognition of her paradoxical position, "I was free and I was not free," rules out an oversimplified feminist reading of the novel's conclusion (241). In contrast to Addie's old-fashioned feminism, contemporary feminists argue either that Del's "experience . . . has disproved that old romantic plot of woman's transformation through sex" or that it has rewritten that plot in a triumphantly self-assertive way (Howells, 84). For example, by "claim[ing] the right to passion for herself," Del has "free[d] her body from . . . symbols that would divide her into parts" and thus "[found] a new wholeness" (Godard, 65, 66). On the contrary, however, by detaching herself from her dangerously transforming sexual experience, Del deliberately divides herself into two parts to regain the wholeness that she has almost lost. Thus, "watching [herself] still," she starts reading want ads to look for a job and makes herself "understand what [she is] reading," an impossible activity while she was still immersed in Garnet's wordless world of the flesh (LGW, 242).

In the Epilogue the split between Del's two parts, the participant who has been experiencing the action of the novel and the observing, retrospective first-person narrator who has been commenting upon her "self-created self," paradoxically both widens and closes (184). Conscious now that her efforts to win a scholarship have been "sabotaged by love," Del is busily planning her novel; thus she actively substitutes fiction-writing for examination-writing (249). In this projected novel she plans to have two main characters, Caroline and The Photographer. Each of these characters, however, is really one aspect of her split self, eager to love and to write.

The character of Caroline is ostensibly a melodramatic metamorphosis of a girl Del had actually known, Marion Sherriff, who, like Elinor Farris, Del's music teacher, drowned herself in the Wawanash River. But it is significant that Marion committed suicide at the age of seventeen, the same age at which Del fights against Garnet's attempt to drown her in the Wawanash, both literally and symbolically. According to rumor, Marion killed herself because she was pregnant, but this is not the most important reason that Del decides to make her character, Caroline, pregnant by The Photographer. As noted in chapter 1, The Photographer metaphorically represents the kind of writer that Del eventually becomes, a writer whose greedily watching eyes see more than the surface reality of the townspeople that he photographs. Instead of being frightened by his penetrating perception, as the other townspeople are, Caroline stubbornly pursues him and offers herself to him "with straining eagerness and hope and cries" (247). He impregnates her, but, when he leaves town and abandons her, she drowns herself. Imagining this plot, Del thinks, "The reasons for things happening I seemed vaguely to know, but could not explain . . . " (248). In an interview Munro has emphasized how "tricky" it is "to write about writers" and, in particular, "about the idea of the novel that [Del has] in her head" in the Epilogue ("Real Material," 26). Although Del eventually rejects this unwritten novel as an "unreliable structure," "the reasons" she "vaguely" senses for the way her plot develops are that the two characters have a double function for her (LGW, 251, 248). Caroline is the participant, and The Photographer is the observer.

On the simplest, literal level, Caroline's eagerness to give herself to The Photographer is the equivalent of Del's eagerness to participate in love and sexual experience. But if Del settled for such experience and nothing more, she, too, would drown herself in the sense of submitting to the side of her that wants to be dominated by Garnet. Such submission, like Miss Farris's suicide, would be the suicide of the artist. Just as putting on the annual school "operetta was [Miss Farris's] passion," so Del's passion is to be a writer, not a participant but an observer (123). Thus, Del is—or at least she very much wants to be—not only Caroline but The Photographer, too. On a second, symbolic level, therefore, the imaginary sexual union of these two characters, for which Caroline is so hopefully eager, closes the gap between Del's participating and observing selves: the girl eager to love and the writer are joined. Del wants love, *and* she wants to be a writer; but, as she complains in "Baptizing," "I felt trapped, stranded; it seemed there had to be a choice where there couldn't be a choice" (181).

Commenting on this crucially difficult choice between love and writing, Munro has expressed her conviction that "a constant state of emotion would be hostile to the writing state," for "[i]f you're a writer, probably there's something in you that makes you value your self, your own objectivity, so much that you can't stand to be under the sway of another person" ("What Is," 19). Insisting on her "essential self," she says "*I* could never lose [that] in total erotic . . . obsession" ("Visit," 13). But she admits that women can fall under another person's sway not only in a love affair but also in a "traditional marriage." A married woman, she believes, "abdicates" because "she is no longer a completely unbiased observer. She has something to defend, ... truths that she sees that she would prefer not to see; that she can't see if she wants to maintain her situation and a writer . . . has to be free of shackles of this sort" ("Conversation," 59). Thus, the woman under a lover's or a husband's sway may lose her essential self and become a kind of prisoner, a subjective participant immersed in her situation instead of a detached observer controlling it.

Before considering the many Munro protagonists struggling for such controlling power, not only against others but also against their own abdicating and ambivalent selves, it is important to note that the key literary questions raised in the Epilogue of *Lives of Girls and Women* are developed and answered much more fully in a later, uncollected story, "The Ferguson Girls Must Never Marry," published in *Grand Street* in 1982.

A very long story, a novel compressed into short story form, as Munro recognized while she was writing it, "The Ferguson Girls" is in several ways very similar to "Epilogue: The Photographer."[10] In both stories the central character is planning a novel that she does not finish and puts away. Del begins and abandons her novel the summer after her last year in high school. Bonnie Ferguson, a television scriptwriter and the protagonist of "The Ferguson Girls," keeps "on a closet shelf . . . the manuscript of a novel she had begun over twenty years ago, and abandoned after about forty pages" (36–37).[11] Since Bonnie is now the mother of a twenty-four-year-old daughter, she, like Del, must have been an adolescent novelist. Both of these aborted adolescent novels are about a family and the house they live in. In addition to The Photographer and Caroline, Del's "black fable" is about the insanity in the Sherriff family (LGW, 248). Bonnie's story of "black magic" is about the "mysterious decline" of the Braddock family ("Ferguson Girls, 43, 37). Del imagines the Sherriffs as residing in a mysterious house that "isolated them, splendidly, doomed them to fiction" (LGW, 244). Similarly, Bonnie's manuscript concentrates on detailed descriptions of the "Braddock house . . . in its last days of neglect and decay," a house that Bonnie feels "was possessed by demons. . . " ("Ferguson Girls," 37, 42). Del abandons her manuscript because she recognizes, during a conversation with Bobby Sherriff as he politely serves her refreshments on his perfectly ordinary porch, that she has exaggerated and distorted the stubbornly complicated reality of the Sherriff family and their home. Bonnie experiences a similar enlightenment, but the meeting that corrects her misconception of one of her central male characters occurs nearly twenty years after she has put away her manuscript. Munro is interested in how "you meet people who were a certain kind of character . . . years ago and they're someone completely different today" ("Interview": Hancock, 89). She not only makes her protagonist, Bonnie, discover such a change in Ted Braddock, her dead sister Nola's husband, but shapes this discovery into a self-reflexive story in which Bonnie's unfulfilled expectations about the ending of her novel also become the reader's.

At he beginning of the story, Nola Ferguson Braddock dies suddenly of the heart disease that seems to run in the family. On the night before Nola's funeral, the assembled characters' dialogue functions to summarize parts of the plot of Bonnie's unfinished novel. The reader thus learns that Ted Braddock grew up with the humiliation of the failure of his family's furniture business. At one time the Braddocks were so poor that "[t]hey sent Ted out to beg for their supper," going from "[d]oor to door" ("Ferguson Girls," 40). Later Ted and Nola were high school sweethearts who, everybody assumed, could never marry because Ted was a Catholic and Nola, an Anglican. Because of this impediment to their union, the young lovers were surrounded by "a melancholy glamour" (49). But after the death of Ted's first wife, Nola and he were married "in the porch" of a Catholic church (50); the location is significant, for neither converted. Ted then devoted his life to restoring the family business, "Braddocks Heritage Reproductions," in which non-unionized workmen produce fake antiques (55). With his profits, Ted built a "baronial hall," as white and icy as "an igloo," in which he and his wife slept in separate rooms and never had any children (61, 43). The seigneurial connotations of this huge "hall" foreshadow the dramatic changes that Bonnie confronts at the funeral.

Arriving at Devlin, her hometown, for the funeral, Bonnie is surprised to discover that the "pale, proud boy" she romantically recalls from high school has become a "thick, and flushed, and hard, and amiable man" (61). This physical metamorphosis sets the stage for the psychological one revealed by the climax of the funeral. Like Ted's conduct in "Accident," this Ted's "implacable" behavior at the funeral suddenly reveals his true personality (57). To the horrified surprise of Nola's family, Ted has his staunchly Anglican wife buried in a Catholic cemetery by a priest. During the funeral Ted looks "a hundred times more in charge of things than the priest" does (57). Initially Bonnie tries to console herself by arguing that she does not care because "a corpse is nothing but a bag of bones . . ."; therefore, "what is done" with it does not "matter" (60). She does not plan to confront Ted, but after the funeral, when she returns to the Braddock home and sees his "look of heat and danger, . . . under terrible control," she suddenly demands an explanation: "Did Nola ever tell you she wanted to be buried there?" Ted replies that she had not, but insists, "I did it to save her soul" (63). This arrogant answer shows the shocked Bonnie that her novel's romanticized conception of Ted's character was a complete distortion of the man he had become. Like Eileen after her nephew's funeral in "Memorial," Bonnie angrily rejects the pious words that Ted is mouthing to exert control over the situation. She cannot think of "impossible" words like *soul*, *heaven*, and *redemption* without mental gagging. She feels them "stuck in her mind like little chunks of bone that couldn't be digested or got rid of" (63). But here again, as in "Memorial," the reader is clearly meant to criticize the critic as well. Ted is not the only person using language fraudulently. The younger Bonnie was doing the same thing in her romantically unrealistic novel about Ted. So was the present Bonnie in her spurious argument that religious ritual means nothing. By saying that a corpse is no longer a person, Bonnie tried to deny her love for her sister.

The climax of the story breaks over Bonnie with a "wave" of pain that she compares to "the big crashing pains of childbirth," an uncontrollable splitting open of the amazed body (64). She realizes that the "surprise ending" of her unfinished novel about the poor, humiliated boy reveals exactly the opposite, a supremely arrogant man: "What things a man like that must take for granted; what means he must think justified; what monstrous, matter-of-fact presumptions were at home in him" (64). The story's title thus acquires a second, ironic meaning. Because of the possible recurrence of the family heart disease, the Ferguson girls feared dying young and leaving behind their grieving husbands and children. But childless Nola, although she dies just as she expected, leaves behind only a bigoted husband who violates their marriage by tricking her in death. "This was the kind of interference Ted Braddock . . . might call love," Bonnie bitterly observes (64).

Thus "The Ferguson Girls" is much more self-reflexive than Del's Epilogue with its criticism of the "lost authority" of her projected novel (LGW, 251). By making Bonnie a middle-aged woman, who in retrospective self-division can abandon her former beliefs and accept her new and painfully "bleak discoveries," Munro shows that the impulse to romanticize reality imposes the wrong kind of control because it distorts the complicated kind of fictionalizing that she wants to achieve ("Ferguson Girls," 47). "[W]hat I most admire," she has told an interviewer, "is where the fictionalizing is as unobtrusive as possible, where there has been as strong an attempt, as honest an attempt, as one can make to get at what is really there" ("Real Material," 6). Looking back on the Epilogue to *Lives of Girls and Women* in an earlier interview, she defined "the Gothic incident," the story of the Sherriff family, as an illustration of the simplistic approach with which both she and Del began. Initially "the town is altered to become this visonary place and later on its reality becomes more and more demanding, its complexity begins to get through" (Untitled, 174).

By incorporating the same type of Gothic distortion into the partially metafictional structure of "The Ferguson Girls," Munro forces her reader to experience the same painfully disorienting jolt that Bonnie does. This distortion is emphasized by the ironic similarity between two outwardly different houses, the Gothic mansion that Bonnie's novel makes out of the Braddocks' old house and the shining new mansion that Ted builds to replace it. When Bonnie learns that "the grand decaying house [is] a commonplace, often seen on paperback covers," she makes fun of her novel, but after the funeral she learns that new mansions can conceal terrible secrets, too (37). This ironic similarity between the two houses is foreshadowed by an artwork that Bonnie remembers seeing with Nola in the Ontario Art Gallery: "There was a table and two chairs, painted white, two intersecting white walls, . . . white curtains blown in- ward . . . . A tape recorder behind the walls released constant, muffled sounds of quarreling voices, with now and then a sharper sound of a glass being smashed or a chair being pushed over" (34–35). Nola asks Bonnie, "Are you supposed to be able to make out what they're saying?" (35). Then, on the night before the funeral, in Nola's house—also full of "high white walls" and "windows behind white curtains"—Bonnie remembers that she resisted "revelations from Nola" about her marriage and her churchgoing (28, 43, 47). Nola confessed that, although she did not love Ted and did not believe in God, she continued to help her husband and her church because she knew they both needed her. At the end of the story, Bonnie has another revelation thrust upon her. She is forced to make out the full significance of what Nola has been saying and of what she herself has been refusing to recognize. Her discovery that Ted does not follow the unwritten script of her novel, but a ritualistically sanctioned script of his own, thrusts her into a total reorientation, symbolized by the childbirth metaphor. As a Ferguson girl, Bonnie has also feared the possibility of "dying, . . . of her heart exploding in a giant pain . . ." (52). But when she feels the "wave coming, like one of the big crashing pains of childbirth," her heart does not die (64). Instead, the love in her heart is reborn in her grief for her sister, betrayed by Ted Braddock.[12]

Since Ted Braddock is much more fully developed than Bobby Sherriff, who is introduced only in the Epilogue of *Lives of Girls and Women*, the difference between the fictionalized character and the true character distorted by the fictionalization is dramatically much more convincing in "The Ferguson Girls," which, in effect, is an epilogue expanded into the main narrative itself. The funeral that occurs in the epilogues of earlier stories, like "An Ounce of Cure" and "Accident," becomes the setting of the main narrative here. Thus, the superiority of "The Fergu- son Girls" to "Epilogue: The Photographer" shows that, when Munro mines the same material by re-exploring a theme, she does not repeat herself. In spite of the basic thematic similarities, she does something quite new, discovers something only glimpsed before. She thus de- monstrates the validity of her own aesthetic: by returning to the same theme, she clarifies her misconception of what she thought was happen- ing and sees what she had not understood in her earlier attempt.

4

The Controlled and the Controllers

Humiliated Characters, Voyeurs, and Alter Egos

Del's struggle to free her body and mind from Garnet's sexual power, which she fears might drown her or bury her alive, and Ted Braddock's imposition of control over Nola's body and soul, by which he literally does bury her, can introduce the long series of Munro protagonists who struggle for power—primarily, though not exclusively, the power to control sexual encounters, love affairs, and marriages. The situations exposing these characters' physical and psychological vulnerability include not only their own sexual experiences and relationships but, in some significant cases, those of others as well. They also include the ultimate humiliation of the flesh, the approach of death, especially, although not exclusively, as it affects sexuality. Beginning with Uncle Bert and Aunt Thelma in "At the Other Place," the characters struggling for power in such situations extend from *Dance of the Happy Shades* to *The Progress of Love* and beyond.

Such characters in *Dance of the Happy Shades* include the narrator of "An Ounce of Cure," already discussed; Lois, used and discarded in "Thanks for the Ride"; Alva, humiliated by a kiss in "Sunday Afternoon"; and Helen Louise, dumped by her lover in "Postcard." In *Something I've*

Been Meaning To Tell You, Edie, the hired girl in "How I Met My Husband," is humiliated by Alice, the jealous nurse, but this story, like "An Ounce of Cure," is a comic story with a happy ending. However, "Tell Me Yes or No" and "The Spanish Lady" are exactly the opposite, painful stories sometimes almost hysterical in tone. The discarded women narrating these stories both try to cope with their humiliation, the first by imagining an alter ego, the second by having one imagined for her.

The imagined alter ego in "Tell Me Yes or No" is objectified into a separate, although imaginary, character, one from whom the narrator can detach herself and therefore watch in her mind. This act of watching to achieve control, an act that the retrospective Del performs through her narration, introduces two types of stories: stories in which the narrator or the protagonist is a voyeur, and stories in which there is an actual alter ego. When the voyeur watches an alter ego, these two types of stories are combined. *Something I've Been Meaning To Tell You* contains three stories in which the protagonist is either deliberately or inadvertently a voyeur. Et Desmond in the title story and Dorothy in "Marrakesh" both gain emotional control by watching other women who have abdicated, in sexual intercourse and in other nakedly revealing situations. On the other hand, Mr. Lougheed, the elderly male voyeur in "Walking on Water," a story that combines the two types, fails to achieve control. Although he watches an alter ego—or perhaps even three of them—he never recognizes them as such. But one of these alter egos, Eugene, is an artist-figure like Del, struggling for control by trying to detach his watching mind from his experiencing body.

"Walking on Water" is linked to "Privilege," the second story in *Who Do You Think You Are?*, by the same scene of voyeurism. The shocking scene of sibling incest that Mr. Lougheed recalls watching is the same scene that Rose remembers watching in "Privilege." The latter story initiates Rose into the humiliations of love, one of the major unifying themes of the linked stories of Munro's second novel. In its fourth story, "Wild Swans," both Rose and the omniscient author become voyeurs to watch the humiliating gratification of Rose's adolescent sexual curiosity. This story is an important story for two reasons. First, it resembles both an earlier and a later story, Del's encounter with Mr. Chamberlain in "Lives of Girls and Women," and a similar encounter in "Jesse and Meribeth" in *The Progress of Love*.[1] Second, in *Who Do You Think You Are?*, "Wild Swans" introduces a dark triad of stories unified by their ironic thematic emphasis upon Rose's social and sexual humiliations as an adult. In "The Beggar Maid" she is a poor college student, humiliated by the social differences between her wealthy fiancé's family and her own. In "Mischief" she is first a wife and later a divorced actress, but she is humiliated twice by the same man; and her second humiliation is, once again, a voyeuristic sexual scene. In "Simon's Luck" the divorced Rose continues to be a very ambivalent voyeur who suffers agonies because she imagines that Simon, a lover, has abandoned her, but finally, after she has struggled free from wanting him, she makes the ironic discovery that she has freed herself from a dead man.

In *The Moons of Jupiter,* this emphasis on the sexual humiliations of aging single women not only reaches its peak but is also intensified by the use of alter egos. In four stories—"Dulse," "Bardon Bus," "Hard-Luck Stories," and "Labor Day Dinner"—the basic situation is much the same: a divorced, middle-aged woman has a love affair with a man to whom she cedes the power to humiliate her. In the first two stories she has already been discarded. In "Hard-Luck Stories," as well as in "Bardon Bus," the ironic conclusion is the narrator's sexual replacement by her alter ego. In "Labor Day Dinner," although the protagonist is still living with the man and masochistically struggling to please him, she fears that their relationship will not last. But in three of these stories, as in "Simon's Luck," Munro stresses that nothing will last permanently, for she links the sexual humiliations of aging women with the approach of death, the final humiliation.

But, as is usually the case with Munro, the end of this procession of voyeurs, alter egos, and humiliated characters is not what the reader might expect. Munro insists, "I don't feel at all pessimistic" ("Interview": Hancock, 102). Although this attitude is not always convincing or even apparent, it seems at least partially confirmed by a group of stories in *The Progress of Love* and by her ironic first novella, "A Queer Streak," also in this collection. In the first of this group of stories, "Eskimo," the lack of pessimism is unconvincing, as the protagonist, a voyeur who watches her alter ego, represses a fully conscious recognition of what this alter ego reveals about her own life. But in "Lichen," written from the alternating double point of view of a middle-aged divorced couple, the voyeuristic man, not the woman, is the most humiliated by love. In "The Moon in the Orange Street Skating Rink," written from the retrospective point of view of an elderly man, the woman exposed to the voyeurs is not humiliated but mysteriously energetic and powerful all through her life. In these three stories, the voyeurs no longer control what they watch. But in "White Dump," the voyeuristic wife derives sexual power from watching her mother-in-law's exposure and her husband's shame. Here the loss of control feared by many earlier characters is transformed into a breakthrough to freedom, but this breakthrough is by no means a mature or permanent resolution, as Munro points out with more than one kind of subtly satiric irony, especially in the revised version of her original *New Yorker* story.

Thus, Munro refuses her female characters "resolutions" because she considers such resolutions "quite ridiculous" ("Interview": Hancock, 102). However, in spite of all their ambivalence and all their humiliation, most of her characters manage to survive and go on, for "the ways people discover for getting through life" are "what every story is about" ("Interview": Hancock, 108). Her emphatic rejection of an interviewer's suggestion that the narrator of "Bardon Bus" "might really crack up and go over the edge," might be insane—"Not in my story she's not!"— reveals the centrality of control in her conception of her characters' activity. "I'm not very interested in crackups," she protests. Although the heroine of "Meneseteung," a later, uncollected story, finally does slip over the edge, Munro is "a lot more interested in survival, in the different strategies for it" ("Visit," 13).

Her characters' most significant method of surviving without crackups is the basic strategy of control that she defined in her commentary on "An Ounce of Cure." Like the narrator of that story and like Del watching her crying face in the mirror, many other characters back off in some way, splitting themselves into two personae, the detached watcher and the experiencing participant. For example, near the end of "Circle of Prayer," Trudy recalls how, two years earlier, she had come to terms with the loss of Dan, her husband, to another woman. She compares her feelings to a moment during her honeymoon when she stood in the darkness outside a window and watched her mother-in-law sadly playing the piano inside. Trudy's physical position outside the building corresponds to her psychological stance inside herself:

> Trudy remembers that so clearly and it seems she stood *outside* her own body, which ached then from the punishing pleasure of love. She stood *outside* her own happiness in a tide of sadness. And the opposite thing happened the morning Dan left. Then she stood *outside* her own unhappiness in a tide of what seemed unreasonably like love. But it was the same thing, really, when you got *outside*. What are those times that stand out, clear patches in your life—what do they have to do with it? They aren't exactly promises. Breathing spaces. Is that all? (PL, 273; emphasis added)

Although this characteristic question remains unanswered, Trudy standing outside her own body is just one of many characters whom Munro splits in this way. The standing outside or split sometimes involves the creation of either an imaginary or an actual alter ego, of two separate characters, the watcher and the watched. In some cases, the watched character is not only observed but also participating in her own right. In other cases, the watcher becomes a voyeur, sometimes able to control what she or he is watching, but sometimes only struggling to do so. These splits occur in both first-person and third-person stories and also in later stories with double and triple points of view; in stories with such multiple points of view, one or more characters are assigned the function of watching. The climax of these splits is the almost pathological split in "A Queer Streak." Violet's moment of crisis, precipitated by the confused combination of a malicious hoax, her own bad judgment, and her fiancé's fears, makes her desperate to dissociate herself from the painfully exposed and humiliated self that wants nothing but instant suicide. She effects this dissociation by a split signalled by an almost schizophrenic auditory hallucination. In this way, convinced that she has been told what to do, she reasserts some sense of control over her life, though it, too, as in "Simon's Luck," eventually proves illusory.

Thus, the manipulation of a split point of view, repeatedly reinforced by splitting metaphors to dramatize the concept of divided or deliberately distanced characters, becomes an exercise in the control, or the attempted control, of humiliation. Although the degree of control fluctuates and sometimes at least partially or temporarily increases in some of Munro's latest stories, control is never permanent because life's constant flux makes permanence impossible.

Dance of the Happy Shades

The three stories about humiliated women in *Dance of the Happy Shades*—"Sunday Afternoon," "Thanks for the Ride," and "Postcard"— differ greatly in some of their superficial aspects. "Sunday Afternoon," first published in the *Canadian Forum* in September 1957, uses both the third-person and the first-person point of view to recollect what Munro has identified as an adolescent experience; "Thanks for the Ride," originally published in 1957 in the *Tamarack Review,* has a retrospective first-person male narrator, a device that Munro defines as "a sort of backing off"; and "Postcard," first published in 1968 in the *Tamarack Review,* is a first-person monologue, delivered by a loquacious narrator, "a *persona* a long way" from Munro's own, and ironically unaware of how much she reveals about herself to the listening reader ("Real Material," 23).

But in spite of these superficial differences, all three stories share two important basic similarities: a poor character suffers humiliation at the hands of much more affluent characters, but this humiliation is controlled. In these stories, as in *Who Do You Think You Are?"* and "Jesse and Meribeth," poverty and femaleness make the characters vulnerable to both social and sexual humiliation. But in various ways the experience of humiliation is nevertheless distanced and controlled. In "Sunday Afternoon" the distance develops from the ironic contradiction between the author's third-person observation of Alva, the central character, and

Alva's first-person voice in a letter to her mother. In "Postcard" the distance is created by the tension between what Helen Louise, the narrator, says and what the reader gradually concludes about her. In "Thanks for the Ride," Dick, the retrospective first-person narrator, humiliates Lois, who is really the protagonist, but too "inarticulate" to say much for herself (DHS, 53). From his temporal distance in the present, he recognizes her inarticulateness as part of her humiliation.

In "Sunday Afternoon" the poor character is Alva, a country high-school girl employed by the wealthy Gannetts as a summer maid. The structure of the story is divided into three major parts. The first and third parts are narrated about Alva from a third-person point of view; the middle part contains a long quotation from Alva's letter, in which she describes what has been happening. Interrupting the third-person narration, the first-person narration of the letter reveals that Alva is not only concealing the facts from her mother but also struggling to conceal them from herself through denial and rationalization. The last word of the story's conclusion, "humiliation," defines the emotion that the entire story explores (171).

In the first part of the story, Alva is "clumsily" preparing Sunday lunch under Mrs. Gannett's condescending eye. Thick-waisted and pale from working indoors, Alva envies Mrs. Gannett's tanned and slender "elegance," her "look of being made of entirely synthetic and superior substances" (DHS, 162–63). Forced to wear the former maid's badly-fitting uniform, Alva feels self-conscious but invisible as she serves lunch to the guests on the patio, on the stones of which her maid's shoes make "a heavy, purposeful, plebeian sound" (164). When lunch is over, she may not leave the house; all she can do for diversion is to read books from her employers' library. In the den, when Mr. Gannett asks her if she gets enough to eat, she borrows *King Lear* to "show him she [does] something besides eat" (166).

But alone in her blistering hot bedroom above the garage, she writes a letter home instead: "Don't worry about me being lonesome and downtrodden and all that maid sort of thing. I wouldn't let anybody get away with anything like that. Besides I'm not a maid really, it's just for the summer. I don't feel lonesome, why should I? I just observe and am interested. Mother, of course I can't eat with them. Don't be ridiculous. It's not the same thing as a hired girl at all" (167). This brave denial of the situation that the narrator has objectively described is effected through the inner separation that Alva tries to create between herself as the participant, the lonesome, downtrodden, subtly humiliated maid, wearing secondhand clothes, and herself as the chipper young observer, detached and "interested" and pretending to read Shakespeare. But she gives herself away by protesting too much, by repeating her insistence at the end of the letter's next paragraph: "I try to take it easy around [Mrs. Gannett] without letting her get away with anything" (167). Without mentioning the heat, she enthusiastically pretends to anticipate her departure with the Gannetts for their island summer home in Georgian Bay: "I will be able to go swimming everyday . . ." (168).

Seeking more immediate relief, she visits her employers' fourteen-year-old daughter in her room. Margaret is getting her summer formals ready for the big weekend dances at a Georgian Bay hotel. Alva, whose envy of Mrs. Gannett's clothes has already been established, now tells herself that she is "not envious" of Margaret's expensive dresses, but of course she is, especially as she imagines all the exciting social activity from which she will be excluded on the island (168). When Mrs. Gannett enters the room, she reprimands Alva for her dirty apron and sends her back downstairs to wash dishes before making dinner.

As she bends over the sink, Alva's thoughts are in sharp contrast to the cheerfully detached observer her letter has described. "[S]he felt heavy . . . with the heat and tired and uncaring, hearing all around her an incomprehensible faint noise—of other people's lives. . . . She could not make a sound here, not a dint" (170). She has become not only invisible, but mute. At this low point, Mrs. Gannett's cousin sneaks out into the kitchen, takes "hold of [Alva] lightly, as in a familiar game," and kisses her lingeringly. After confiding that he, too, is going to Georgian Bay, he leaves, "moving with the graceful, rather mocking stealth of some slight people" (170).

Filled with instinctive sexual gratitude, anticipation, and renewed self-confidence, Alva imagines that her whole situation has somehow been altered. However, the last sentence suggests that perhaps she is mistaken, but reluctant to admit her naive mistake quite so soon: "there was something she would not explore yet—a tender spot, a new and still mysterious humiliation" (171). The scenario suggested by this ironic conclusion is reminiscent of the social inequities taken for granted in an Ibsen drama or a Freudian case history. The cousin will seduce Alva, the maid, who will eagerly acquiesce in her own humiliation until she realizes too late that the young man was simply taking advantage of their social inequality to have some fun.

A sharp social difference also separates the two main characters in the other two stories. In "Postcard" Helen Louise, the first-person narrator, is a department store clerk, and Clare MacQuarrie, her lover, is a wealthy businessman, the son of a member of Parliament. The central irony of the story is that Helen Louise, Clare's mistress for many years, is baffled when he suddenly marries another woman, but the reader is not. Helen Louise describes him as "an unexplaining man," but through the ironic distance that Munro maintains from her narrator, she shows the reader that the narrator herself is the explanation for Clare's unexpected marriage: her first-person dramatic monologue reveals her mercenary motives and her blindness (146).

When Helen Louise first meets Clare, twelve years her senior, she is still "in a stupor over Ted Forgie," her first love, who has left town: "When [Ted] went away I just turned into a sleepwalker" (135, 134). In this somnambulistic state she becomes Clare's mistress because, she reveals, she is eager to acquire the advantages that marriage will bring her after his invalid mother dies. Clare has already bought Helen Louise a car and clothes, and confidently expecting to move into the McQuarrie mansion, she secretly gloats over Mrs. McQuarrie's linen, silver, and china, and fantasizes about future shopping trips as his wife, flaunting her new position in the department store where she is now employed. Her description of Clare during coitus is the most dramatic revelation of her blindly mercenary attitude. With a detachment that anticipates Del's commentary on Mr. Chamberlain in the throes of his self-induced excitement, Helen Louise becomes the clinical voyeur of Clare's passion: "I used to look down at his round balding head and listen to all his groaning and commotion and think, what can I do now except be polite?" (135). Like a bored but docile wife, she silently "let[s] him" do what he wants, a phrase she keeps repeating, but she crassly reminds him that if his "commotion" damages her coiffure, he will have to pay for her beauty salon appointment (135, 138).

When she reads the newspaper announcement of his sudden marriage during a trip to Florida, her reaction is the same as it was when Ted Forgie left town. So sleepy that she goes to bed, she literally shuts her eyes to the whole situation. But in the final scene of the story, she drives to the McQuarrie mansion to demand an explanation from her lover, returned with his new wife.

Sitting in her car in front of the house, Helen Louise leans on the car horn and yells his name. She can vent her humiliation in this way because she feels split into two parts, the yelling participant and the detached observer of her *own* emotions now: "I felt as if I was watching myself, way down here, so little, pounding my fist and yelling and leaning on the horn" (143). When Clare comes out, she is still separate from her participating self: "I sat there waiting to hear what I would say to him" (144). But she does not say anything, and Clare simply sends her home with the night constable, who assures her that people survive public humiliations like hers by continuing on with their lives.

She is convinced, however, that there is something mysterious about the man whom she has been watching for so long, something that even he cannot explain. She is also convinced that the townspeople "understood what had happened and perhaps had known it was going to happen and [she] was the only one who didn't know" (142). This partial insight brings her to the realization that, even while watching him, she has not "paid attention" to Clare (145). But she never quite realizes that she has not paid attention to her own blindness, that *she* is the explanation that he cannot give her. Disapproving of their sexual relationship, her mother scolds, "You destroyed your own chances" (142). This comment is accurate, but not in the sense that her mother intended. Helen Louise destroyed her chances not by physically participating in intercourse, but by not participating in it emotionally (Noonan, 172).

In "Thanks for the Ride," the title itself is a reference to intercourse (Dahlie, "Alice Munro and Her Works," 232). The retrospective first-person narrator, Dick, the son of a chartered accountant, is just out of high school when the action takes place. While his mother is vacationing at a beach resort, Dick and George, his cousin, pick up two poor local girls, Adelaide and Lois, for casual sex in a barn. Dick thus becomes the agent of Lois's humiliation, and his narration interprets it for the reader because Lois cannot do it herself. Therefore, in contrast to the situation in the two preceding stories, here the articulate observer and the inarticulate participant are two separate characters.

After being picked up on the street, Lois insists on going home to dress up elaborately for her "date." While she does so, Dick meets her mother and sick grandmother, and is appalled not only by the stale poverty of their house but also by the heterogeneous revelations of the mother's conversation. Almost in the same breath, Lois's "slovenly" mother confides that her husband has been decapitated in an industrial accident and that Lois had "a nice boy friend" who used to spend the night when he wasn't staying at his parents' cottage (51). Her grandmother, less permissive, roughly warns Dick to use contraception.

Later, during the preliminaries of drinking in the car, Dick wants to talk to Lois. But, although she will let him use her body—she has been with many other men—she will not talk: "talk was not so little a thing to her as touching," he realizes (53). Dick's observation of this distinction defines the basic difference between the two characters' roles in the story. But as they walk in the fields, he begins to question her; and although she protests, "I don't have to answer you," she does reply (55). Naively "startled" by the bitter hostility of her outburst, he learns that she has left school to work in a glove factory and that the young men vacationing at the beach sleep with her and with girls like her during the summer (54). But by winter, she complains, "those guys have forgotten even what [the girls'] names were" (56). Defiantly determined to impress all these forgetful "guys," she boasts about the wardrobe she is accumulating on her factory pay. When Dick protests that she should not have worn her stiff, shiny dress, high heels, and rhinestones in the fields, she bursts out, "I wanted to show you guys!" (55). This is all she says, but Dick describes and interprets her behavior for the reader: "The drunken, nose-thumbing, toe-twirling satisfaction could not now be mistaken as she stood there foolishly, tauntingly, with her skirt spread out" (55).

After losing his virginity in the barn, Dick, feeling sad and confused, remembers part of the Latin aphorism, "*Omne animal . . . . Triste est*" (56, 57). He observes that Lois reflects his mood, for she is "cold and rumpled and utterly closed up in herself" (57). Still eager to talk to her, however, but now to establish some kind of communication between their "chilled and shaken" bodies after their "headlong journey," he realizes that he cannot find any words that would seem "even half-true" (56, 57). So he just takes her home, but, as he drives away, he hears her calling after him in a "loud, crude, female voice, abusive and forlorn: 'Thanks for the ride!'" (58).

Although the defiant Lois does not intend anything but a mocking, contemptuous politeness here, both the sexual and the slang connotations of "taking someone for a ride" color the narrator's memory of what he has done. Like all the other young men, Dick has taken Lois for a ride: he has used her body, then dumped her. His present narration is his mode of controlling his full realization of that fact. His consciousness of having inflicted humiliation humiliates him, for looking back over his later sexual experiences from his present point of view as a mature man, he grasps something that the just-initiated adolescent certainly could not have known: "There are some people who can go only a little way with the act of love, and some others who can go very far, who can make a greater surrender, like the mystics. And Lois [was] this mystic of love . . ." (57). The intensely involved Lois, therefore, is the exact opposite of the detached Helen Louise. This thematic definition of Lois's role reinterprets Dick's initial observation of the difference between them: just as language is his medium of communication, so touching is hers. Neither is a little thing, as Munro later makes Del discover with Garnet. Because the adult narrator feels guilty about his adolescent irresponsibility in using, observing, and humiliating a "mystic of love," he narrates Lois's story much more than his own.

But the first-person male narrator here does not sound totally convincing. Although Munro does not make the mistake of trying to describe Dick's first sexual experience from the male point of view, it is difficult to believe that an adolescent who had gotten "strangely drunk" and who had just had his first girl would think of a Latin quotation afterward, no matter how appropriate (57). This quotation seems to be projected back into the past instead of occurring in the narrator's mind at the time. Munro has defined "Thanks for the Ride" as "a given story," "told" to her by "a friend." While she was writing it, she "heard [the friend's] voice" and tried "to use him." She recognizes that it is "a bit of a surface story" (Untitled, 180).

Something I've Been Meaning To Tell You

In contrast, the two stories about humiliated women in *Something I've Been Meaning To Tell You* are anything but surface stories. In both of them, first-person female narrators use writing to try to control their humiliation. "Tell Me Yes or No" is actually a letter addressed by a discarded woman to her silent lover, who no longer writes to her. She suspects that her past love letters may be one reason for his present silence. Although she carefully pretended that her "gigantic hope" for his love would not overwhelm him, he was quick to recognize her letters as "humiliating charades" that made him "a good deal ashamed for [her]" (114, 115). Similarly, the discarded wife in "The Spanish Lady," a professional translator of short stories, also writes letters, addressed to Hugh, her husband, and to Margaret, the mutual friend he is in love with, but she never mails them. Therefore, both narrators use writing to distance themselves from their painful emotions.

In fact, the entire story in "Tell Me Yes or No" illustrates Munro's definition of the writer's attitude, as formulated in her comment on "An Ounce of Cure": the narrator splits herself into an observer and a participant by inventing an alter ego, another woman in exactly the same situation that she is in. This maneuver is as psychologically necessary to her as her initial invention, the pretense that her lover has died. She begins the story by announcing to him, and thus to the reader, "I persistently imagine you dead" (106). Her purpose in doing so is to kill him in her heart, just as his silence has killed their relationship. For her, this ending is like a death, a gravelike "hole [she] fall[s] into" (117). To escape from it, she invents his death, a much more tolerable rationalization than the admission that she, like many other women, has merely been discarded by her lover. At first these other women are just women in general, whose "[c]ase histories" she reads in women's magazines to discover how "they managed to [free] themselves" from their bondage of delusion about casual love (117). Ironically, this story was first published in the March 1974 issue of *Chatelaine*, a Canadian women's magazine, and Munro has mentioned reading "through a lot of rubbishy articles in magazines like *Cosmopolitan*," where such material can also often be found ("Conversation," 57). All the women whose case histories the narrator reads share certain deplorable characteristics. They "build their castles on foundations hardly strong enough to support a night's shelter; . . . [they] deceive themselves and uselessly suffer, being exploitable because of the emptiness of their lives and some deep—but indefinable, and not final!—flaw in themselves" (117). But in an interview Munro *has* defined this flaw as a "tendency in women" caused either by "a conditioned fear of being on our own or . . . a deep biological need," and has also significantly suggested that "the more militant feminists are afraid to look at this latter possibility" ("Great Dames," 38).

By reducing and solidifying such self-deluding women into a specific woman, a character in her imagined story, the narrator cures herself of her own delusion. As Margaret Gail Osachoff points out, this alter ego functions to distance the narrator's suffering and thus to deny its reality (79). The narrator imagines visiting her lover's "widow" in another city and being given a bag crammed with love letters. At first she thinks, "I knew I would find my letters," but then the denial begins to function. Looking at the letters, she insists, "These letters are not mine, they were not written by me" (121). But when she begins to read them, the parallels between the imaginary "Patricia" and the narrator are obvious. Like her, this woman has been bombarding her reluctant lover with frantic letters: *"I must know whether you love me and want me any more so please, please, tell me yes or no"* (122). Like the narrator when she first met her lover, this woman is the mother of a young daughter. When the narrator returns "Patricia's" letters to the "widow," she repeats her denial, "I didn't write these letters," and when the "widow" asks, "Aren't you her?" the narrator replies, "No. I don't know who she is. I don't know" (122). Thus, through her insistent denials, she has deliberately divorced herself from her past self. But after she leaves the imaginary widow, she also imagines her alter ego's attempts to overcome her grief, which include sex with another man—a device that the narrator has already tried with such frenzy that her unsuspecting partner urged her to consult a psychiatrist.

Now, in effect, the narrator has become her own psychiatrist, for with this final parallel with her fictional alter ego in place, she can calmly admit to her still-living lover exactly what therapeutic effect she has been aiming for by creating Patricia "in this city of [her] imagination": "When I think of her I see all this sort of love . . . as something going on at a distance . . ." (124). Thus she concludes: "I invented her. I invented you, as far as my purposes go. I invented loving you and I invented your death. I have my tricks and my trap doors, too. I don't understand their workings at the present moment, but I have to be careful, I won't speak against them" (124). In the *volte-face* of this characteristic conclusion, deprecating her "tricks" and insisting that she does not understand how they function, the narrator paradoxically explains exactly why they *do* work: because they fulfill her purposes in controlling her humiliation through a distancing alter ego.[2]

In "The Spanish Lady" (1974), the alter ego of the Canadian narrator, a betrayed wife going home to Vancouver by train, is the imaginary Spanish lady of the title. On the train the narrator meets a Rosicrucian, who tells her that he remembers her from a previous incarnation in which she was a twenty-one-year-old Spanish lady whom he left behind in Spain when he set out for Mexico with the conquistadors. In his unhappy present life, which, like the narrator's, includes a broken marriage, the Rosicrucian derives consolation from the idea of having more than one life, of being reincarnated and getting a "fresh start" (188). But when the narrator arrives in Vancouver, the Rosicrucian "has vanished as if [she] had invented him" (189). The narrator's idea of inventing the inventor of an alter ego links this story to the preceding one.

The narrator also recalls several different selves from her actual life: the nervous young mother burdened by small children; the unsuspecting and self-confident friend of Margaret, the woman with whom her husband, Hugh, is now in love; and the sexually dissatisfied young wife who solidified her "explosive" erotic "fantasies" in several love affairs of her own (182). Therefore, because she, too, has been unfaithful, she admits that "it is not so simple, not so plain a case as [her] grieving now, [her] sure sense of betrayal, would lead anybody to believe" (182). But in spite of this candid admission, when the narrator arrives at the Vancouver station, the self that she remembers most poignantly is the young bride who arrived at the same station twenty years earlier and was met by Hugh, bearing a bouquet. Now she is met by no one.

In her roomette on the train, she has been trying to control her humiliation by writing letters to Hugh and Margaret, but this device does not work. She imagines them *"laughing at"* her, a masochistic scenario of ridicule that links this story with the credo of Del's aunts (176): "The worst thing . . . that could happen in this life was to have people laughing at you" (LGW, 38). Later the narrator imagines Hugh and Margaret in bed together: "perhaps I go into the bedroom and . . . grab and tear the bedclothes and kick the mattress and scream and slap their faces and beat their bare bodies with the hairbrush" (SIB, 180). But this voyeuristic fantasy of hysterical revenge fills her with such pain that she "howl[s]" out loud in "protest" (181). Her pain is intensified by her memory of Hugh's silent refusal to answer her agonized questions about Margaret: "He reads whenever I speak to him" (187).

In the climactic scene in the Vancouver station, these earlier episodes—the conversation with the invented Rosicrucian about other selves, the painful howling in the roomette, and the narrator's memories of Hugh's sexual coldness and his self-defensive reading—are all pulled together and dramatically unified. The narrator hears "a real cry," not of her own grief, as she initially suspects, but "a cry . . . like that of an invader, full of terrible grievances," and sees that an old man has risen from a station bench "to let out this cry, . . . more a cry of rage, of conscious rage and terrorization, than a cry of pain" (189–90). As she watches, he falls to the floor, twitches, and dies, much like the shot and quivering horse that the narrator secretly watches in "Boys and Girls." However, "the other old men sitting on the bench. . . . hardly look at [the dying man], but continue reading the papers . . . " (190). The parallel between the narrator's howls and the old man's is intensified by the second parallel between the reading Hugh and the reading old men on the bench. That the sufferers cannot evoke any recognition of their suffering, any emotional response from the others, suggests that the worst thing that can happen in this life is not to have people laugh at you, but to have people ignore you. And this double parallel between the narrator and the old man links the sexual humiliations of the flesh, about which she has been raging, with the final humiliation of death. This is the same terrible link that Del sees in her vision of humiliation at her uncle's funeral. But this old man's dying rage seems directed not against the other men's indifference but against death itself and its finality. The narrator's painful recognition of this finality—one self is all there is and that self dies—forces her to conclude:

> By [the old man's] cry Hugh, and Margaret, and the Rosicrucian, and I, everybody alive, is pushed back. What we say and feel no longer rings true, it is slightly beside the point. As if we were all wound up a long time ago and were spinning out of control, whirring, making noises, but at a touch could stop, and see each other for the first time, harmless and still. This is a message; I really believe it is; but I don't see how I can deliver it. (190–91)

Here again, the narrator paradoxically protests that she cannot really conclude her story—the tightly unified climax *has* concluded it—but the reason for her protest is much more painful than in "Tell Me Yes or No." Here there is no other self, no tricky trap door through which to escape, and the old man's death, unlike the lover's, is very real.

This concluding scene in "The Spanish Lady" blurs the distinction between the observer and the participant, for in different ways they are both powerless. The old man dies, and the watching narrator, overwhelmed by his powerlessness and "spinning out of control" herself, insists that she cannot deliver her message. The watching child-narrator of "At the Other Place," ignorant about sex and horrified by her dying aunt's powerlessness, says, "[I] did not know Death to see it . . . " (132). But this adult narrator knows only too well about both sex and death and is struck mute by the painful irony of her knowledge.

In contrast to "The Spanish Lady," the dividing line between observer and participant sharpens and solidifies in the title story of this collection and in "Marrakesh." In both of these stories the role of the observer intensifies into that of the deliberate voyeur, watching those who are powerless. These two stories are both about a woman who watches others; and, although they are narrated from the third-person limited point of view, Et and Dorothy, the two point-of-view characters, function as witnesses on the periphery of the main action rather than as protagonists in its center. But *because* they are witnesses, they subtly control what happens to those in the center. In both cases the characters in the center are humiliated by their helplessness in sexual love, and this helplessness, as in the climax of "Baptizing," is equated with drowning.

"Something I've Been Meaning To Tell You" (1974) is defined in its first two paragraphs as a story of sadistic watching. Et Desmond begins by speaking of Blaikie Noble's ability to fascinate women; she then looks at her sister, Char, who—the reader later learns—was so in love with Blaikie thirty years before that when he left town to marry someone else she attempted suicide. The second sentence reads: "She could not tell if Char went paler, hearing this . . . ." Not quite sure of Char's reaction, "Et pressed on" (1). This punning phrase means that she continued not only to talk about Blaikie but also to press on the old wound of Char's unhappy love affair.

Later, in a flashback to the summer of 1918, when Char and Blaikie fell in love, the two sisters go downtown to meet Blaikie. "'Isn't he stuck on himself?' said Et to Char, watching" (9). From childhood on, Et, the plain younger sister, has been intensely jealous of Char's almost legendary beauty, which makes two men fall in love with her, the first man twice. Because Et never marries, her corrosive jealousy turns her into a sharp-tongued, sharp-eyed woman viciously searching for everybody's Achilles heel. She enjoys catching people at a disadvantage and spends her whole life maliciously capitalizing on the opportunities to exercise the controlling power generated by these insights. Munro twists Et into such a person to make her role as a lifelong voyeur psychologically credible. Although Et the voyeur is not the narrator, her jealous watching is often reminiscent of Sir Laurence Olivier's film portrayal of Shakespeare's Richard III. As the twisted Richard, Olivier stands in the foreground and watches his victims. This is what Et does, too.

In the thirty-five-year period that the story covers—Munro condensed it from an abandoned novel that "wasn't working at all"—Et watches the key events in Char's life with her lover, Blaikie, and with her husband, Arthur Comber, Et's high school history teacher ("Real Material," 27). In his obsession with Char, Arthur never even notices that Et is in love with him. Et catches Char and Blaikie together, just before or just after they make love; she watches Char attempting suicide after Blaikie's marriage; Char trying to conceal her furious contempt for Arthur, a clumsily earnest man who repeatedly calls himself "a fool"; and Char inadvertently disclosing the abrupt end of their sexual life (SIB, 16, 17).

Even Et's role as the town dressmaker defines her function as the voyeur. When her customers are trying on their new dresses, they call her "a terror. She had them at a disadvantage, she had them in their slips and corsets. Ladies who looked quite firm and powerful, outside, were here immobilized, apologetic, exposing such trembly, meek-looking thighs squeezed together by corsets, such long and sad breast creases, bellies blown up and torn by children and operations" (18–19). The unmarried Et, who has presumably escaped some of these physical problems, much like those of Aunt Moira in "Heirs of the Living Body," reveals what she is up to in the entire story when she warns her half-naked customers against men "peeking" in "to get an eyeful." When the customers protest that Jimmy Saunders, the man Et is accusing of trying to be a voyeur, "has a wooden leg," Et coarsely replies, "He hasn't got wooden eyes. Or anything else that I know of." The women's chorus, "Et, you're terrible," suggests what Munro is showing through her character's act of projection: that Et's voyeurism contains a sexual component (19).

This component is most clearly illustrated in the 1918 scene in which Et surprises the two young lovers in the summer grass. Going out into the dark backyard to retrieve a dress drying on the line, Et turns on a light that reveals Char and Blaikie "still tangled together," with "their mouths . . . big and swollen, their cheeks flattened, coarsened, their eyes holes" (10). Et runs back inside, and the next morning she is careful to let Char believe that she has not seen anything. "That way, Et was left knowing more; she was left knowing what Char looked like when she lost her powers, abdicated. Sandy [their dead little brother] drowned, with green stuff clogging his nostrils, couldn't look more lost than that" (11). Like Munro's later narrator in "Miles City, Montana," Et remembers "her father carrying the body . . ." (7). Thus, Et's knowledge of Char's abdication of power equates sexual helplessness with the utter helplessness of a drowned corpse. And when Et witnesses Char's suicide attempt, her secret knowledge is deepened. Seeing her sister vomiting and groaning after taking poison, Et knows how completely Char has handed over her power to Blaikie; thus, she acquires a subtle power to control her sister's obsessed life.

One way that Et controls Char, in addition to watching for inadvertent revelations of Char's vulnerability in her unhappy marriage, is through increasing this vulnerability by exposing her to public criticism. Et is described as keeping Char "beautifully dressed," but when the town criticizes Char for dressing "too elegantly" for a teacher's wife, Et's motivation immediately becomes suspicious. Of course Et blames Arthur for letting his adored wife "do anything she liked," but it is Et the dressmaker who literally exposes Char by making her a "backless" evening gown for a high-school dance (19). Once again, Et is projecting.

Another way that she controls Char is not as clear, for, as John Orange notes, it is deliberately disguised by Munro's method of narration (91). But in the key paragraph Et momentarily becomes the narrator, and this fact in itself arouses the reader's suspicions, for Et is not to be trusted. Et says that Char alternates between dieting and eating binges, after which, "pale and horrified she took down Epsom salts, three or four times the prescribed amount. For two or three days she would be sick, dehydrated, purging her sins, *as Et said*" (20; emphasis added). That Arthur never knows about Char's bingeing or self-dosing, but believes that she is merely dieting, is also suspicious. "Nobody but Et knew it all," and she blandly assures him that his wife "won't do herself any harm," a statement that reverberates with verbal irony because *Et* will do Char harm (19, 20). Et originally suspects Char of slowly poisoning Arthur with a completely tasteless poison, but, as already shown, Et repeatedly projects her own behavior onto others. At the climax of the story, the possibility that Et has been slowly poisoning Char grows much stronger.

Et's biggest opportunity to control Char comes when Blaikie returns to town thirty years later and the two former lovers renew their old relationship. Once again, Et watches them jealously: "Et looked at Char and Blaikie. . . . They sat apart but shone out together. *Lovers*" (14). When Blaikie leaves town for a few days, Et lies to Char by telling her that he has gone off to get married, just as he had back in 1918. Then, to rip open the painful wound even farther, she tells the old story, minus Char's suicide attempt, to Arthur. At this point Char either takes poison or, weakened by the poison with which Et has been dosing her for a long time, suffers a fatal heart attack, precipitated by the shock of Et's viciously cruel lie. The latter interpretation seems more consistent with the genesis of this story as a condensed novel and with its subtly sadistic tone and point of view because, in sharp contrast to the sudden, visible eruption of violence in "Executioners," "Royal Beatings," and "Fits," the murder here is not a single act but the slow, invisible, corrosive poison of a lifetime of repressed jealousy.[3]

Char's death gives Et exactly what she wants: the life with Arthur that she could enjoy only sporadically in the past. For example, whenever Char was incapacitated by her alleged purging, Et cooked for Arthur and dined with him. The story's conclusion clinches the control that Et's voyeurism has finally achieved for her. She and Arthur live together, and "[i]f they had been married, people would have said they were very happy" (23). At the end of her life, Et is finally in the center of the action she has been jealously watching.

In "Marrakesh" (1974), Dorothy, a seventy-year-old retired school-teacher, is also at the end of her life. Like Et, she is on the edge of the action, but watching and subtly controlling it from there. In spite of her age, Dorothy still possesses a "strong curiosity," a conviction that "everything" contains "something to be discovered," a feeling that "pin[s] her" down in the "irritable, baffled concentration" of a watcher (162, 163). Munro has defined this conviction as central to her own attitude toward life ("Interview": Hancock, 101). Her character, Dorothy, watches her visiting granddaughter, Jeanette, and wonders about her sixties-style wardrobe and behavior. Although the "thirtyish" Jeanette is a college professor, she has "the figure of an eleven-year-old child," emphasized by her "little childish print dresses" (159). At first Dorothy simply comments on Jeanette as an illustration "of this new type of adult who appeared to have discarded adulthood" (160). But when Jeanette sunbathes in her grandmother's backyard, Dorothy sits upstairs and watches her, "look[ing] down for some time from her bedroom window at her granddaughter's spare brown body, as if it were a hiero-glyph on her grass" (166). Because Jeanette is wearing only a bikini and is unaware that she is being watched, Dorothy's concentration on the puzzle of the "hieroglyph" is intensified.

This first watching scene prepares for the climax of the story, which Dorothy subtly engineers by bringing together her unmarried grand-daughter and her neighbor, Blair King, whose hospitalized wife is dying of cancer. During their long and increasingly intoxicated conversation on Dorothy's porch, Dorothy is full of satisfaction that the situation is developing just as she has intended. She has served liquor to loosen the two participants' tongues, and, as Jeanette and Blair nearly finish a bottle of gin, she listens to them very attentively: "This was what she had been counting on—that Blair King might turn out to be more the sort of person Jeanette was used to, that she could talk to, and that she herself listening to this talk could get a better idea of what Jeanette was like than she had been able to get up to now. So she sat concentrat-ing . . . " (167–68).

As Jeanette and Blair discuss their European travels, Jeanette refers to the inconvenience and importance of "[o]ne's baser needs" (168). Although she is ostensibly referring to Mediterranean lavatories, Dorothy detects an undercurrent completely different from Jeanette's superficial "anima-tion," "something quite still . . . , something not playful, but acquiescent, almost forlorn" (169). And when Jeanette tells a long and lurid story, "all like a play," about being robbed and almost raped at knifepoint in Marrakesh, Dorothy becomes very suspicious and skeptical (171). "What is there here that is not being told? thought Dorothy. She had had a great deal of experience listening to the voices of children who were leaving things out" (171). By presenting Dorothy's unspoken thoughts as a constant counterpoint to the spoken dialogue of Jeanette and Blair, Munro emphasizes Dorothy's role as the watching and listening witness.

In the story's climax, this role becomes that of the voyeur. Glimpsing her reflection in a mirror, Dorothy describes herself as "an old Norse witch," an image of sinister power confirmed by her reaction in the story's climax (172). Just like Et in the preceding story, Dorothy goes outside and, standing in the darkness outside Blair's illuminated porch, watches Jeanette and Blair suddenly strip and start to make love. This revelation suggests the second, secret meaning of Jeanette's earlier reference to "[o]ne's baser needs" (168). As Dorothy watches the copulating couple "[f]launting themselves in the light," they, too, become actors in another play, on a brightly lit stage (173). She realizes that "this was what" she "had set in motion," and as she continues watching them from the dark, she experiences exactly the same reaction that Et does when she turns on the light and illuminates Char entangled with Blaikie (173). "Bold as they were," Dorothy thinks, "they looked helpless to her, helpless and endangered as people on a raft pulled out on the current" (173). Once again the voyeur observing the participants in a sexual scene emphasizes that their acquiescence to desire has made them as powerless as those about to drown. Although Dorothy's actions are certainly not as vicious as Et's, she, too, deliberately locates and exposes another person's sexual vulnerability and thus deciphers the hieroglyph of her granddaughter's mystery. Jeanette's deceptively childish dresses conceal the forlornly needy body of a woman who has not been able to discard the sexual desires of adulthood. Her clothes, therefore, are a disguise that she sheds in a double sense when she strips for Blair. When Dorothy returns home, she is trembling, but the story's conclusion emphasizes her concentrated control and her gratitude for the knowledge of Jeanette that she has acquired as a result: "Strength is necessary, as well as something like gratitude, if you are going to turn into a lady peeping Tom at the end of your life" (174). In a sense, therefore, both Et and Dorothy can be seen as writer-figures, watching and manipulating much more than participating.

But the elderly Mr. Lougheed in "Walking on Water" (1974), another story set in the 1960s, is not such a figure, although he, too, is a peeping Tom at the end of his life. In this gallery of humiliated women, he is one of the two humiliated men struggling for control. In his case, however, his loss of power is caused not by sexual desire but by the ultimate humiliation of the flesh—aging and the approach of death. But Munro uses a sexual scene to dramatize his humiliation.

When Mr. Lougheed inadvertently catches Rex and Calla, a pair of hippies, "tangled up with each other," copulating in the hall of the house where he lives, they do not feel helpless or embarrassed (70). On the contrary, just as Mr. Chamberlain eagerly watches Del, they gleefully watch him watching them. Their "laughter" is "not only unashamed but full of derision. He was apparently the one to be laughed at, for having witnessed, for being shocked at, their copulation" (70). Although he cannot forget their mocking laughter and even imagines obscene sound effects to accompany it, he wants to protest that he is not shocked by public sex because, as a child, he paid to watch a brother and sister copulate in the toilet of his rural school. What he objects to, therefore, is not the sexual act itself but the "showing off," which he sees as part of a much larger pattern that subtly mocks his poor farm background. He hates the hippies' self-congratulatory artificiality, their ridiculous pretense of farming, their role-playing in "costumes of striped overalls and underwear with holes" (71).

Munro assigns Mr. Lougheed not only the rural background of her own childhood but also the same experiences and opinions that she gives to characters in several other stories. First, Rose watches a similar scene of sibling incest in "Privilege" (1977), a story Munro has repeatedly identified not only as "the most autobiographical thing" in *Who Do You Think You Are?* but as one that originated in her "almost documentary desire" to record her experiences at the school she "actually" attended ("Interview": Hancock, 93; "Real Material," 21). "I almost thought of ["Privilege"] as an autobiographical piece, not fiction at all" ("Who," 6). Second, Mr. Lougheed's angry criticism of hippie costumes is repeated by characters in three other stories. In "Memorial" Eileen criticizes trendy 1960s types who "appropriate serious things for trivial uses" and "mock things by making them into fashions" (SIB, 211). In "The Progress of Love" (1985) Phemie, the farm-bred narrator, remembers the hippie commune that rented her dead parents' farm and lashes out against "the men . . . with holes in their overalls that [she] believed were cut on purpose" to "mock" her parents "and their life and their poverty," even though she has to admit that the hippies were quite unfamiliar with her parents' poverty-stricken life (PL, 24). Similarly, in "White Dump" (1986) the elderly Sophie considers costumed hippies self-centered "playactors," even though she vigorously defends their right to wear whatever "weird" costume they wish (PL, 291). The similarities between Mr. Lougheed and these characters suggest that he embodies one attitude toward control, the emphasis on rigid self-control that constituted a primary value of Munro's rural upbringing. By her repetition of the pejorative "mock," she reveals her partial identification with this background and her sympathy with Mr. Lougheed, whose origins in such a rural tradition show why the radical shift in values illustrated by the hippies' behavior makes him doubt his ability to comprehend or control anything.

But, in spite of his negative reaction against the hippie generation, Mr. Lougheed not only shares Dorothy's stubborn desire to understand these bewildering young people but also discerns a dim similarity between their generation and his own. In the scene that gives the story its metaphorical title, Eugene, a twenty-eight-year-old philosophy student, tries to walk on water, while two groups of eager spectators, "all over sixty or under thirty," watch on the pier (85). Observing the old people and the young hippies, Mr. Lougheed muses: "Two groups with more in common than they knew. . . . Neither would have admitted that. But didn't their expectations run along the same lines? And what was it . . . that prompted such expectations? It was despair, it was being at the end of the track. Nevertheless pride should forbid one" (87). Through this explicitly defined similarity between the two age groups, Munro sets up a unifying thematic parallel, as she does in "Executioners" and "Royal Beatings," between the two characters' experience. Both Mr. Lougheed and Eugene are desperately trying to achieve control, but, because Eugene's conception of control is very different from Mr. Lougheed's, their attitudes toward possible failure also differ. The story dramatizes the tension between these two types of control.

The first time that Mr. Lougheed hears about Eugene's plans for walking on water, his informant remarks, "There's nothing you can't control if you set out to. So [Eugene] says" (68). When Mr. Lougheed later asks Eugene about this plan, Eugene insists that "[t]he world . . . [of] external reality . . . . responds to more methods of control than we are conditioned to accept," and argues that "the mind can work in some way to control matter . . . " (75, 76). He wants to test this principle by trying to walk on water: "Now suppose I step out on the water and my apparent body—*this* body—sinks down like a stone, there is a possibility that my *other* body will rise, and I will be able to look down into the water and watch myself." Mr. Lougheed scornfully replies, "Watch yourself drown" (77).

Both Eugene's description of splitting himself in half to watch himself and Mr. Lougheed's reply recall not only the drowning metaphors in the two stories just discussed but also two drowning scenes in *Lives of Girls and Women*, Miss Farris's drowning in "Changes and Ceremonies" and the drowning scene in "Baptizing." In contrast to the literally drowned Miss Farris and the metaphorically drowned Char, Jeanette, and Blair, Del does *not* drown in the river. As the retrospective narrator, she splits in half to watch herself win her underwater struggle for control. Her split suggests that Eugene's vaguely mystical conception of control is, in fact, analogous to hers and to that of many other Munro characters. By trying to split into an observer and a participant in order to watch his own suffering, by trying to catch a glimpse of what is hidden under the surface of external reality, Eugene becomes the writer-figure in this story, a metaphor for the artist attempting the tricks and miracles of impossible control. Miss Farris, the passionately devoted music teacher, is another such artist-figure. When she goes skating, her activity is symbolically analogous to Eugene's. The solid surface of the frozen river supports her weight as she displays her "schoolteacherish . . . skill" and her homemade but theatrical skating costume (LGW, 122). Her walking on water thus takes the symbolic form of skating. But when she later drowns herself, she plunges through the no-longer solid surface and is found "floating face down, unprotesting" (141). Like her earlier counterpart, Miss Abelhart, who drowns figuratively when she is laughed at and left "alone in a bottomless silence," Miss Farris is also laughed at, and the "exhausting effort" of her "unrequited love" evokes a permanent response only from Del, the embryonic artist ("The Dimensions of a Shadow," 10; LGW, 141). Thus, if Eugene succeeded, if he literally walked on water, it would be either a trick or a miracle. At this point, he, too, is simply laughed at.

So, although impressed by the breadth of Eugene's scholarly reading, Mr. Lougheed ridicules his ambition to walk on water. But when Eugene replies, "Road to Emmaus," his biblical allusion draws a parallel between Mr. Lougheed's inability to believe in miracles and the initial inability of the disciples of Christ—Who actually did walk on water—to believe in His resurrection (76).[4] That Mr. Lougheed nevertheless warns Eugene against making a fool of himself links him in yet another way with the rural values of older Munro characters, such as Del's aunts, who anxiously warn Del, the budding writer, against incurring public ridicule. The crucial difference between the two characters seeking control is that Eugene does not share Mr. Lougheed's fear of humiliation.

Thus, when his public attempt to walk on water fails, Eugene simply apologizes to the spectators: "I haven't reached the point I hoped I might have reached, in my control" (87). If this apology sounds like an ironic parody of the apologies of Munro's self-conscious first-person narrators, protesting to their readers that they are not sure that they can control their material, it is because Munro's metaphorical definitions of the writer's activity echo what Eugene has quite literally been trying to do. She defines the writer as a person "who work[s] daringly out in the public eye" (SIB, 27), and her own writing as "a way of getting *on top of* experience" and "getting control" ("Alice Munro," 245; emphasis added). Thus, despite Munro's sympathy with old Mr. Lougheed and despite Eugene's youthful irrationality, Eugene is the character closest to being a Munro persona in this story. The tension between the two types of control that Munro explores through her old and young characters is suggested by her ironically self-reflexive position between them. Neither old nor young, she explores her own ambivalent attitude toward control. Like Del's old aunts and sometimes like Munro herself, Mr. Lougheed considers Eugene's, or the writer's, obsession with artistic control either a trick or a dangerous delusion about reality. Thus, when Eugene later disappears, Mr. Lougheed begins to fear that Eugene's "mind" may be "disturbed" and that he might have tried walking on water again and drowned in the attempt, or deliberately drowned like Miss Farris (91).

Mr. Lougheed's fear is fed by his recurring dream about an event of his rural childhood. By symbolically relating his past to his present, this dream unifies his associative memories into a thematic pattern that the reader, unlike the confused dreamer, can comprehend. Mr. Lougheed remembers that, when Frank McArter, another disturbed young man like Eugene, murdered his parents and later perhaps drowned himself, the men in the community went out to search for him, Mr. Lougheed tagging along with his father. In his recurring dream about this search, he has an urgently growing sense, so common in anxiety dreams, "that there was something they were going to find" (82). In the story's climax, he suddenly recalls standing on a broken bridge and looking "down" at "a boy's body spread out, face down," in the river below, but he does not know whether he is remembering what he actually found as a boy or only what he dreamt (90). This image of watching a drowned corpse then keeps appearing in his mind, as it also does in Munro's, for the narrator of "Miles City, Montana," a woman writer like Munro, has a similarly confused memory of a drowned boy. But there is a significant difference in "Walking on Water": the remembered image is analogous to the image of miraculous control that Eugene hoped to achieve, looking down into the water and watching his *own* body floating below him. Thus, unlike Et and Dorothy, who see *others* figuratively drowning, Mr. Lougheed sees himself. For the drowned male figure of his dream is not only Frank and perhaps Eugene but also a symbolic projection of himself, his alter ego, split off from him. Neither disturbed young man, Frank or Eugene, could walk on water because it is a totally alien environment, impervious to mental control. In the turbulent 1960s, the elderly Mr. Lougheed is confronted by an equally alien environment; therefore, he is also disturbed. Because *lough* in Irish means a bay or an inlet, Munro may have intended to link his name with the story's title and the impossibility of control that it connotes. Therefore, watching his alter egos does *not* give Mr. Lougheed any control because he never consciously recognizes what his persistent dream might signify. His lack of recognition adds a second layer of meaning to Eugene's allusion to Emmaus. Although the resurrected Christ appeared to His disciples on the road to Emmaus, "their eyes were kept from recognizing him" (Luke 24:16). In the same way, Mr. Lougheed's eyes are kept from recognizing the similarity between himself and this persistent image of the drowned figure. He cannot understand his present experiences or control his memories of the past. Only the writer confronting her obsessive images in story after story and thus metaphorically "walking on water" can try to do that. Neither can Mr. Lougheed allay his anxiety about Eugene's fate. He can only remember watching images of sex and death, images of his rural childhood, now irrevocably gone.

Who Do You Think You Are?

In "Privilege," the second story in *Who Do You Think You Are?*, Munro returns to these images of her own rural childhood. In spite of the graphically horrifying description of Franny McGill, howling and "jerking" under her brother's body, Rose is psychologically detached from the experience of watching this act of incest in the boys' toilet (26). This detachment is emphasized in two ways. When Flo, Rose's stepmother, disgustedly calls incest *"a performance,"* Rose childishly imagines it as something theatrical occurring on "some makeshift stage, . . . where members of a family got up and gave silly songs and recitations" (25). When she actually sees it later on, her detachment is also reflected in her description of the scene. What she and the audience of jostling, "hollering," and "giggling" children watch, "interested but not alarmed," has "no bearing on what could happen to anyone else" (27). And because of this voyeuristic detachment from her experience, Rose actually learns from it, both as a child and as an adult, although in very different ways.

The adult Rose, narrating these incidents to people "in later years," stresses that as a schoolchild she acquired a tough, practical wisdom about how to survive in an environment where such acts as incest were possible (27). And as an adult, Rose uses this memory of Franny, the abused sister, as a grimly realistic yardstick for measuring the romantic nonsense of men's "books and movies" about "the figure of an idiotic, saintly whore" (26). Although the story opens with the narrator's ironic criticism of her protagonist, of Rose's self-consciously calculated purpose in regaling people with stories about her childhood, "queen[ing] it over them" because they "wished they had been born poor, and hadn't been," Rose's indignation about men's literary laundering of girls like the "stunned, bewildered" Franny is savagely sincere (23, 26). What she—and through her Munro—are criticizing here is the authorial detachment from such characters that their being cleaned up and canonized implies. The men who create such characters in their books and movies are self-deluding cheaters because, to achieve literary control, they detach themselves not only from the girls' very real suffering but also from

their own sexual complicity, "refusing to take into account the aphrodisiac prickles of disgust" aroused in them by real-life Frannies (26).
As Del shrewdly notes in *Lives of Girls and Women*, "disgust" and "enjoyment" can be "inseparable," but Rose feels that to derive vicarious
sexual pleasure from other people's suffering is shameful (148, 149).[5]

The unifying link in "Privilege," entitled "Honeyman's Granddaughter" when it was published in *Ms* in October 1978, is the honeyman,
or honey-dumper, the man who cleans up the most disgusting places,
privies. From the story's opening section, with its description of privies
with knotholes through which "[a]ll the little girls squatted to see" an
evacuating old man as he "sagged through the hole," Munro moves to
Cora, the honeyman's granddaughter, one of the "big girls" in Rose's
school (24, 25). When Rose develops an obsessive crush on Cora, Munro
demonstrates that in love no self-deluding detachment, no face-saving
control, is possible.

Uncontrollably obsessed with the beloved, the lover finds it impossible to grasp her real essence or to render it permanent, for the beloved
is mortal. Rose's crush on Cora involves her in the funeral game of "the
last look," which is very much like Uncle Craig's funeral scene in "Heirs
of the Living Body" (33). While Cora pretends to be the coffined corpse,
Rose, along with the other little girls, lines up to take the lingering last
look. This "funeral-play" resembles the real funeral in two important
ways.[6] First, the act of seeing is once again charged with significance.
When it is Rose's turn to cover Cora's "corpse" with lilacs and she can
get close enough to the beloved older girl to look at her with "crazy
concentration," she vainly tries to control her obsession by struggling
to get every detail of Cora's physical appearance and to define "her real
smell" (34, 33). Obsessed with pinning down these details, Rose feels
an "impotence and hopelessness" that introduce her to the double
humiliations of the flesh (34). Like Del's "crazy, heartbreaking" greediness to record every impermanent detail of Jubilee (LGW, 253), Rose's
hopeless urge is another manifestation of Munro's documentary drive
to "fight against death" by recording everything because she "can't
stand to have things go" ("Alice Munro," 243). Second, by occurring at
the imaginary funeral of the beloved Cora, Rose's introduction to humiliation once again links sex and death.

The retrospective omniscient narrator of "Privilege" emphasizes the
humiliations of sexuality. Like the voyeurs Et and Dorothy, this generalizing narrator equates Rose's childish crush with the overwhelming erotic
feelings, "[t]he high tide" and "the flash flood," that have threatened
to drown Rose ever since (WDY, 33). As Del recognizes when she refuses
to yield in her symbolic underwater struggle with Garnet, as Et recognizes when she compares the besotted Char to Sandy's drowned corpse,

and as Dorothy realizes when she sees the "helpless" lovers as "people on a raft pulled out on the current," there is more than one way to drown, and the metaphorical way is in one sense more dangerous because it can be repeated (SIB, 173).[7] When Rose steals candy for Cora from Flo's store and Cora returns this "clownish" love-offering to Flo, Flo sarcastically berates her stepdaughter, not because she suspects any latent lesbian tendencies but because Rose's idea of love "sicken[s]" her (WDY, 34, 35). "It was the enslavement, the self-abasement, the self-deception. That struck her. She saw the danger all right; she read the flaw" (35). This definition of the dangers of love is clearly reminiscent of Mrs. Jordan's lecture on self-respect and also of the magazine articles read by the narrator in "Tell Me Yes or No," who deplores exactly the same traits in the self-deceiving and therefore exploitable women whose case histories she studies. Such women are all abdicators, all potential drowning victims. Looking back on Flo's recognition of these dangerous characteristics, Rose sees that her stepmother was "trying to warn and alter her," but at the time she was no more willing to listen than Del was (36).

Thus, all these characteristics appear full-blown in the stories about Rose's courtship, marriage, and adult love affairs. Although eight of the ten stories in *Who Do You Think You Are?* were originally published separately, the collection constitutes an organic whole, and the humiliations of love are one of the major themes integrating and unifying it into Munro's second "open-form" novel (Struthers, "Alice Munro and the American South," 123). What is significant in "Privilege" is that Munro dramatizes even a childish, homoerotic crush as an exposure of humiliating helplessness. The adult Rose sees that to participate in love, to come even temporarily under the sway of another person of either sex, is as dangerous as drowning. This is why the observer must pull away from her participatory self, struggling in "the flash flood," and try to keep her head above water (WDY, 33). And this is why Munro is so swift to recognize a similar attempt in male writers who distance themselves from their female characters, for they, too, are trying to deny, and thus to escape from, their own sexual feelings.

The trickiest trap doors for escaping from the participatory self are the ones that Munro constructs in "Wild Swans," the fourth story in *Who Do You Think You Are?* This story is similar not only to "Lives of Girls and Women" but also to "Jesse and Meribeth," a story about adolescent sexual curiosity in *The Progress of Love*. In all three stories, the fantasizing, sexually curious adolescent girl is involved with a much older, but basically childish man who substitutes some kind of perverse sexual dramatics for the normal act. As I have already shown, one manifestation of this character is the father in "Royal Beatings," who gets and gives pleasure by beating his daughter, Rose. Later I will show that the same type of character reappears, as the grey-haired, theatrical Clifford in the epilogue of "Mischief," and, with a significant difference, as another middle-aged but very exciting lover in "White Dump."

But in spite of the similarities between "Lives of Girls and Women" and "Wild Swans," there are important differences between them, not only in the degree of the protagonists' involvement but also in Munro's manipulation of point of view and other key elements in the second story. These manipulations conceal Rose's involvement not only from her but also from the reader. Del is not involved. Watching Mr. Chamberlain masturbate, she says, "It did not seem to have anything to do with me" (LGW, 170). Although at first she is "violently anxious to know what would be done to" her, what Mr. Chamberlain does to himself does not happen to her in any sense except the visual (169). Discussing male Peeping Toms, Rosalind Coward notes, "Peeping Toms can always stay in control. Whatever may be going on, the Peeping Tom can always determine his own meanings for what he sees. Distanced he may be, but secure he remains" (77). Forced to be a female Peeping Tom, Del remains secure because she is distanced.

But exactly the opposite is true in "Wild Swans," where Rose is not secure because she participates. Just as she plays both a passive and active role in "Royal Beatings" when her father beats her, so she now becomes both "[v]ictim and accomplice" when a similar character, a middle-aged "minister," manipulates her while they are seated side by side on a train (63). This episode, like the one with Mr. Chamberlain, is introduced by an emphasis on the adolescent girl's sexual curiosity. Just as Del spins excited erotic fantasies about being seen naked by Mr. Chamberlain, so Rose, as she feels the man's encroaching hand on her leg, concealed by both her coat and his carefully spread-out newspaper, remembers her sexual fantasies about "mature" men and admits, "She had a considerable longing to be somebody's object. Pounded, pleasured, reduced, exhausted" (61). The possible fulfillment of this fantasy fuels her "[c]uriosity. More constant, more imperious, than any lust. A lust in itself, that will make you draw back and wait, wait too long, risk almost anything, just to see what will happen" (62).

Paradoxically, however, just as Del is initially ambivalent about seeing, so every key element in this story—incident, point of view, and ironic allusion—disguises the act of seeing "what will happen." As Rose is about to depart for Toronto on the train, Flo warns her about white slavers disguised as ministers. The man whom Rose meets on the train says that he is a minister, but is not wearing his "uniform" (60). Very confused by this double disguise, at the end of the story Rose remembers that "Flo had mentioned people who were not ministers, dressed up as if they were. Not real ministers dressed as if they were not. Or, stranger still, men who were not real ministers pretending to be real but dressed as if they were not" (64). Flo also tells Rose about the retired undertaker who, much like Rose stealing candy for Cora, buys chocolate to lure women into his hearse, which he supposedly uses as a kind of mobile bordello. When Flo speculates about what happens inside the "purple" plush interior of the hearse, the erotic suggestiveness of this soft and disguised setting for sex links it with both the disguised "minister" and his own mobile setting, the train in which he operates to satisfy his lusts (57). And because undertakers and ministers often work together, there is a natural association here, which once again links sex and death and funerals. In addition, Rose's purpose in making the trip is to shop secretly for cosmetics, jewelry, and clothes, all to disguise herself: "She thought they could transform her, make her calm and slender and take the frizz out of her hair, dry her underarms and turn her complexion to pearl" (58).

In addition to these examples of transforming disguises, Munro also manipulates point of view to disguise what happens during the actual encounter on the train. Although this story, like all the Rose stories, is written from the third-person point of view, the narrative voice here does not remain constant. Hallvard Dahlie points out that "Munro's verb-tense modulations confuse" what is going on ("Alice Munro and Her Works," 250). They do, but so do the modulations in her pronouns. These shifts separate the participating Rose from the observing and generalizing author-narrator, who refers to herself in the *first*-person plural. At first Rose is thinking in the simple future: "[h]er legs were never going to open" (62). Then in the next paragraph, she begins to use the conditional future: the man's invading "fingers would not hesitate, but would go powerfully and discreetly to work" (63). It appears to be Rose who thinks, "This was disgrace, this was beggary," but in the next sentence the point of view suddenly shifts to authorial generalization in the first-person plural (63).

In one way these authorial comments sound very much like Del's first-person singular comments on masturbation in *Lives of Girls and Women*. Just as she compares her "[g]reedy eating" of "sickening[ly]" sweet food to "masturbating," and just as Rose's greedy eating of chocolate cookies in "Royal Beatings" is suggestive of masturbation, so the same equation between two kinds of physical greed, subtly introduced by the undertaker's seductive use of chocolate, recurs here (LGW, 184). The narrator excuses Rose's masturbation by asking and answering rhetorical questions about greediness: "But what harm in that, we say to ourselves at such moments, what harm in anything, the worse the better, as we ride the cold wave of greed, of greedy assent" (WDY, 63).

Just as Del reads about European "peasants" masturbating "with carrots," so here the narrator rationalizes that, after all, everybody masturbates somehow: "A stranger's hand, or root vegetables or humble kitchen tools that people tell jokes about; the world is tumbling with innocent-seeming objects ready to declare themselves, slippery and obliging" (LGW, 184; WDY, 63). Thus even objects are suddenly perceived as operating in disguise. But the crucial difference between the two sets of narratorial comments is that in "Wild Swans," because the comments come from a narrator who is *not* the same person as Rose, these arguments ironically emphasize all the falseness and all the slippery projections and evasions of Rose's excitedly rationalizing mind.

The narratorial disparity of these tricky shifts in point of view is also reinforced by allusions to two Yeats poems to emphasize the theme of a sexual encounter experienced in disguise. Here, as in "Baptizing," it is important to recognize the function of Munro's allusions in developing not only this story but also its relationship to others in *Who Do You Think You Are?* As a university student in "The Beggar Maid," Rose writes an essay on Yeats (80). In "Wild Swans" the obvious allusion is to "The Wild Swans at Coole," but a much more important parallel, both verbally and thematically, is "Leda and the Swan."[8]

The allusion to the first poem is introduced when the "minister" strikes up a conversation with Rose by referring to "*snows,* a poetic-sounding word," and then describing "[a] whole great flock of swans," "[a] very fine sight," the scene described by the speaker in "The Wild Swans at Coole" (59, 60). Later, when Rose reaches either a real or perhaps only an excitedly imagined orgasm as the train passes the Toronto Exhibition Grounds, the allusion continues: "the painted domes and pillars floated marvelously against her eyelids' rosy sky. Then flew apart in celebration. You could have had such a flock of birds, wild swans, even, wakened under one big dome together, exploding from it, taking to the sky" (63). This passage echoes the second stanza of "The Wild Swans at Coole," in which the swans "all suddenly mount / And scatter wheeling in great broken rings / Upon their clamorous wings" (Yeats, 129). The Yeatsian image becomes Rose's explosive sexual metaphor.

But the events leading up to her climax are described in language that echoes "Leda and the Swan" in the same ironically deflating type of classical allusion that Munro uses in "Executioners." As the man's fingers on Rose's legs gradually get her legs to open, she thinks, "Her legs were never going to open. But they were. They were" (WDY, 62–63). These contradictions ironically echo Yeats's description of Leda and the swan: when Leda feels "her thighs caressed / By the dark webs . . . ," the speaker in the poem asks, "How can those terrified vague fingers push / The feathered glory from her loosening thighs?" (211). If the "exploding" swans signal Rose's climax, she feels the same "shudder in the loins" that Leda feels when Jupiter, disguised as the swan, "engenders" Helen in her (212). Unlike Jupiter, the "minister" is not a god; he doesn't even speak of God, as Rose initially expects him to. Nevertheless, like Jupiter, he too is disguised, and he too engenders something permanent in Rose, something that causes almost as much trouble as the legendary Helen does.[9]

The disguise theme links the poem to the story's conclusion, in which Rose thinks of the man's minister-disguise and then of a good-looking friend of Flo who pretended to be a movie star in disguise. Rose decides, "it would be an especially fine thing, to manage a transformation like that. To dare it; to get away with it, to enter on preposterous adventures in your own, but newly named, skin" (WDY, 64). "Leda and the Swan" concludes with the question, "Did she put on his knowledge with his power . . . ?" (212). The answer to this question in Rose's case is definitely yes. In a flashforward, the omniscient narrator reveals Rose's future discovery of the knowledge that, like the "minister," she, too, in the disguise of her imagination has often transformed a situation. She recognizes the role of the "minister" in her future sexual relationships with "husbands or lovers" (64). Even though, like Mr. Chamberlain, he lacks "grown-up masculinity," in her erotic imagination she keeps him "on call, . . . for years and years, ready to slip into place at a critical moment . . ." (WDY, 63–64). By doing so, she makes him one of her trap doors of escape from reality.

Escaping from reality into fantasy is also the theme of "Jesse and Meribeth," a revision of "Secrets Between Friends," published in *Mademoiselle* in November 1985. The two friends mentioned in the original title, Jessie and MaryBeth, who are very much like Del and Naomi in "Lives of Girls and Women," change the spelling of their names to glamorize them. But this transformation is only the beginning. Jessie, the retrospective first-person narrator, remembers herself as another adolescent girl with a fantastic imagination and an intense sexual curiosity. So she regales her friend with erotic fantasies about her employer, Eric Cryderman, a character who resembles both Art Chamberlain and the "minister" in "Wild Swans." As the Crydermans' maid, Jessie is in a situation analogous not only to Del's and Rose's but also to Alva's in "Sunday Afternoon." Mrs. Cryderman is older than her husband and heavily pregnant. Mr. Cryderman, just like the man in "Sunday Afternoon," makes passes at Jessie in the kitchen, and Jessie, like Alva, gets quite excited. However, she makes no connection between the possible consequences of her own sexual excitement and Mrs. Cryderman's pregnancy.

But the "secrets" of the original title suggest not only the secrets that

Jessie makes up about Mr. Cryderman but also the concealment of the consequences of sex, pregnancy. In "Jesse and Meribeth," in sharp contrast to "Lives of Girls and Women" and "Wild Swans," a revelation about pregnancy significantly precedes the climactic encounter between the erotically fantasizing adolescent girl and the older man. This revelation occurs in a scene that is a self-reflexive echo of "Images," where the pregnant body of the mysteriously metamorphosed mother remains hidden "under the covers," and where Mary, who comes to nurse her, remarks, "[Y]ou'll be worse before you're better!" (DHS, 33). When Mrs. Cryderman uncovers her blotched and swollen abdomen to show Jessie the baby kicking inside, she makes the same comment: "I'll be worse before I'm better" (PL, 171). Munro's repetition of this euphemistic allusion to labor pains emphasizes the important difference between these two stories: in "Jesse and Meribeth" one layer of concealment is split to reveal the hidden reality of advanced pregnancy. When Mrs. Cryderman exposes her abdomen, Jessie is horrified to see Mrs. Cryderman's "navel" protruding "like a cork ready to pop," and is nauseated to see the baby's movements, "not a flutter on the surface but an underground shifting and rolling of the whole blotchy mound" (180). This "underground shifting" is a physical parallel to the metaphorical earthquake that Robert mentions in "Fits." When the cushion covering Mrs. Cryderman's genitals suddenly falls off, the nauseated Jessie rushes out into the kitchen, but she is pursued by Mrs. Cryderman's taunting question: "Jessie, what are you scared of? I don't think one of them ever came out that way yet!" (180). The subtly implied connection between the mother's uncovered genitals and the "way" the baby *is* going to come out is the second layer of reality, which remains unrevealed, but the potential violence of that inevitable earthquake makes Jessie break out in a sweat and admit, "I felt a hard ball of disgust pushing up in my throat" (180).

Yet this disgust is not sharp enough to puncture Jessie's fantasies about Mr. Cryderman or to make her fear sex. On the contrary, when he invites her into an almost subterranean place of revelation, his low-roofed, "secret," and "shady" summerhouse, she enters eagerly, hoping for a "passionate attack" (182, 183). However, just like Del with Mr. Chamberlain—the two male characters' surnames are significantly similar—Jessie is disappointed, for the revelation she receives is not what she anticipated. What she gets instead is a confusing and ironic mixture: some of the same sexual pawing that Rose gets from the "minister" and, simultaneously, a paternal lecture about being "hot-blooded" and self-centered instead of being concerned for his pregnant wife (184). Mr. Cryderman's reference to his impending fatherhood alerts the reader to the psychological effect of Munro's revision at this point. In the original version, "Secrets Between Friends," Jessie's reaction in the summer-house is described in the past tense, but in the revised version, her reaction leaps into the dramatic present as the retrospective narrator relives an intensely disturbing experience. This technique, reminiscent of the beating scene in "Royal Beatings," reveals Mr. Cryderman's role as another sexually arousing father-figure:

> His hand rouses and his words shame me, and something in his voice mocks, mocks endlessly, at both these responses. I don't understand that this isn't fair. . . . I feel shame all right, and confusion, and longing. But I am not ashamed of what he's telling me I should be ashamed of. I'm ashamed of being caught out, made foolish, of being so enticed and scolded. And I can't stop it. (184)

Although Mr. Cryderman, like Mr. Chamberlain, Rose's father, and the "minister," is observed only from the outside, Munro uses Jessie's internal monologue to develop his character. The paradoxical combination of his stroking, enticing hand on Jessie's leg and his superior, mocking voice suggests a deeply ambivalent man who can communicate two diametrically opposed messages at the same time, especially to an adolescent girl whom he considers his social inferior. Thus both characters are split in half, not only Jessie in her shamed confusion, but Mr. Cryderman, too.

But when he tells her that she must acquire the "difficult" art of considering the "reality of other people," her sexual excitement suddenly evaporates: she *can* "stop it," after all (184). "Pride hardens . . . over the nakedly perceived fault," the retrospective narrator generalizes (184). And Jessie *has* been stripped naked—but psychologically, not in the exciting physical way that she has desired. She suddenly realizes that Mr. Cryderman has penetrated her fantasy world. "Isn't it true that all the people I know in the world so far are hardly more than puppets for me, serving the glossy contrivings of my imagination?" she sternly asks herself (184). Although the same recognition occurs in the flashforward at the end of "Wild Swans," here it occurs at the climactic moment, and its result is quite different. Unlike Rose, who keeps the "minister" permanently on call in her erotic imagination, Jessie angrily rejects any further humiliation. In a passage added to the story's revised version, she thinks: "What do I want with anybody who can know so much about me? In fact, if I could wipe him off the face of the earth now, I would" (184).[10] Sensing this sudden internal change in his now recalcitrant accomplice, Mr. Cryderman stops stroking Jessie's legs and sends her home.

In an epilogue four years later, Jessie recalls her "abysmal confusion in the summerhouse," but in spite of that scene and the scene with the naked Mrs. Cryderman, at this point she is still naive (187). She still believes that she can be free of the consequences of her own behavior, that she can evade reality and live in her imagination, "unaccountable" and "tumbl[ing] through the world scot-free" (188). When the retrospective, first-person narrator recalls this nineteen-year-old's youthful illusion about escaping from reality, her ironic tone is exactly the same tone that the third-person narrator takes toward her protagonist, Rose, in "Wild Swans." These two stories show not only that Munro continues to develop a basic situation and redefine a basic theme but also that the distance she maintains between her observing narrator and her participating character is the same in both the split third-person and split first-person points of view.

Rose's most important escape from adult reality is her career as an actress. As a child, Munro fantasized about becoming a movie star (Mallet, F3). The motives behind Rose's choice of an acting career constitute one of the unifying factors in the novel. Although there are only a few scenes in which she is actually acting, she is nevertheless "an actress to the marrow of [her] bones" (WDY, 157). As Susan J. Warwick has shown, Rose is almost always acting, in a broader metaphorical sense, and also watching herself and others act (211). In addition, the omniscient narrator ironically watches Rose and periodically interjects her comments, as the retrospective adult Del does in Munro's first novel. This narrator functions like a drama critic in the audience of the real-life plays in which Rose is constantly performing. With a superior watcher thus observing a self-watching actress, the manipulation of the split point of view develops this central dramatic metaphor by emphasizing Rose's oscillation between the helpless humiliation of a participant and the controlling power of an observer. In "The Beggar Maid" her social humiliations arise from her poverty and from her initial uncertainties about Patrick, but the balance of power tips to her side at two points, when she breaks their engagement and then when she ill-advisedly renews it. In "Mischief" and in "Simon's Luck," Rose is again repeatedly humiliated, but in the latter story she regains control by deliberately rejecting love, much as Del rejects Garnet and regains control at the end of "Baptizing"; however, this rejection turns out to be ironic. This triad of stories about Rose, therefore, constitutes not only a thematic unity in Who Do You Think You Are? but also a transition to the stories in The Moons of Jupiter about women who allow themselves to be humiliated in sexual relationships.

In "The Beggar Maid," originally published in the New Yorker on 27 June 1977, Munro's emphasis on the painful social symbolism of clothes recalls both "Thanks for the Ride" and "Sunday Afternoon." Like Alva envying Margaret's expensive wardrobe, Rose, a poor freshman on a scholarship at the university, envies the affluent students' collegiate blazers and is self-conscious about her own cheap, homemade suit. Needing a job to supplement her scholarship, she miserably imagines herself as a student waitress, toiling in a "green cotton uniform, her face red and her hair stringy from the heat." She realizes that "[p]overty in girls is not attractive unless combined with sweet sluttishness, stupidity. Braininess is not attractive unless combined with some sign of elegance; *class*" (WDY, 71). Stuck with precisely the wrong combination, "publicly proclaimed braininess and poverty," the stigmata of the outsider, she feels "bitterly superior and despondent" (71). Later, when Patrick Blatchford, her wealthy fiancé, takes her home to meet his family on Vancouver Island, she assembles a costume: she borrows a raincoat, which is too long for her, and she sells blood to buy a new sweater. She is aware that Patrick, in his masculine ignorance of the obvious social symbolism of women's clothes, plans to try to conceal her poverty from his family. But upon meeting his mother and his sisters, she realizes her failure to fit into this new role: she is humiliated not only by her "cheap and imitative" clothes, "a small-town girl's idea of dressing up," but also by her sharp consciousness of the difference between her social exposure and the protective cocoon woven for the Blatchfords by their comfortable affluence (84, 83): "Patrick and his sisters behaved as if things could never get at them. . . . They had never had to defer and polish themselves and win favor in the world, they never would have to, and that was because they were rich" (76).

When Rose and Patrick become lovers, she fears sexual, as well as social, humiliation. "She was terrified . . . that there was a great humiliation in store, a great exposure of their poor deceits and stratagems" (81). Although she initially feigns passion, she soon begins to experience sexual pleasure, only partially alloyed by her double bind, the necessity of continuing to pretend in order to conceal her initial pretense from Patrick. But her social humiliations are much more persistent. She becomes increasingly confused and miserable about the social differences separating her lover from herself and, after a visit home to introduce Patrick, acutely ashamed of the reasons for her confusion.

In the midst of her protagonist's shameful confusions, the omniscient narrator interjects one of her typically ironic flashforwards. It occurs after the visit, when Patrick criticizes Flo, Rose's stepmother, by suggesting that her "real mother" must have come from "a more genteel background," and Rose gets angry, both at him and herself (87). "What a coward he was, . . . but she knew that she herself was the coward, not knowing any way to be comfortable with her own people. . . . Years later she would learn how to use it, she would be able to amuse or intimidate right-thinking people at dinner parties with glimpses of her early home" (88). The distance here between the narrator and her protagonist is very wide, emphasized by a tone that echoes the ironic opening of "Privilege." The irony springs from the narrator's verbs, *use*, *amuse*, and *intimidate*, and from her mockingly self-conscious anticipation of the malleable reactions of the "right-thinking people," whom a more sophisticatedly calculating Rose, quite at ease "at dinner parties," "would learn" to manipulate to her social advantage. Then the narrator pulls back to her protagonist in the present—"[a]t the moment she felt confusion, misery"—only to pull away again to dissect the understandable, if not exactly admirable, reason for Rose's sudden "loyalty" to her background: "Now that she was sure of getting away, a layer of loyalty and protectiveness was hardening around every memory she had . . ." (88). As earlier, the narrator's interruptions of her protagonist's narrated monologue introduce ironic complications and subtleties into the readers' opinions of Rose's honesty and motives, but without lessening either their sympathy with Rose's difficulties in her rapidly changing role or their recognition of the candidness of Munro's self-criticism.

To end this confused misery, Rose suddenly breaks her engagement. Taunting Patrick with being a poor lover, and sensing his total vulnerability to her, she humiliates him with "great pleasure" and "energy" (92). This is one of the few situations in which she feels that he is completely exposed to her. Another occurs later when she deliberately creeps up on him, unaware of her presence, as he is studying in his carrel in the university library. As she stands there, "looking into his carrel," and watching him silently from the darkness in the stacks, "free of him, invisible to him," she becomes a kind of voyeur (96). She is "free" not only to "look at him as she would look at anybody," without any emotion, but also to imagine herself split off into a separate self, "running . . . into Patrick's carrel" and giving herself back to him (93, 94). The imagined scenario, in which she embraces him and repeats "*I love you*," is somewhat like the actual love scenes witnessed by the two female voyeurs standing silently in the dark in "Something I've Been Meaning To Tell You" and "Marrakesh" (94). And this one, too, becomes an actual love scene at the pivotal moment when Rose abandons her controlling position as the nonparticipating observer and rushes onto the stage. The many possible reasons for her turnabout are analyzed in a long retrospective epilogue, years after her disastrous marriage and divorce.

Like the flashforwards already mentioned, the epilogues in the Rose stories afford sufficient temporal distance to separate the observing narrator from the participating protagonist. One reason that Rose offers in this epilogue, but later rejects, is that she was unable to "resist such a test of [her] power" (95). Later still, in "Simon's Luck," she equates freedom with power when she recalls that only with Patrick "had she been the free person, the one with [the] power" to say *"Come here . . .* or *go away"* (169). That Rose possesses this freedom and power only during the precariously poised, critical moment when she is secretly watching Patrick in his carrel and imagining "the possibility of happiness" corroborates once more the idea that the voyeur is in a controlling position precisely because she is not participating (95). But as soon as Rose runs into his carrel, she loses this freedom by fusing with her imagined self to become a participant in the play. Thus, Patrick becomes "a person she was bound to . . . " (96). Even nine years after their divorce, she still feels bound to him. Munro has commented that "everything can be foreseen" in this story, "the whole inevitability, inescapableness of the wrong choice . . . "("Interview": Hancock, 89). Remembering her moment of mistaken choice in the library, Rose thinks, "She should have left Patrick there" (WDY, 96).

In "Mischief" it becomes clear that doing so would have been better for both of them. Because this story, first published in *Viva* in April 1978, is one of Munro's most ambiguous and ironic stories, it deserves detailed analysis. The mischief begins to develop early in the marriage, when Rose is so humiliated by her husband's pompous and prejudiced harangues at a party that she walks out of the house and into the rain. But there, when she is romantically consoled by Clifford, her friend Jocelyn's husband, she immediately feels "transformed, invulnerable" (WDY, 109). The narrator later comments sarcastically, "She wanted tricks, a glittering secret, tender celebrations of lust, a regular conflagration of adultery. All this after five minutes in the rain" (112). These desires are much the same as the first-person narrator's erotic fantasies in "The Spanish Lady," but by presenting them from the third-person point of view and by having her narrator mock the fantasizing protagonist, Munro creates an ironic distance missing from her earlier story of a sexually dissatisfied young wife.

Rose's relationship with Clifford, however, involves much more than a simple search for sexual excitement. She is also trying to erase two different but closely related social humiliations. Both Patrick and Jocelyn come from affluent backgrounds, and both treat Rose with snobbish condescension, making her feel once again like an outsider. They both lecture her on her social *faux pas,* and although resentful, she listens and learns. But when she discovers that Clifford, like her, comes from a poor family, she jumps to the conclusion that the two of them are natural allies against their spouses: their "weariness, suppleness, deviousness, meanness, common to a class" make them "both shifty pieces of business" and endow them with a guileful power that Patrick and

Jocelyn lack (111). Convinced that she understands Clifford much better than his wife does, Rose also feeds her self-confidence by maliciously observing that after two babies Jocelyn has lost her figure and "become spectacularly unkempt" (119). But the expectations based on this double-barreled self-confidence, both social and sexual, become painfully ironic when Rose and Clifford arrange a secret tryst to consummate their relationship in an out-of-town hotel. For Rose's attempt to erase her humiliations produces only more humiliation.

Waiting for Clifford's arrival, she visits a public library; but, just like Del under the spell of Garnet's power, the sexually excited Rose discovers that she cannot read. She "went in and looked at the titles of the books, but she could not pay attention. There was a fairly incapacitating though not unpleasant buzzing throughout her head and body" (120). Neither can she fully admit to herself what she is doing. In this mental dodging, she is like the earlier Rose of "Wild Swans." Although she has packed a diaphragm and has deliberately dressed in "dramatic sexually adver-tising clothes," she dissociates herself from the specific purpose of these preparations by calling her clothes "a disguise" (119). When some men yell at Rose from a car, the narrator describes her reaction with subtle irony. "She saw her own reflection in store windows and understood that she looked as if she wanted to be stared at and yelled at" (119). Annette Kolodny has defined "reflexive perceptions" like this one as an important stylistic device used by "contemporary women writers" to describe the reactions of a female character "depicted discovering herself . . . in activities she had not planned or in situations she cannot fully comprehend" (79). The irony here is that because Rose *has* planned this activity, her reaction to how she looks is disingenuous. She behaves as if only her reflected alter ego were wearing tight pants, a tight black sweater, and heavy makeup. But Rose's lack of real control, subtly foreshadowed by her inability to read and by her division from her disguised self, is soon disastrously confirmed.

When Clifford arrives, he announces that he cannot hurt his wife and calls the whole thing off. Much like the unexpected return of Mrs. Storey, whose arrival cuts short her son Jerry's adolescent experiment with Del, Jocelyn's reinstatement in Clifford's guilty conscience aborts his plans for adultery. He does not possess the deviousness and guile that Rose has mistakenly attributed to him. In a painfully comic scene, her whining and nagging attempt to persuade him to shed the role of the "dutiful" middle-class husband to which he has reverted only deepens her final humiliation (WDY, 122).[11] When she phones Clifford's hotel room in the middle of the night, her humiliation reaches its peak. She begs him to talk to her, but he just keeps repeating, "That's okay, Joss" (125). Rose cannot decide whether he is "pretending" that she is his wife or "so sleepy" that he believes she is (125). But the ambiguity of his sleepy repetitions suggests his anxiety to reassure his wife of his fidelity. Rose's resulting "shame" is "like a whole wall crumbling in on her, rubble choking her" (123). Full of "mashed pride and ridiculed fantasy," she cries all the way home (130). There she tries to recover her pride by announcing to Patrick that she and Clifford have "had an affair" (131). The motive behind this lie is reminiscent of Del's "furious" brooding after her fiasco with Jerry: "I would never get a real lover" (LGW, 206). Rose's adolescent self-dramatization reduces her husband to grieving "silence," which she, egotistically engrossed in her own humiliation and still expecting a phone call from Clifford, resents as "ill-timed" and "unfair" (WDY, 131). In retrospect, however, backing off from both her lie and her humiliating rejection, she comforts herself by deciding that the humiliation "was necessary, . . . the start of wrecks and changes" leading to her divorce (130).

But the epilogue, set some twenty years later, brings fresh and more ironic humiliations when Rose renews her friendship with Clifford and Jocelyn, who both give the appearance of having changed radically. They have become rich and trendy, and, like June in "Memorial," they spout psychobabble. Thus Clifford blithely explains that he never has been able to decide whether he wants to leave his wife or does not—"It's a static contradiction"—and that he has never been comfortable "with the adult male role" (128, 129). The latter observation is immediately reinforced by Rose's observations that Clifford is now gray, but "[h]is waist and hips [are] narrow as a twelve-year-old's," and he is wearing a T-shirt with the adolescent slogan *"Just passin thru"* (129). Although Clifford's appearance is "something theatrical," and although his self-analysis is couched in the kind of jargon that Munro obviously rejects, both how he looks and what he says fit the personality he demonstrated in his on-again, off-again relationship with Rose twenty years earlier (129). He was just "passin thru" with her then, too. He also accuses his wife of wanting to play mother: "You want to be the grownup" (128). Jocelyn agrees that this may be so, but she defines the permissive-ness of her maternal role in her anecdote about listening to her adult son, living in the apartment below his parents', make love to an audibly reluctant partner. Although Jocelyn says she was embarrassed, she did not actually interfere. This significant conversation among the three characters prepares for the post-party scene in which the old relationship between Rose and Clifford is consummated while Jocelyn watches.

Like her hosts, Rose is "fairly drunk" and "feeling a remote and wistful lust; a memory of lust, maybe" (132). This old and unfulfilled desire, which suggests that she has not really changed either, prevents her from protesting when Clifford casually suggests intercourse. By making love to Rose in front of his wife, Cliffords acts out his "static contradiction," and by "hover[ing] above them making comforting noises of assent," Jocelyn gives him reassuring maternal permission to do so (128, 132). This episode thus becomes a perverse theatrical performance, not only like Mr. Chamberlain's performance in front of Del but also—because of the sexual triangle—very much like the sadomasochistic family farce in "Royal Beatings" and like Rose's childish image of incest as a family stage show. There is a clear element of voyeurism not only in Jocelyn's position as the mother but also in that of Rose. Split between active sexual participation and observation, Rose feels "curious, disbelieving, hardly willing, slightly aroused and, at some level she [is] too sluggish to reach for, appalled and sad" (132). But clearly the hovering Jocelyn is the observer who controls this situation, while Rose can only attempt to control it, for Rose's confusing mélange of curiosity, disbelief, and reluctance is fixated at the same adolescent level as in "Wild Swans." Just as she describes the gray-haired "minister" as lacking "ordinary grown-up masculinity," so the childish Clifford, now also gray-haired, makes her react in much the same way (64). Paradoxically, both immature men are sexually arousing father-figures. And just as the sexy outfit Rose wears for her abortive tryst with Clifford is not a disguise, neither of these two men is disguised, either: the "minister" wears ordinary clothes because he is not a minister, and Clifford's teenage T-shirt proclaims what he actually is, another arrested adolescent like Rose. Therefore, this is not only one of the "critical" sexual moments that the narrator anticipates at the end of "Wild Swans" but also one in which Rose is relegated to performing a minor part in Clifford's adolescent drama rather than starring in her own (63).

The next morning Rose realizes that this encounter has revived her "cold and hurtful need" for a man, "which for a while she had been free of" (132). Thus, once again, what she is trying to get rid of boomerangs in her face. The sharp hunger of her renewed appetite makes her very angry with Clifford and Jocelyn because "they had made a fool of her, cheated her, shown her a glaring lack, that otherwise she would not have been aware of" (132). But later, cautiously backing away from her indignation, she decides to continue her friendship with them and tells herself that "she needed such friends occasionally, at that stage of her life" (132). Lawrence Mathews asks whether we should "deplore [Rose] for needing Clifford and Jocelyn, or . . . applaud her for having the maturity to recognize that she does need them" (189). Neither is correct, for Rose's rationalization only veils her recognition that an indignant, self-righteous fuss would just expose her to further humiliation. Once again, as in "Wild Swans," she has been both victim and accomplice.

Thus, Rose's second encounter with Clifford does not disrupt the story. On the contrary, the ironic psychological parallels between her two climactic encounters with him unexpectedly unify the epilogue with the main part. Although his sexual behavior in these two episodes is radically different, the startling double irony is that neither his personality nor his disappointing effect upon Rose has changed. When he does not make love to her, she feels "betrayed"; when he does, she feels "cheated" (WDY, 125; 132). Another static contradiction, this emphasizes the paradoxical similarity of her two experiences and thus the ironic circularity of the story's action. Rose has not really reached a new "stage of her life," any more than Clifford has (132). On the contrary, she has done the same humiliating thing twice. Therefore, out of all this protracted mischief, Munro points out, Rose gets not a "love affair," but only "a way out of her marriage" ("What Is," 19). However, that way out is at least partially based on her self-dramatizing lie to Patrick; and after that, her highly uncomfortable knowledge of her sexuality produces only her very gradual and erratic transformation from Patrick's wife into a woman uncertainly trying to control her own life.

The difficulties of achieving such control in the face of her persistent and paradoxical desire for love are further developed in "Simon's Luck," an even more tightly unified and ironic story.[12] It begins with another image of Rose as a voyeur, a "lonely" woman walking down a dark street and looking "in the lighted windows" and "warm . . . rooms" of homes where other people are enjoying "family suppers" and parties. As an actress she feels that she could participate in any of these dramas, and in her loneliness she wants to participate. "It's no good telling herself she wouldn't be long inside there . . . before she'd wish she was walking the streets" (152). This initial ambivalence about where she really wants to be—inside or outside a warm house—subtly foreshadows the story's major conflict.

In the next scene, although she has been invited to a party, she still feels "doomed to hang around the fringes of things . . . " (154). When she tries to participate in the conversation by telling the guests about her cat, who died because he "liked to jump" into the warm clothes dryer, a guest remarks, "It was warmth he was seeking in the dryer. It was love" (154, 155). This symbolic equation of warmth and love defines what Rose is seeking from Simon, the professor who comes to her rescue after a drugged student insults her: "Now you won't be able to fuck the cat anymore" (155).

Rose immediately identifies Simon, a Polish Jew, as a man with "a richer and more complicated masculinity than the masculinity to be found . . . where she had grown up" (155–56). Her definition is confirmed when they leave the party to go to her home and make love.

But making love is only the first way in which Simon provides the warmth that she seeks. His practical advice on how to make her chilly house warm, by insulating it and getting the furnace filters cleaned, links this scene with the opening one in which Rose yearns for warm houses. Delighted with this "warm" man in "the widespread sunlight of the moment," she is already convinced that he is "the man for [her] life" (164). His warm love also includes advice about the student's insult, about which she keeps brooding compulsively. When she tells Simon that, without his comforting presence, she "would have been in a state of humiliation" about it, he replies, "That's a pretty small thing to get into a state of humiliation about." Although Rose admits that it is, she defines the vulnerability of the typical Munro heroine when she adds, "It doesn't take much with me" (163).

Simon's advice, "[l]earn not to be so thin-skinned," seems particularly appropriate for a man with his background (163). As a Jewish child sent to France during World War II, he twice eluded the Nazis and also survived a serious infection. At this point, therefore, the reader accepts the title, "Simon's Luck," at face value: Simon is a very lucky man. And his warning of mortality, *memento mori*, seems at first to be linked only to these wartime childhood traumas. Rose, who attributes her own role-playing to him and therefore believes that he is pretending to be some "Old Philosopher," finds this imagined play-acting one more appealing trait in his personality (161). He is the direct opposite of that perverse male trio, Mr. Chamberlain, the "minister," and Clifford. Instead of disappointing or exploiting Rose, Simon is wise and protective.

But when he fails to return the next weekend, after the excited Rose has made elaborate preparations for his visit, she imagines herself ejected into the cold and dark again. Working herself into a frantic humiliation, she remembers all the "mortifications" that she has suffered before in such situations and predicts future mortifications even if Simon does return to resume their relationship (168). Sooner or later, she fears, he would find her unattractive and reject her in bed. Munro has admitted that she has always considered it "very important . . . to be attractive" and has emphasized that it is very "difficult for [a woman] to take sexual rejection" ("Writing's," E1; "Great Dames," 38). Here, through Rose's fears, she dramatizes this difficulty in the most painfully humiliating terms:

> She would lie there wishing she had some plain defect, something her shame could curl around and protect. As it was, she would have to be ashamed of, burdened by, the whole physical fact of herself, the whole outspread naked digesting putrefying fact. Her flesh could seem disastrous; thick and porous, grey and spotty. His body would not be in question, it

never would be; he would be the one who condemned and forgave and how could she ever know if he would forgive her again? (169)

In this masochistic fantasy, in which all the power is automatically imputed to Simon, Rose becomes an observer separated from herself and examining her exposed body, almost as if she were looking at a photograph, full of close-up clinical detail, or the center of a freeze-frame in a film. Painful as it is, this distancing helps her begin to struggle free from Simon, to reject the possible bondage that she fears their future relationship might involve. This scene is therefore parallel in function to the scene at the end of "Baptizing," in which Del watches her crying face in the mirror and by doing so is able to imagine that her suffering self is "not [her] at all" (LGW, 241). Here the actual mirror image is replaced by an imagined photographic image in which Rose sees herself as she fears Simon might see her in the future. As Rosalind Coward says, "Photographic ideologies convince us that we can be both self and other. We can see ourselves and see how others see us." Convinced of this paradoxical split, we can therefore adopt "the position of the other who judges and records" (49; 53).[13]

To avoid the imagined humiliation of Simon's judgment and rejection, which she expects simply because he is the male, Rose leaves her job and her chilly rented house and drives westward, struggling to "leap free" of the ambivalent feelings about Simon that keep tempting her to turn around and go back (169). This vacillation recalls not only her initial uncertainty about whether she wanted to be inside or outside a warm house, but also the very similar ambivalence of the first-person narrator of Munro's earlier story "The Office."[14] Comparing these two stories clarifies the experiences of Rose and of later Munro characters in analogous situations.

The woman writer in "The Office," first published in the *Montrealer* in September 1962, explains that she needs an office to write in because, unlike a man, she cannot work in the house. "She *is* the house; there is no separation possible" (DHS, 60). But no sooner has the narrator explained all the highly convincing reasons for the frustrating fusion between her and the house than she suddenly admits that sometimes a rather frightening separation *does* occur:

> At certain times, perhaps on long spring evenings, still rainy and sad, . . . I have opened the windows and felt the house shrink back into wood and plaster and those humble elements of which it is made, and the life in it subside, leaving me exposed, empty-handed, but feeling a fierce and lawless quiver of freedom, of loneliness too harsh and perfect

for me now to bear. Then I know how the rest of the time I am sheltered and encumbered, how insistently I am warmed and bound. (DHS, 60–61)

The ambivalence suggested by these paradoxical pairs of participles, "sheltered and encumbered," "warmed and bound," produces the narrator's conflict. Identifying this story as "the most straightforward autobiographical story [she has] ever written," Munro defines her narrator's internal tension as a "contradiction . . . in the woman *herself . . .* [b]etween the woman who is ambitious and the woman who is . . . traditionally feminine, who is passive, who wants to be dominated, who wants to have someone between her and the world" ("On Writing," 259; "Conversation," 59). Thus, just as Munro's characters experience a conflict between two kinds of language, a conflict that she herself has experienced, so, as already illustrated by Del, who wants to be loved *and* to become a writer, Munro's characters also experience a sharp conflict between dependence and ambition.

In addition to acknowledging this conflict within herself—"I know *I'm* like this. I have the two women"—Munro notes that ambition may also cause conflict with hostile men ("Conversation," 59). For the woman writer, ambition connotes the threatening possibility that men will criticize her as "sexually unappealing" and "unwomanly." At the beginning of her career, Munro carefully concealed her ambition because she was "afraid of" such criticism (Kolson, 4C). Her fear sprang from her "very complicated . . . need" to be liked by men: "You can't go too far or they won't approve of you; they think you're a castrating bitch . . . " ("Alice Munro," 262).

Thus, the narrator's confusingly candid self-description in "The Office" is echoed not only by the opening image in "Simon's Luck"—the lonely Rose standing outside the warmly sheltering family houses—but also by the spatial metaphors that Munro repeatedly uses to describe "The Office" and the difficulties of the woman writer. These spatial metaphors objectify the writer's ambivalence. Munro has described "The Office" as a story "about a woman's particular difficulties in *backing off* and doing something lonely and egotistical" ("On Writing," 261; emphasis added). These difficulties occur because "[t]he *detachment* of the writer, the *withdrawal* is not what is traditionally expected of a woman, particularly in the man-woman relationship. . . . There's the desire to give, . . . [to play] in many ways . . . a quite traditional role, and then of course the writer *stands right outside this,* and so there's the conflict right there" ("Alice Munro," 250; emphasis added). The feminine conflict, therefore, is wanting to split in half, wanting "to be both kinds of women" ("Great Dames," 38).

Rose obviously wants to be two women, too. Filled with the "low, steady hum of uneasiness, fatigue, [and] apprehension," she wants to be dominated by the warmly protective Simon, but when she recognizes her desire for such total domination, she is even more apprehensive (WDY, 158). "Nothing would do any more but to lie under Simon," she ironically observes; "nothing would do but to give way to pangs and convulsions" (165). Thus, just as Del has to struggle against part of herself to get free from Garnet, under whom she has very pleasurably given way to "pangs and convulsions," so Rose has to struggle against the part of herself that, like the narrator of "The Office," wants the protective warmth of a man and a sheltering house. Freedom and ambition, therefore, mean not only independence and fulfillment, but also the cold and loneliness of exposure.

But on her drive west, Rose finally achieves the same experience as Del does in "Baptizing": she rediscovers the world. Breakfasting in a restaurant, she realizes that "the world had stopped being a stage where she might meet [Simon], and gone back to being itself" (170). The dramatic metaphor in this statement signals Rose's rejection of her earlier self-dramatization; however, this rejection also becomes ironic later on. But at this point, Rose, like Del, realizes that "love removes the world for you, and just as surely when it's going well as when it's going badly" (170). This removal is, in a way, like the death of Rose's cat, for in seeking warmth and love, the cat literally lost the world. Now Rose deliberately rejects not just "the disappointment, the losses, the dissolution," but also their "opposite, . . . the celebration and shock of love, the dazzling alteration. Even if that was safe, she couldn't accept it. Either way you were robbed of something—a private balance spring, a little dry kernel of probity" (170). But then, as in "Memorial" and in "Accident," the ironic narrator interjects her wry comment, "So she thought," thus implying the possibility that Rose's wholesale rejection of love might, after all, be a mistake (170).

This possibility subtly prepares the reader for the epilogue, which is set a year later. Once again Rose is outside, trying to get warm. Acting in a television series, she is on a "freezing" British Columbia ferryboat where a scene is being filmed (171). As she goes to "the sheltered part of the deck" to get a coat and some coffee, she meets a woman who had also attended the party at which Rose met Simon (171). This woman informs her that he has died of cancer, from which he had suffered for a long time. This completely unexpected "disarrangement" of Rose's conception of Simon's power reveals that his stories of his wartime childhood and his repetition of the grim reminder, *memento mori*, constitute the central irony of the story and of its title: Simon's luck has run out (173). In retrospect, Rose's lament about *her* humiliatingly powerless body not only intensifies this irony but also emphasizes her egotistical self-dramatization. Her lament thus becomes a subtle parody of the feminist protest against the exacting standards of sexual attractiveness men apply to women but never to themselves.[15] The conclusion stresses this point: "It was preposterous . . . that Rose even at this late date could have thought herself the only person who could seriously lack power" (173). To render Rose's misjudgment of Simon plausible, Munro makes it impossible for her to see that he is terminally ill. However, his energetic lovemaking, furnace-inspecting, cooking, and gardening, all crowded into one weekend after a party, seem rather implausible for a seriously sick man.

But this ironic epilogue, as unexpected as the epilogue of "Mischief," produces what can be read at least on one level as an anti-feminist story. The conclusion shows that Munro's emphasis on female humiliation does *not* make her a feminist "injustice-collector" ("What Is," 13). The ambivalence of her heroines and their self-dramatizing complicity in their own victimization repeatedly vitiate the polemicists' stereotyped contrast between all-powerful male victimizers and helpless female victims. For Munro the conflict is never ideologically simple, but always complicated by a confusion of many paradoxical factors. The complications in this story include Rose's deep ambivalence about exactly what she wants; Simon's unselfish kindness to her, heightened by the irony of his complete powerlessness; her trivial complaints about the student; and her narcissistic lamentations about her body. In an even deeper irony, Rose's protracted psychological struggle to free herself from Simon, to regain that "little dry kernel of probity," though undeniably crucial to her conception of herself, turns out to be a fight to free herself from a dead man (170). Thus, "Simon's Luck" is an ironic reversal of "Tell Me Yes or No," in which the narrator pretends that her lover is dead to free herself from her emotional dependence upon him. Simon would have saved Rose the trouble. But in thus making her character confront the fact that all human beings, *not* just women, lack power simply because they are mortal, Munro is emphasizing more than the final impossibility of controlling life. She is not merely restating the theme of "Heirs of the Living Body" and "The Spanish Lady." Indirectly, she also seems to be insisting on her unwillingness to subscribe to any kind of feminist ideology. She repeatedly refuses to fit her paradoxes to the proverbial Procrustean bed: "I'm a feminist in all kinds of practical ways, but I don't think fiction is anything you make serve any cause at all" (Mallet, F1, F3). "I back off my party line," she says elsewhere, "even those [sic] with which I have a great deal of sympathy, once it gets hardened and insisted upon. I say to myself that's not true all the time. That's why I couldn't write a straight women's lib book to expose injustices. Everything's so much more complicated than that" ("What Is," 15).

The Moons of Jupiter

Complexity is also one of the major unifying themes of *The Moons of Jupiter*, insistently reiterated in thematic definitions in almost every story. In "Prue" (1981) the central character, who "presents her life in anecdotes," seems to be a Munro persona, for "it is the point of most of her anecdotes that hopes are dashed, dreams are ridiculed, things never turn out as expected, everything is altered in a bizarre way and there is no explanation ever . . . " (MJ, 129). If "short stories" are substituted for "anecdotes," Munro's explicit definition of her character's narrative "point" paradoxically explains the lack of explanation; thus, Munro is exerting the control that her earlier narrators protest they cannot have. This definition is, of course, also a self-reflexive description of the structural irony in both "Mischief" and "Simon's Luck." Similarly, at the end of "The Stone in the Field" (1979), the first-person narrator refuses to fictionalize what she knows about the mysterious Austrian hermit who lived and died in a shack on her aunts' farm. Although she has heard about this man from her father and has also read a newspaper article about him, she insists that she cannot attempt to solve his mystery. "If I had been younger I would have figured out a story," she says. But "[n]ow I no longer believe that people's secrets are defined and communicable, or their feelings fullblown and easy to recognize. I don't believe so" (35).[16] This constitutes another thematic statement. In two other stories in this collection, the narrators adopt the same attitude toward the characters that they observe. In the conclusion of "Hard-Luck Stories" (1982), the narrator recognizes the impossibility of trying to understand Douglas Reider, a former lover: "I could be always bent on knowing, and always in the dark, about what was important to him, and what was not" (197). And the retrospective narrator of "The Turkey Season" (1980) analyzes an adolescent experience three times: at the time where it occurred, "later, when [she] knew more, at least about sex," and "later still" (74). At the center of this experience is Herb Abbott, who may have been a homosexual. But the narrator insists that defining him as such is unimportant. "He is not a puzzle so arbitrarily solved" (65).

The persistent psychological puzzle of women's masochistic complicity in their own humiliation is the core of four of the stories in this collection, but Munro returns to this theme in a somewhat different way, both thematically and technically. Just before the publication of *The Moons of Jupiter*, she defined its subject as "the whole subject of what men and women want of each other" ("Interview": Hancock, 112). She wrote *Lives of Girls and Women* unself-consciously, simply because she knew "a great deal" about women, but in *The Moons of Jupiter* she is much more "consciously interested in the way women live" and the "way things are different for men and women at middle age, ... the particular conflicts between men and women . . . at a middle-class educated level" ("Interview": Hancock, 112, 113). In "Dulse" the forty-five-year-old divorced Lydia, full of "loneliness and pain," tries to figure out how she can continue her life without her lover ("Interview": Hancock, 108). In "Bardon Bus" the first-person narrator, another middle-aged woman, tries to regain her lover but is replaced in his affections by her friend. A similar replacement occurs in "Hard-Luck Stories." In both of these ironic stories, the narrators' friends function as their alter egos, mirroring their situation, and in "Hard-Luck Stories" the first-person narrator's friend becomes a second narrator, telling her own story. In "Labor Day Dinner" Roberta, like the protagonists of the three preceding stories, is an aging woman who feels humiliated by her lover. In this story, however, Munro exploits a triple point of view, a technique that she introduces in *The Moons of Jupiter.*[17] She presents Roberta not only through her own third-person point of view but briefly also through her lover's and her daughter's points of view. In her journal entries about her mother, the daughter becomes a first-person observer. In these last three stories, Munro's new techniques—actual alter egos and multiple points of view—develop her theme of the humiliations of middle-aged women in new ways.

Because we now see from more than one angle of vision, these devices multiply the confusion that was limited to one protagonist in the earlier stories. They also intensify the protagonists' confusion because, in contrast to earlier protagonists, these characters are much more firmly rooted in the main time frame of the action, their middle-aged present. Although there are frequent flashbacks, they are usually to the quite recent past. The only exception is the second narrator's section in "Hard-Luck Stories." Similarly, the endings of this set of four stories are not far removed in time from the main narrative action. In "Hard-Luck Stories" and "Labor Day Dinner," for instance, the main action is limited to one day. These characters, therefore, do look back, but since the conclusions follow immediately or soon after what has happened, the sense of retrospective distance created by the epilogues and by the ironically omniscient narrators in earlier stories is either absent or assigned to one of the characters in the story. In this way, Munro emphasizes the present and the future rather than the past. The present is full of the humiliations of the flesh that combine the same two elements so disturbingly juxtaposed in "At the Other Place" and in Del's vision of humiliation at her uncle's funeral: sex and death. The humiliations of sexuality now become the humiliations of aging and of approaching death, especially in "Bardon Bus" and "Labor Day Dinner."

In both of these stories, as in "The Spanish Lady" and "Simon's Luck," the looming future means the inevitability of death, the ultimate humiliation of the flesh. In struggling against this inevitability, the characters are once again concerned with possessing controlling power, but—just as before—it is their own deep-seated and painfully paradoxical ambivalence about such power that undermines their efforts from within.

With the paradigmatic clarity of a psychiatric case history, "Dulse" dramatizes self-destructive ambivalence. First published in the *New Yorker* on 21 July 1980, this story contrasts Lydia, the devastated protagonist, and Mr. Stanley, an elderly American she meets in a guest house on an island in the Canadian Maritimes. The purpose of Munro's contrast is to show the two different kinds of "shelter" that these characters construct to help them get through the rest of their lives (59). Mr. Stanley finds shelter by "worshipping" Willa Cather, whose work he has admired "for over sixty years" ("Interview": Hancock, 109; MJ, 39). Lydia's shelter is the much less reliable recourse of having love affairs. Abandoned by Duncan, her lover, she is trying to understand what happened between them. This contrast between Lydia and Mr. Stanley is emphasized by the structure of the story: flashbacks to the recent past in Kingston, Ontario, when Lydia and Duncan were still living together, alternate with scenes set in the present on the island.

In the flashbacks Lydia's retrospective point of view allows her to back away from herself and analyze her relationship with Duncan in two ways. She remembers what happened, and, in flashbacks within flashbacks, she also discusses Duncan with a psychiatrist. After her final futile phone call to Duncan, Lydia sees herself reduced to "something like an egg carton, hollowed out in back" (41). Although she tries to explain what happened, she very typically distrusts her own explanation and wants, instead, to "cover her head and sit wailing on the ground" (50). That is almost exactly what she does: she makes an enormous psychic effort to buy herself some food, but then she leaves her groceries on the floor and sits in the hall, unable to move or eat. Completely powerless, "[s]he asks herself what gave [Duncan] his power? She knows who did. But she asks what, and when—when did the transfer take place, when was the abdication of all pride and sense?" (50). In trying to answer her own questions in this anguished internal monologue, she remembers her "gigantic efforts to please" Duncan, efforts comparable to the muscle-straining exertions of "a dancer on her toes, trembling delicately all over, afraid of letting him down on the next turn" (53, 54). This metaphor reverses the usual male and female roles in a ballet. Although Lydia, like Char in "Something I've Been Meaning To Tell You," has abdicated, has handed over all her power to her lover, the ballet metaphor shows that, instead of expecting his emotional support, *she* feels compelled to support *him*. In trying to do so, she listens masochistically as he enumerates "his calm and detailed objections" to "those things about her person and behavior which he did not like. He listed these things precisely. Some were very intimate in nature and she howled with shame and covered her ears and begged him to take them back or to say no more" (53). These sadistic objections, which Duncan delivers with deeply thrilling "satisfaction," suggest the same kind of criticism that Rose expects from Simon, but here, because the criticism actually occurs, Lydia's humiliation is painfully real, not imaginary and completely self-induced (53).

After describing this situation to the psychiatrist, Lydia asks him, "Suppose it's the humiliation, I want to be humiliated? What good will it do me to know that?" (55). In both "Memorial" and "Mischief," Munro derides psychiatrists, but here, despite Lydia's resistance, the psychiatrist serves the important function of emphasizing Lydia's paradigmatic characterization. She exemplifies what Karen Horney defines in *Neurosis and Human Growth* as the "self-destructive character. . . . in the condition of morbid dependency" (118–19). In her analysis of the behavior of such a character, Horney lists almost everything that Lydia does in her relationship with Duncan, including her "secretly welcom[ing her lover's abusive] behavior and most actively collaborat[ing] with him" (239–58, 251). Although I do not mean to suggest that Munro is deliberately basing her character on Horney's theories—any more than she based the character of Rose on Freud's—she clearly emphasizes Lydia's intuitive recognition of the painful paradox of her behavior. Recognizing that she might want to be humiliated and that the sadist and the masochist make a monstrous symbiotic couple, Lydia acknowledges that "[s]he made [Duncan] a present of . . . power, then complained relentlessly to herself and finally to him, that he had got it" (MJ, 55). This acknowledgment is like Del's dismayed recognition in the drowning scene that she had "granted" Garnet "powers" over her (LGW, 238). It is also like Rose's role as the willing victim of a procession of males with whom she actively collaborates—her sadistic father, the "minister," and Clifford. Lydia is thus fighting against the same self-destructive ambivalence that splits these earlier characters but, since she is older and therefore somewhat less resilient, with notably less success.

In the scenes set in the present, Lydia meets three other men besides Mr. Stanley, and, after much talk about sex on the island, she speculates about them as possible lovers who might assuage her loss of Duncan. But Munro has defined her character as someone who "would rather speculate than act" ("Interview": Hancock, 109). So when one of these men, Eugene, invites Lydia to his bed, she declines. "Things had changed for her; she refused adventures" (MJ, 50). But when Vincent, another man, gives her a present of a bag of dulse, a type of seaweed eaten as a local snack, she is pleased by his attention.

The climax of this alternating pattern of past and present scenes is an argument between Mr. Stanley and Lydia about Willa Cather, who used to have a house on the island and who once advised a local woman about a marriage proposal.[18] Mr. Stanley insists that, although Cather may have lacked "experience," she could give such advice because she "knew things as an artist knows them." But Lydia, although a writer herself, angrily disputes Cather's knowledge of marriage: "Willa Cather lived with a woman" (57). What Lydia really wants to know about Cather, but cannot ask Mr. Stanley, is the same thing she wants to know about her own lonely life: "How did she live?" (58). In a way, therefore, despite her lesbianism, Cather becomes an alter ego of the writer-protagonist, but there is no answer to Lydia's question.

The conclusion connects this story with the emphasis on shelter and warmth in "The Office" and "Simon's Luck." Lydia thinks of Mr. Stanley's admiration of Cather as "a lovely, durable shelter he had made for himself," one that he cannot be deprived of (58). Although she has lost her temporary shelter with Duncan, she feels "warmed" by Vincent's gift (59). Reminiscent of the conclusions in *Dance of the Happy Shades*, this neat ending offers a pointed thematic summary: the two characters represent the respective consolations of art and love.

In contrast to "Dulse," both "Bardon Bus" and "Hard-Luck Stories" focus on a pair of female characters. In each case the first-person narrator's friend mirrors the narrator's own characteristics. Thus, instead of looking at herself in a mirror, as Del does at the end of "Baptizing" when she observes herself suffering, each of these narrators observes reflections of herself in the other woman. The subjective observer-participant split in Munro's earlier narratives has now been objectified: the narrator observes not only herself but also another participant in the same situation that she is in—no longer an imaginary participant as in "Tell Me Yes or No," but another actual woman.

In "Bardon Bus" (1982) the narrator and Kay, her friend, who share a Toronto apartment, are both "getting over" love affairs and encouraging each other in their attempts to recover (117). Their former lovers, also friends, are both anthropologists. Both women are described as going through the same stages of a love affair—from the initial euphoria through the anguished struggle to free themselves from their humiliating emotional dependence on men who no longer want them. Observing the many repetitions of this process in Kay, who "survives without visible damage," the narrator concludes, "the spectacle of her life is not discouraging to me" (117). Then she narrates the stages of the same process in her own life. But her comment about the lack of "visible damage" in Kay is subtle dramatic irony, for Munro deplores the damage that women inflict upon themselves when they let themselves drown, totally immersed in a series of love affairs: "I've watched the lives of friends who are always either falling in love or recovering from a love affair and then going into the next one. There is no time or emotional energy for anything else" ("Great Dames," 38).

Both the narrator and Kay also use clothes as erotic costumes to attract a man. Munro has explicitly criticized this behavior, too. She has defined the tone of "Bardon Bus" as a "feeling of hysterical eroticism. Very edgy and sad. . . . a feeling about the masquerades and attempts to attract love" ("Interview": Hancock, 82). After a brief Australian affair with Alex, her anthropologist, the narrator, alone again in Canada, is "half convinced that a more artful getup would have made a more powerful impression" on him, that "more dramatic clothes" than the casual ones she wore in the Australian heat "might have made [her] less discardable" (MJ, 124–25). So she shops "feverishly" for a "devastating" new outfit that will win Alex back when he also returns to Canada (124, 125). The irony of her attitude toward clothes is revealed at the end of the story. Paradoxically, she is both right and wrong. Masquerading as a "kinky" schoolgirl in a tunic with nothing underneath, *Kay* snares Alex (128).

But the irony of this story is shaped by something much more complicated than either the parallelism between the two women or the unexpected ending. While writing a story, Munro likes to "discover. . . . ambiguities in the situation," to "keep finding out more and more about it" ("Interview": Hancock, 84–85). Both the irony and the ambiguity of this story arise from the tension of the narrator's enormous ambivalence about her experience with Alex. The dramatic irony generated by the numerous contradictions between the thirteen short sections of the story reveals the civil war splitting the ambivalent narrator in half. What she says and what she feels are often very different. In fact, what she says is a struggle against what she feels, for, like Del and like Rose, she is acutely aware of "the threat" of seeing "herself slipping under" (MJ, 115). She is another potential drowning victim.

One of these contradictions between saying and feeling appears in a parallel pair of successive scenes. The first scene is set in the past in Australia, where the narrator and Alex invite his friend, Dennis, to dinner; the second is set in the present in Toronto, where Dennis takes the narrator out to dinner. In both of these dinner scenes, Dennis is brutally rude to the narrator, but as long as she is with Alex she can be brave and spunky. Dennis compares Alex's women—he has been married three times—to the standing army of terra cotta soldiers excavated in Sian, China.[19] But the narrator jauntily insists that "the comparison's a bit off" because the women "came along and joined up of their own free will and some day they'll leave. They're not a standing army. Most of them are probably on their way to someplace else anyway" (120). At the end of this feminist declaration of sexual independence, Alex choruses, "Bravo" (120).

But when Dennis has the narrator alone in Toronto, she is psychologically unprotected against his brutality. The underlying reason for her vulnerability is, as in many earlier characters, her ambivalence about what she really wants. At this point Munro suggests this uncertainty by an ironic contrast between the narrator's memory of herself as a young nursing mother and a recent dream. The narrator remembers the nursing mother as "[f]at and pink on the outside; dark judgments and strenuous ambitions within" (118). But her dream undercuts both these undefined ambitions and the fervent force of her Australian speech about independent women. Sometime before the Toronto dinner, she has a wish-fulfilling dream about Alex in which he tells her "he did not want to interfere with [her] life but he did want to shelter [her]." She comments, "I loved that word." Then she awakens: "The word shelter was still in my head. I had to feel it shrivel" (114).

At the Toronto dinner, she shrivels horribly. She naively expects Dennis to bring her a message from Alex, but Dennis's only message is his cruel reminder that, although older men can always get younger women and "start all over," the reverse is not true. "A woman your age can't compete" (121). To define the impossibility of this competition, Dennis then goes into far more clinically explicit and humiliating detail than anything imagined by Rose or inflicted upon Lydia: "The uterus dries up. The vagina dries up" (122). In an interview Munro has defined "the ultimate horror" as "getting to a stage where one still has sexual feelings but is no longer considered a possible sex object" ("Great Dames," 38). Rubbing the narrator's nose into this horror, Dennis watches her maliciously to see just how she will react to being stripped emotionally naked. Tongue in cheek, he argues that because "women are . . . . forced to live in the world of loss and death," they are "the lucky ones!" But he insists that they "won't get any happiness by playing tricks on life. It's only by natural renunciation and by accepting deprivation, that we prepare for death and therefore that we get any happiness" (122). This cruel speech is a much grimmer version of Simon's *memento mori*.[20]

Stunned into silence by this sadistic attack, the narrator is nevertheless not ready for renunciation. So, hoping to disguise her aging body, she sets out on a shopping expedition. In defining this story's tone of "hysterical eroticism," Munro located its source in her own expeditions to "women's dress shops," where she has observed not only the clothes but also the shoppers, "all sorts of ordinary women, like shop girls and typists," who dress "like prostitutes" and who make "their faces up in brilliant and very artificial ways. Also, there are old women dressed the same way, made up the same way" ("Interview": Hancock, 82). During her search of the dress shops, the narrator sees two people masquerading: a fat old woman, ridiculous in buttercup yellow, and a transvestite, "a pretty boy dressed up as a lady" (125). Just as Simon's reminder of death grows much rawer in Dennis's mock praise of sexual deprivation, so the disguise theme of "Wild Swans" grows much darker in the narrator's description of these two figures, neither of whom succeeds in being what she or he pretends to be. The narrator imagines that the fat woman, deluding herself about her desirability, sees herself "in the mirror" as a yellow "flower" surrounded by a "lovely buttery light" (125).

Through the ironic repetition of yellow as the key color in the narrator's compulsively relived memories of a love scene with Alex, the fat woman's dark self-delusion dyes the narrator, too. When she and Alex had intercourse, she wore a yellow nightgown and their bedroom was filled with the "golden twilight of love" (124). The full significance of this love scene emerges from a comparison with the opening section of the story, for these two sections, just like the two dinner scenes with Dennis, suggest ironic contrasts that develop the narrator's ambivalence about Alex and sexual love. In the opening section, the narrator imagines herself as "an old maid, in another generation," a rural woman whose only emotional nourishment comes from a "lifelong dream-life" about a pathetically unconsummated love affair in her past (110). The "center of [her] fantasy" as this spinster is "the moment when you give yourself up, give yourself over, to the assault which is guaranteed to finish off everything you've been before" (111). But the narrator sarcastically ridicules this fantasy, just as she later ridicules Dennis's analogy of the standing army. Imagining the spinster in her lonely bed, with nothing but a "hot-water bottle . . .clenched between [her] legs," she mocks her "stubborn virgin's belief . . .in perfect mastery; any broken-down wife could tell you there is no such thing" (111).

Coral Ann Howells praises this mocking passage as a "critical scrutiny" of "romantic" female "fantasy," but she ignores the contradiction in the love scene with Alex that the narrator keeps reliving (86). In that scene, the narrator is anything but critical. On the contrary, her attitude toward such sexual "mastery" is exactly the opposite. She keeps remembering this scene because in violently passionate intercourse she and Alex "almost finished each other off" (124). The repetition of this key phrase, *finish off*, links the spinster's fantasy with the love scene, and everything about the narration of this sexual memory reinforces the narrator's belief not only that such sexual experience *is* possible but that she has actually had it.

In her memory she sees herself as if in an imaginary photograph or film, and the moment she sees is one of complete physical and emotional helplessness, just after orgasm. Initially she delights in reliving these memories, but gradually, deprived of Alex, their source, she begins to be tormented by them: "All they did was stir up desire, and longing, and hopelessness, a trio of miserable caged wildcats that had been installed in me without my permission . . . . The images, the language, of pornography and romance are alike; monotonous and mechanically seductive, quickly leading to despair" (123). The tormentingly intense reality of the scene that she now hates to remember, "but . . . can still slide deep into," is emphasized by the use of the present tense, with the events in the remembered scene synchronized with the narration (123). But at the same time, her separation from this past is suggested through the sudden shift from the first-person to the third-person point of view. This combination of the present tense and the third person produces the paradoxical equation of pornography and romance to reduce the narrator to a helpless voyeur compelled to watch *herself*:[21]

> On the bed a woman lies in a yellow nightgown . . . pulled off her shoulders and twisted up around her waist. . . . A man bends over her, naked, offering a drink of water. The woman, who has almost lost consciousness, whose legs are open, arms flung out, head twisted to the side as if she had been struck down in . . . some natural disaster [,] . . . rouses herself and tries to hold the glass in her shaky hands. (123)

That this woman has suffered an assault that has finished off everything she was before, precisely the assault that the mocking narrator earlier insisted was impossible, is underlined when her lover, laughing with "amazement . . . not far from horror," says, "We almost finished each other off" (124).

All this tremendous ambivalence about how she feels, combined with her separation from her compulsively remembered past, impels the narrator to try to argue herself out of her humiliating confusion. But once again, she is ambivalent. In a series of brief scenes set in the present in Toronto, she keeps assuring herself that since she has now hit bottom she will soon recover. But she then recounts another dream about Alex, "a movie-dream of heaven." In this dream the two of them "were wearing innocent athletic underwear outfits, which changed at some point into gauzy bright white clothes, and these turned out to be not just clothes but [their] substances, [their] flesh and bones and . . . [their] souls." When these souls embrace, their passion is "transformed . . . into a rare state of content" (127). Just as Rose in "Mischief" denies what she is doing when, meeting Clifford, she pretends that her sexy clothes are really a disguise, so this dream denies what the narrator has been trying to do by shopping for clothes to disguise her body. Thus, like her first dream about Alex, in which she yearned for shelter, this dream also functions as wish-fulfillment, for it insists that clothes *are* the body, not disguises separate from it, and that bodily passion can somehow be transmuted into something spiritual. Thus with sinuous subtlety it denies the humiliations of aging female flesh.

When the narrator is awake, she tells herself, like Rose in "Simon's Luck," that she has to make up her mind: "What you have to decide . . . is whether to be crazy or not, and I haven't the stamina, the pure, seething will, for prolonged craziness" (127). She also insists that there's "a pleasure in taking into account . . . everything that is contradictory and persistent and unaccommodating about life" (128). One of these contradictory elements is that "misplacement is the clue, in love, the heart of the problem, but like somebody drunk or high I can't quite get a grasp on what I see" (128).

Such *misplacement*, which is clearly both a thematic and a structural definition of the story, sounds like the *disarrangement* that Rose discovers and defines when she is informed of Simon's death (WDY, 173). But until some point beyond the last scene of this story, the narrator's intense ambivalence makes her incapable of grasping the misplacement that she herself is constantly engaged in, paradoxically positioning herself on both sides of her internal argument. The differences between her dreams and her compulsive sexual memories, on the one hand, and her waking actions and consciously formulated beliefs, on the other, emphasize this tension very sharply. Munro has defined the internal conflict in this story as "the tension between erotic hysteria and the survivor's common sense," and the joltingly unexpected last scene shows why she argues that "the survivor's common sense wins . . ." ("Visit," 13). Even though Munro does not indicate her narrator's reaction when she discovers the irony of her protest against the standing army of Alex's women, Dennis's cruel comparison was not "off," after all. Alex has not only returned to Toronto without contacting the narrator but has already initiated a new affair with Kay. This sudden turn of events seems to imply that the whole humiliating process will now repeat itself in the mirror of Kay's experience. Therefore, the spectacle of Kay's life *will* be discouraging to the narrator because now it will reflect her own hysterical behavior and thus restore her to common sense at some point after the end of the story. The structure of this story, like that of "Mischief" and "Simon's Luck," emphasizes, once again, that, although "things never turn out as expected," the reasons that they do not have just as much to do with the ambivalent characters' often subliminal emotions as with unknown information about other people (MJ, 129). Alex and the narrator are another symbiotic pair.

In "Hard-Luck Stories," as in "Bardon Bus," the parallelism between the two mirroring characters involves their relationship with the same man. Both the primary first-person narrator and Julie, her friend, have affairs with Douglas, one after the other. But in this story the parallelism between the two characters becomes even more explicit in Julie's role as an additional first-person narrator, telling her "hard-luck" stories in two long flashbacks within a flashback. Her eagerness to have an exciting extramarital affair, reminiscent of Rose's in "Mischief," is satirized in her involvements with a mental patient and then with a highly unprofessional psychologist. These stories are then followed by the primary narrator's. And both narrators' stories illustrate the same disappointing point: that neither woman inspires a man's irrational passion. But that, the primary narrator insists, is the kind of love that everybody really wants, not the calmly intelligent and rational kind. Discovering this disappointing lack in herself "was so humiliating" that she "couldn't stand it," especially because this "revelation" occurred in the home of the woman with whom her own lover was obsessed, and about whose new lover he kept up a furiously jealous tirade "[b]efore, during, and after making love" to the narrator (196, 195, 194). But her willingness not just to listen to his tirade in such a situation but even to reveal it in detail to others identifies her as yet another character who is an accomplice in her own humiliation. Both narrators tell these self-exposing stories to the same listener, Douglas, who chants an appropriately mocking introduction to their revelations: "'Back and side lay bare, lay bare . . .'" (191). Their confessions are the psychological equivalent of the physical self-exposure of such characters as Mr. Chamberlain and Mrs. Cryderman.

Unlike the unexpected ending of "Bardon Bus," the ending here occurs at the beginning. In a self-reflexive opening scene, the two narrators discuss the irony of their both having affairs with Douglas. They insist that "that isn't the way things happen" (182). But a series of flashbacks within a flashback demonstrates that they are wrong: that *is* the way things happen, after all. Douglas becomes Julie's lover, too. The contrast between Julie's appearance in this opening scene, in which she is joyously meeting Douglas, now her lover, and her appearance in the major flashback, in which the narrators tell their stories, shows that Munro is mocking the same game of erotic masquerade that the two women play in "Bardon Bus." In the flashback scene in which Julie is introduced to Douglas, she is wearing denim and hiking boots; but in the chronologically later opening scene, she has transformed herself from this briskly practical and androgynous woman into "a southern belle's romantic notion of herself" ("Interview": Hancock, 82). She is wearing a pink and white dress and a Scarlett O'Hara picture hat "with a pink rose under the brim" (MJ, 181).

The ending of the major flashback, like the endings of "The Spanish Lady" and "Simon's Luck," functions as a somber corrective to the primary narrator's self-centered absorption in her own humiliations. After the narration of the stories, the two women and Douglas stop in a country graveyard to "soothe" their "spirit[s]" and to amuse themselves by idly reading the inscriptions on old tombstones. The primary narrator reads one aloud:

Afflictions sore long time she bore
Physicians were in vain,
Till God did please to give her ease,
And waft her from her Pain. (196)

Coming immediately after the narrators' tales about sex, this grim description of physical suffering and death once again juxtaposes the two humiliations of the flesh. But the primary narrator is jarred by the sharp contrast between real pain and the trivialities that she and Julie have been complaining about. Suddenly separated and distanced from her egotistically complaining self, she makes the kind of critical comment that the omniscient narrator makes about the protagonist in *Who Do You Think You Are?*: "Then I felt something go over me—a shadow, a chastening. I heard the silly sound of my own voice against the truth of the lives laid down here. Lives pressed down, like layers of rotting fabric, disintegrating dark leaves. The old pain and privation. How strange, indulged, and culpable they would find us—three middle-aged people still stirred up about love, or sex" (196). This split, in which the self-critical narrator recognizes the culpability of her own behavior, is yet another illustration of the analogous functions of Munro's first-person and omniscient third-person narrators.

A similarly jarring ending occurs at the climax of "Labor Day Dinner," originally published on 28 September 1981, in the *New Yorker*. On their way home from a Labor Day dinner party, Roberta, her lover, George, and her two daughters are nearly killed. In this story the forty-three-year-old Roberta's humiliations are once again those of a divorced, middle-aged woman; but here, by combining the points of view of three characters, Munro introduces a new technique to criticize her protagonist. Instead of showing "the other characters . . . only through the eyes of the main character," her usual technique, here Munro shows Roberta, the main character, first from her own third person point of view and then briefly from her lover's and her older daughter's ("Interview": Hancock, 112). In this way these two characters fulfill the critical function of the omniscient narrator in earlier stories and also become much more important as characters in their own right.

Dressing for the dinner party, Roberta puts on a halter top, but when George remarks, "Your armpits are flabby," she scurries into "something with sleeves" and hides her weeping behind dark glasses. She is convinced that George, six years her junior, "is disgusted by her aging body" (MJ, 137). Munro has defined her own attitude toward aging and clothes as a recognition that "there is a cutoff point in a woman's life where you have to realize you just can't go on trying to be 19 anymore so what are you going to be like?" Although "it's liberated not to care what you look like, . . . I'm not going to be able to stop" ("Great Dames," 38). Roberta echoes this confusion about knowing when to stop: "Now the payment is due, and what for? For vanity. Hardly even for that. Just for having those pleasing surfaces once, and letting them speak for you; just for allowing an arrangement of hair and shoulders and breasts to have its effect. You don't *stop* in time, don't know what to do instead; you lay yourself open to humiliation" (MJ, 137; emphasis added). But she backs off enough to recognize these feelings as "self-pity—rising and sloshing around in her like bitter bile" (137).

The disadvantages of middle age are also stressed by the contrast between Roberta and her two lovely young daughters, Eva and Angela, the latter a teenager so beautiful that people compare her to a goddess. All three of them live with George in his farmhouse. Being in love in this situation makes Roberta resemble two earlier Munro characters, Del, who cannot study, and Rose, who cannot read, when they are in love. Roberta, an illustrator, cannot do her work. "Roberta meant to keep busy illustrating books. Why hasn't she done this?" She answers her own question with a series of self-defensive rationalizations: "No time, nowhere to work: no room, no light, no table. No clear moments of authority, now that life has got this new kind of grip on her" (141).

This "grip" is George. But, in the two sections of the story narrated from his point of view, he is very critical of Roberta's inability to work. "Roberta does do some work, though she has done nothing to earn money as far as he knows; she hasn't been in touch with her publishers, and she hasn't worked on ideas of her own" (144). He is also very critical of her as a mother. But, although he wants to make reparations for his remarks about her appearance, he cannot help wondering at the radical transformation that being in love with him has produced in Roberta's behavior. When they met, Roberta "seemed to him courageous, truthful, without vanity. How out of this could come such touchiness, tearfulness, weariness, such a threat of collapse he cannot imagine" (150).[22]

Between these two sections narrated from George's point of view is also a section from Angela's point of view. Five years older than Eva, Angela remembers a happy time with her parents when her mother was pregnant with Eva. Now this happy childhood memory is implicitly contrasted to her mother's present condition as "a person who doesn't ask for anything" (147). In excerpts from Angela's journal, the point of view switches from the third person to the first to reveal her recorded observations of her mother. Like George, Angela is critical of how love has altered her mother's behavior: "I have seen her change . . . from a person I deeply respected into a person on the verge of being a nervous wreck. If this is love I want no part of it" (147). The "if" reveals that this stern adolescent critic, like Del before she falls in love with Garnet, has no personal experience on which to base her opinions. Nevertheless, she continues: "He wants to enslave her and us all and she walks a tightrope trying to keep him from getting mad" (147). This acrobatic metaphor of obsequious tension links Roberta to Lydia in "Dulse," trembling on her toes in her unsuccessful efforts to please her critical lover. Like Lydia, Roberta "doesn't enjoy anything and if you gave her the choice she would like best to lie down in a dark room with a cloth over her eyes and not see anybody or do anything. This is an intelligent woman," her daughter grumbles, "who used to believe in freedom" (147).

First by revealing Roberta's panicky overreaction to George's remark about her armpits and then by having both George and Angela criticize her helpless disintegration, Munro creates still another drowned character whose "emotional life" has become "so overwhelming" that she has no "time for work or anything else . . ." ("Great Dames," 38). Even worse, Roberta's attitude has affected not only her own behavior but her daughters' also. Already aware of Angela's scathing opinions, for she has read parts of the journal, Roberta also overhears Eva discussing her "silent fights" with George and realizes that "she has instructed [her daughters], by example, that he is to be accommodated, his silences respected, his joking responded to" (MJ, 151). Thus, Roberta is apprehensive not only for her powerless self but also for her children if George should somehow reject them. During the dinner party she gets intoxicated enough to think to herself, "Sexual abdication is not enough . . . " (156). The choice of the word *abdication* to describe the helplessness of her sexual relationship echoes Char's besotted helplessness when she had "lost her powers, abdicated," and thus resembled a drowned corpse (SIB, 11).[23]

But the dinner-table conversation about a widower mourning his wife, who uncomplainingly wore a colostomy bag on their last shared vacation, gradually modifies Roberta's self-perception. Because she is not a dying woman, she begins to feel that she can accept her aging "matter-of-factly" instead of whining about it (MJ, 154). Driving home in this increasingly self-confident mood, she is convinced that George no longer controls their relationship. "She has power. But the minute she begins to value it it will begin to leave her" (158).

Then suddenly, on the dark country road, a speeding "ghost car" silently "flashes before them" and nearly kills them (159, 158). Like the narrator in "The Spanish Lady," for whom the death of the old man in the Vancouver station makes everything else "slightly beside the point," the adult occupants of the car, when they finally reach home, "feel as strange, as flattened out and borne aloft, as unconnected with previous and future events as the ghost car was . . ." (SIB, 190; MJ, 159). And like Rose in "Simon's Luck," who realizes that the total power of death silences all her egocentric arguments about the sexual balance of power, Roberta is jolted by Eva's sleepy, uncomprehending question, "Are you guys dead?" (159). Grazed by death, the surface has split open to illuminate the terrifying reality underneath the concealing darkness.

The Progress of Love

In addition to "Jesse and Meribeth," already discussed in this chapter, four other short stories in *The Progress of Love* and the novella, "A Queer Streak," examine characters struggling to control humiliating situations. The first two of these stories, "Eskimo" and "Lichen," make significant comments on "Bardon Bus": "Eskimo" dramatizes a much darker example of the same basic ambivalence, but "Lichen" reverses the sexual situation of "Bardon Bus." The next two stories, "The Moon in the Orange Street Skating Rink" and "White Dump," also introduce important thematic reversals in the power struggle of the sexes. In the novella, the question of who possesses power, about which Rose was so ironically mistaken in "Simon's Luck," becomes even more ironic, and the answer to this question thus becomes much more explicitly satirical.

In addition to these thematic parallels, these stories, as well as later ones, are also unified by Munro's continued use of alter egos, voyeurs, and splitting metaphors. Alter egos appear in "Eskimo," "The Moon in the Orange Street Skating Rink," "A Queer Streak," and "Oh, What Avails" (1987).[24] "A Queer Streak" contains two pairs of alter egos, who not only structure the parallel plots but also double their satirical thrust against oversimplified concepts of control. Voyeurs appear in "Eskimo," "Lichen," "The Moon in the Orange Street Skating Rink," "White Dump," "Meneseteung" (1988), and "Oranges and Apples" (1988); but with the exception of "White Dump" these characters no longer control what they are watching, not even the voyeur who watches another voyeur in "Oranges and Apples" (46). Splitting metaphors also recur, surrealistically in "Eskimo," almost schizophrenically in "A Queer Streak," and self-reflexively in "White Dump." In both the novella and "White Dump," the splitting produces a temporary illusion of control, but later events in both works dispel this illusion to demonstrate that continued control is impossible.

Just as the double alter egos in the novella produce a greater complexity of characterization, so the manipulation of point of view in all these works also involves an increasing complexity of technique. "Lichen," like the earlier "Accident," uses an alternating point of view, but it is much more fully developed. The two-part novella also has a double point of view; in addition, an argumentative narrator engages the reader in a confrontational dialogue. "White Dump," however, exhibits the most significant technical breakthrough in Munro's use of a multiple point of view. She not only narrates the story from the overlapping viewpoints of three major protagonists but also criticizes them through the comments of an ironic narrator. A comparison of the original *New Yorker* version of this story with its revision in *The Progress of Love* reveals Munro's increased emphasis on the critical opinions of this distanced narrator.

In addition to using both alter egos and point of view in more complicated ways, in this collection and in later stories Munro also employs male protagonists with increasing frequency. In both "Lichen" and the novella, one of her two protagonists is a man; the central character who observes the action in "The Moon in the Orange Street Skating Rink" is a man; and, as already shown, two other stories in this collection, "Fits" and "Monsieur les Deux Chapeaux," also have male protagonists. The same is true in two later stories. "Oh, What Avails" has a male protagonist as well as a female one, and the central character in "Oranges and Apples" is a man. Thus, Munro cannot be classified as a feminist writer who programmatically limits herself to female narrators or protagonists or who presents the struggle of the sexes only from the feminine point of view.[25] But neither does she always present her male characters sympathetically.

Like "Bardon Bus," "Eskimo," originally published in the December 1985 issue of *Gentlemen's Quarterly*, is a very ironic story about a woman who is deeply ambivalent about her relationship to a man and who has an alter ego that reflects her situation. But the alter ego, a sixteen-year-old Eskimo girl, is superficially so different from Mary Jo, the protagonist, that Mary Jo is able to repress her incipient recognition of the psychological parallels between them. When this recognition begins to surface in her conscious mind, she deliberately goes to sleep—just like the narrator of "Postcard"—to prevent the process from continuing. The gradual stages of this process of consciousness-raising, the confused scene of voyeurism that precipitates a glimmer of recognition, and the nightmare that follows it are all striking illustrations of the development of Munro's technique since "Bardon Bus." Although she has basically the same pair of characters, a very ambivalent woman and her alter ego, and uses dreams again to dramatize her protagonist's ambivalence, this story, written from the third-person limited point of view, is much more dramatic in a surrealistic way and much more tightly unified; therefore, the concentrated effect is much darker in tone.

In a jet flying from the West Coast of Canada to Tahiti, Mary Jo is on a holiday trip paid for by Dr. Streeter, a married cardiologist who is both her employer and her lover. She thinks of how he and his wife take vacations together and how she has exaggerated her excitement about her lonely trip to impress her sisters, "whom she suspects of thinking she doesn't have much of a life . . . " (PL, 192). But she tells herself that she loves Dr. Streeter "with a baffled, cautious, permanent love" (203). For ten years she has served him faithfully, both in the office and in her apartment over the office. She "loves the office," where she is an unliberated factotum, brewing coffee and watering the plants (196). One reason that she may be content to limit her life to the building in which she lives and works is that she started out as a poor, small-town girl who had to borrow money for her education. When she got her first nursing job, she was overjoyed to be able to afford cosmetic dentistry, to have "her eyeteeth pulled and [her] front teeth filed" (193). This description of her teeth links her with the Eskimo girl who now sits across the aisle from her on the plane and whose "front teeth are missing, all across the top" (197). The Eskimo girl's traveling companion is an older man, a Métis (a man of mixed French and Indian ancestry), whose expensive clothes remind Mary Jo of Dr. Streeter.

But initially Mary Jo does not know these passengers' nationality and so dissociates herself from them. Imagining them to be Afghans, like the ones that she has seen on a television program, she thinks of the man as an exotic foreign "Khan" with a harem and plans a humorous letter about him to Dr. Streeter: "If he asks me to join his harem, I promise I won't agree to any such weird procedures!" (197, 198). But when the couple begin a drunken quarrel and the girl crosses the aisle to sit with Mary Jo, she tells Mary Jo that she is an Eskimo and the man, a Métis. Startled to realize that they are not foreigners at all, but "[f]ellow-Canadians," Mary Jo does not understand exactly what the girl wants when she confides in her "as if . . . confessing something—a shameful secret, a damaging mistake" (200). Although she offers her assistance to the frightened teenager, the girl finally returns to her own seat and, in the darkened cabin, begins to make love to the man she has just been complaining about.

Mary Jo "cannot stop herself from watching" this scene, which develops another parallel between Dr. Streeter and the Métis man (204). Mary Jo remembers how the doctor always keeps his eyes closed during coitus, "a fierce but solitary relish" that excludes her (194). Similarly, the man across the aisle keeps his eyes closed while the Eskimo girl "kisses him" and "licks him all over his face . . . . in a trance of devotion." This is a "ritual that takes every bit of her concentration and her self but in which her self is lost" (204). Compulsively watching this scene for "an immeasurable amount of time," Mary Jo feels "sick with revulsion," but, as soon as she stops watching, she feels exactly the opposite, a sudden rushing avalanche of sexual desire (204–5). This voyeur is clearly not distanced from what she watches.

Her erotic response makes her imagine the doctor's voice saying that the "girl's teeth were probably knocked out. In some brawl" (205). And she realizes that this comment, charged with "a sly and natural satisfaction," is a prejudiced and arrogantly self-satisfied remark, just like the other opinions that she has often heard him express and that Rhea, his feminist daughter, has described as characteristic of "the mind of a dinosaur" (205, 190). Although Mary Jo has not agreed with Rhea's description before, she now begins to sense that the Eskimo girl's "shameful secret" is analogous to her own (200). "She feels a physical shame and aversion," and "disgust, . . . worse than pain." For a moment, she realizes that she hates Dr. Streeter, but she immediately tells herself that she has manufactured her hatred. "If such a feeling became real, if a delusion like that got the better of her, she would be in a state too dreary to think about" (205).

To avert this danger, she falls asleep, but she has a very Freudian nightmare, in which she first sees the Eskimo girl "on the floor" with her head attached to her body only by an "elastic band" and later sees "[a] large figure entirely wrapped up in bandages . . . carried" into Dr. Streeter's office (206, 207). This headless alter ego and this helpless, concealed figure in the familiar office both suggest the truth that Mary Jo cannot force herself to face: that her abject devotion to Dr. Streeter makes her just as pitiable as the toothless Eskimo teenager licking her indifferent lover's face. Rhea has derided Mary Jo's devotion—"Mary Jo, you think he's God!"—a worshipful attitude illustrated by Mary Jo's inability to think of him as anything but "Dr. Streeter," even in the privacy of her own sexual memories (191). This devotion has deprived her of motherhood. Earlier in the story, her irritated disgust with the two young families sitting near her on the jet suggests her subconscious envy of parents with children to love. But in her nightmare she tells the Eskimo girl to "think clearly" and to decide "how she [can] save herself," advice that she herself has already received in Rhea's scornful assessment of her relationship with the doctor (206, 207). Then another dream-figure, a woman dressed in a sari, assures Mary Jo, "You'll get a chance to choose your own" (206). The nightmare ends with this woman asking Mary Jo a confusing question: "The court is in the garden?" In the dream, Mary Jo thinks that "the word 'court' may refer to Dr. Streeter. The woman may mean 'count,' being mixed up in her spelling. If that's so, she intends to mock him" (207). But it is Munro who intends to mock her protagonist, for the word *count* echoes Mary Jo's earlier memory of the "Khan" on television and thus subliminally suggests that Dr. Streeter also has a harem, his wife and the faithful Mary Jo, who agreed to the "weird procedure" ten years ago by becoming his mistress. Her restricted life in the doctor's building is almost analogous to a concubine's in purdah, but the ironic difference is that, unlike a Moslem woman (somewhat inaccurately suggested by the sari-clad figure), Mary Jo has already had her chance to choose and has chosen this life for herself.

When Mary Jo wakes up, "lifted to the surface" after her descent into an underworld of nightmarish revelations, "she can't get back . . . to the clear part," can't comprehend what her dream about her split alter ego has told her about herself (207). Her lack of comprehension echoes her ironic insistence to Rhea, "No man is wrecking my world," a true statement because *she* has let Dr. Streeter wreck it (190). Mary Jo's consciousness thus has not been raised far enough, for she cannot accept the effects of what she has chosen to do with her life. Munro believes that "some people don't admit their discoveries and turn aside from them," especially if their discoveries are painful ("Interview": Hancock, 102). If Mary Jo admitted her discovery about the doctor and herself, she would split in half, just as the Eskimo girl is nearly decapitated in the dream. There is an additional layer of irony here in that, unlike Del, Rose, and Roberta, Mary Jo *can* do her work because a nurse's work traditionally defines her role as secondary to a man's. Thus Munro uses the traditional doctor-nurse relationship as a paradigm of the secondary position of some of her earlier characters.

In its dramatization of ambivalence, "Eskimo" resembles "Bardon Bus." But "Lichen" (which first appeared on 15 July 1985 in the *New Yorker*) is exactly the opposite of that earlier story about an aging woman. Her ability to accept the inevitable effects of aging distinguishes Stella, the female protagonist of "Lichen," from David, her ex-husband. The ironically alternating points of view through which Munro develops these two contrasting characters reverse the sexual situation in "Bardon Bus." In that story, Dennis confidently insists that men can always start all over again with younger women and thus renew themselves. But this time it is the aging man who, in repeatedly trying to achieve this rejuvenation, exposes himself to exactly the same humiliations as those experienced by aging women trying to hold on to their lovers. This thematic reversal makes David the second humiliated man in Munro's procession of humiliated characters.

By beginning "Lichen" from David's point of view, Munro introduces his angry, misogynistic attitude toward Stella. Coming to visit her with

Catherine, one of his lovers, David sees Stella as "a short, fat, white-haired woman" not wearing any underclothes "to support or restrain any part of her." He fumes to Catherine, "Look what's happened to Stella . . . . She's turned into a troll" (PL, 32). When Catherine defends Stella, David turns his misogyny inside out and projects it: he is convinced that Stella's appearance deliberately dramatizes older women's defiant hatred of men. "There's the sort of woman who has to come bursting out of the female envelope at this age, flaunting fat or an indecent scrawniness, sprouting warts and facial hair, refusing to cover pasty veined legs, almost gleeful about it, as if this was what she'd wanted to do all along" (33). He is equally critical of Catherine, whose attempts to camouflage her approach to forty he considers unsuccessful. But he feels confident that he has resisted the effects of age. When he and Stella later meet a retired man who urges David to keep up his interests, David agrees that doing so "keeps you young," and he surreptitiously shows the man a photograph, commenting, "One of my interests" (38, 39). Later, to suggest the nature of this interest, he ostentatiously sings, "O, Mistress mine, where are you roaming? / O, stay and hear, your true love's coming" (39).

The narrative point of view then switches to Stella's. In this section David echoes Dennis's sadistic remarks in "Bardon Bus." Speaking of Catherine, David confides to Stella, "You know, there's a smell women get . . . . when they know you don't want them anymore. Stale" (40). Unknown to Catherine, David has already replaced her with Dina, a twenty-two-year-old "little witch" who "torments" his "soul" (42). David then shows Stella the photograph that he has shown the retired man, a pornographic shot of Dina's fully exposed genitalia. To maintain her composure, Stella refers to "the dark blot" of Dina's pubic hair as "lichen" (42, 41). As David continues gloating over Dina, "Oh, she's a bad girl!," Stella watches him and silently listens to his voice: "His voice when he talks about this girl seems . . . peculiarly artificial. . . . This special voice of his is rather high-pitched, monotonous, insistent, with a deliberate, cruel sweetness. Whom does he want to be cruel to—Stella, Catherine, the girl, himself?" (42). One answer to this unspoken question is David's outrageous request that Stella keep Dina's photograph so he won't yield to his temptation to show it to Catherine: "It's not that I want to hurt her" (43). He no longer bothers about not hurting Stella; in fact, he obviously derives deep sadistic pleasure from forcing her to be a secondhand voyeur.

Part of the reason for his behavior is revealed in the next scene, also narrated from Stella's point of view. Left alone together, Stella and Catherine discuss David, and Catherine tells her that he dyes his hair, something Stella has not noticed. "Every time he'd think of it," Catherine explains, "he'd tilt his head back, so you couldn't get too close a look. I think he was afraid you'd say something. He's slightly afraid of you. Actually, it looks very natural" (44). Ironically, Catherine believes that David dyes his hair to keep her love. But the next scene, once again narrated from his point of view, reveals that he is desperately struggling to hold on to Dina.

Trying in vain to telephone Dina, David is frantically afraid that she has betrayed him with a younger man. Now the jaunty song he sang earlier becomes an ironic comment on his inability to reach his mistress and make her hear: he knows that she is roaming, but he doesn't know where. His "innards" are "bubbling" with "craziness" as he thinks, "Of course she has betrayed him. She betrays him all the time" (46, 49). If she answers the phone, "he could howl at her, . . . he could plead with her" (49). Like so many of Munro's female protagonists humiliated by love, David now splits into two selves to try to control his humiliation: "He knows . . . and observes himself," the craziness of his own "suffering," the lack of "dignity" in his "bouts of desire and dependence and worship and perversity . . ." (50, 49). But "such knowledge and observation has no effect at all on his quaking gut, zealous sweat glands, fierce prayers" (50). The pornographic photograph of Dina thus shows that David has become a voyeur in his frantic scrabbling for the power to control his humiliating dependence. He has reduced Dina to her genitalia and those to an object that he can look at, control, and thus possess permanently. "To photograph is to appropriate the thing photographed," as Susan Sontag has remarked (4).

The difference between David and Stella is shown in yet another way when they visit her blind old father in a nursing home. Stella describes her father as having "reached the stage where . . . his big recreation [is] fixing up the past so anything he wishes had happened did happen" (52). Ironically, David, in his desire to rejuvenate himself by effacing the past he has shared with his wife, reveals himself to be like this old man. Looking back on their marriage, which his constant philandering sabotaged, David is sure that Stella is the only obstacle that prevents him from experiencing the psychic victories that he is still capable of enjoying. She "drag[s] so much weight with her" and is so "bloated" with her long-term and intimate knowledge of him that he can "never feel any lightness, any secret and victorious expansion . . ." (54). Nevertheless, to comfort Stella after the visit, he embraces her; but when a pretty young nursing-home aide sees them together, he feels embarrassed to be seen embracing someone so old. When Stella immediately senses his unspoken reaction and comments upon it, his conviction that she knows him too well for comfort is dramatically confirmed. Such a confirmation is one of the advantages of the alternating point of view Munro uses here.

In the conclusion, Stella discovers that David, like an adolescent who leaves a pornographic pinup for his mother to find, has left the photograph behind. Forced to see it again, she feels "the old cavity opening up in her," but in spite of her awareness that this familiar pain will recur, she knows that her activities, will keep the "flow" of her "days and nights . . . going" (55). These activities, which significantly include writing articles for "the historical society and the local paper," give her the control that the desperately struggling, self-deluding David lacks (35).

When compared to "Bardon Bus," "Lichen" shows Munro's characteristic insistence on complexity. She has remarked, "There's something about aging when you're a woman [that makes] you feel you can't win," and even if Alex's new affair jolts the narrator back to sanity, "Bardon Bus" clearly illustrates this pessimistic conclusion ("Great Dames," 38). But "Lichen" just as clearly illustrates the opposite, or rather that an aging man "can't win" either, and for much the same reasons. David's narcissistically dyed hair is analogous to the seductive outfit the narrator of "Bardon Bus" hopes will regain her lover. Her obsessive thoughts about the humiliations of love are also very much like David's. She thinks: "I can't continue to move my body along the streets unless I exist in his mind and in his eyes. People have this problem frequently, and we know it is their own fault and they have to change their way of thinking, that's all. It is not an honorable problem. Love is not serious though it may be fatal" (MJ, 126). Similarly, David thinks, "People don't have any patience with this sort of suffering, and why should they? The sufferer must forgo sympathy, give up on dignity, cope with the ravages" (PL, 49). In an interview, Munro has argued that, although life devoid of romantic love "is uninviting," nevertheless "there's something not serious about [such suffering]. It is not worthy somehow, not a proper kind of suffering" ("Writing's," E1). By assigning a similar self-critical lamentation to both of her characters, Munro sounds almost as if she were insisting to her reader, if you assume that only women suffer in this way, think again. Men can be drowned by love, too.

A similarly ironic reversal of the reader's assumptions about male and female roles occurs in "The Moon in the Orange Street Skating Rink," originally published on 31 March 1986 in the New Yorker. Like "Walking on Water," "Wood," "Fits," and "Monsieur les Deux Chapeaux," this story is written from the third-person point of view of a male protagonist. In the main time frame of the story, Sam Grazier, a retired Victoria businessman, is a sixty-nine-year-old widower visiting Gallagher, the small Ontario town where he and his cousin, Edgar, attended business college fifty years before. Edgar and his wife, Callie, still live there, and most of the story is a long flashback to Sam's memories of the relationship among the three of them when he and Edgar were boarders at Miss Kernaghan's boardinghouse, where Callie, perhaps their landlady's illegitimate daughter, drudged away as a pitiful little domestic slave. Sam and Edgar, both farm boys, felt very much out of place in town and at the college: they were outsiders because their clothes were wrong and their appetites too big. Nevertheless they felt very superior to Callie, "a little slavey, forever out of things, queer-looking, undersized, . . . compared to [whom] they were in the mainstream, they were fortunate. They could be mean or kind to her as they pleased, and it pleased them to be kind" (PL, 142). But the main event of the plot ironically demonstrates that the two boys' condescending appraisal of Callie as the quintessential outsider completely misinterprets her true character. At the end of the story, which returns to the present, Sam, visiting Edgar and Callie, still does not understand why things happened the way they did. His bewilderment confirms his story-telling role as a typical Munro persona, and it is now "[f]ifty years too late to ask" (160).

The first indication that the two farm boys misinterpret Callie is that she figures out a way to get the three of them into the Orange Street Skating Rink free. Although actually nineteen, she looks about twelve, and dressed like a boy in "ragged, ill-fitting . . . clothes," Callie climbs a tree, drops from it to the skating rink's roof, crawls through one of the air vents in the roof, jumps down to a platform inside the rink, and secretly admits the boys through a snow door (141). Her cleverness, her monkeylike agility, and her completely changed expression when she is disguised as a boy, "thoughtful but independent, alert for possibilities, ... sober and self-respecting," all suggest that Callie's tomboyish character is like the shifting effects of the "moon" installed in the skating rink roof (143): "The moon . . . is a yellow bulb inside a large tin can, a syrup tin, from which one end has been cut away. The other lights are turned off when the moon is turned on. A system of wires and ropes makes it possible to pull the tin can this way and that, creating an impression of shifting light—the source, the strong yellow bulb, being deeply hidden" (140).

This "impression of shifting light" characterizes not only the subject of the story but also its manipulation of point of view and narrative time. Sam's role in the story contributes to this pattern of wire-pulling and light-shifting because he does more than simply figure in his memories of the past. At times he functions like a third-person narrator, answering the questions of an imaginary auditor in the future. For example: "Why did others not manage the same trick [of sneaking into the rink], Sam might be asked on those occasions, years and years later, when he chose to tell the story, and he always said maybe they did, he wouldn't know about it. . . . And why was Callie not noticed? Well, she was very quick, and she was never careless; she waited her time" (141). These flashforwards to introduce retrospective commentary, like the omniscient narrator's interjections in *Who Do You Think You Are?*, effect the same split in the point-of-view character, who is both participating in the story in the past and narrating it in the future.

The second sign that Callie's personality is as changeable as the moon is a scene in which she temporarily sheds both her disguise as a drudge and her tough little-boy persona and reveals herself to be female, but only up to a strangely confusing point. Both Sam and Edgar attempt intercourse with her, but to no avail. Sam becomes a voyeur as he watches dubiously while Edgar, who pretends to be sexually experienced, takes the first turn, removing Callie's bloomers and bossily giving her irritated instructions. Then Sam himself takes over, with "jabbing and prodding and bafflement. Callie lay beneath them each in turn, half-grudging, half-obliging, putting up with them and not complaining that anything hurt" (146). Sam feels that he needs to learn what a naked girl looks like, but he is confused by his introductory anatomy lesson: "Callie was so thin her hipbones stood up, yet she seemed quite extensive to Sam, and unwieldy and complicated. . . . When he thought of this afterward, he still wasn't sure that he had found out what girls were like. It was as if they had used a doll or a compliant puppy" (146). He apologizes, but Callie, "[c]old and sticky" with spilled semen, scornfully dismisses the whole fumbling fiasco as "that stupid business" (146).

Up until this point in the flashback, Sam and Edgar are each other's alter egos. Both seventeen, the two country bumpkins are mistaken for brothers. Their similarity is symbolically emphasized by their performance of acrobatic stunts in which they "welded themselves together, . . . eliminating to an astonishing degree their separateness . . ." (135). But after their failure to shed their virginity, "a wedge" begins to develop between them (139). This wedge gradually pushes Sam to the periphery of the main action and reinforces his role as a third-person observer. When Edgar gets sick and stays behind at the boardinghouse, Sam continues to attend college. While they are thus separate, Edgar evidently achieves with Callie what the two boys could not do together, but terrified that consummation might also mean conception, he and Sam secretly take the train to Toronto.

At first Sam does not notice that a third passenger boards the train with them, an "absurd and dirty and ragged pretend-boy," Callie in her skating-rink disguise (155). Not only has she figured out where the boys are going and how, but she has also stolen money from Miss Kernaghan to buy her ticket. Tremendously impressed by her cleverness, Sam and Edgar are convinced that "she was exercising powers that didn't fall far short of being miraculous" (155). Sam suddenly realizes that Callie is not at all what the boys, in their simpleminded male superiority, have imagined her to be. "At that moment he saw power—Callie's power, when she wouldn't be left behind—generously distributed to all of them. The moment was flooded— with power, it seemed, and with possibility" (156–57). Munro's repetition of her key word, *power*, emphasizes this climax as the comically ironic reversal of what the boys believed. Callie is not a doll or a puppy nor the helpless little drudge, casually impregnated and left behind to suffer the permanently humiliating consequences—as Miss Kernaghan most likely was, although she has denied it very dramatically. On the contrary, Callie is an enterprisingly energetic "boy" who escapes to freedom with them. At this climactic moment, her cleverness and determination gleam like "the strong yellow bulb" of the skating-rink moon (140). Although Edgar's fears are groundless, for Callie is not pregnant, he marries her in Toronto, anyway. But their triumphant escape, with which "Sam's story . . . always ended," very typically turns out to be deceptive (157). Although Sam becomes a successful West Coast businessman, the young couple return to Gallagher, where, after inheriting Miss Kernaghan's money, they lead a fairly prosperous but restricted small-town life.

In the story's concluding section, which returns to the present time of its beginning, Sam observes that Edgar, although he has suffered a debilitating stroke, is well cared for by his still-energetic wife, who polishes him as if he were a Christmas-tree "ornament" (158). Callie's expression Sam now reads as a revelation of "a lifetime of fairly successful efforts and calculations," probably the result of her applied power (161). But he still does not understand why Edgar married Callie, "did what nobody was making him do, took what he had run away from" (160). He wonders if Edgar felt "compunction," but he still remembers his amazement at Edgar's unexpected decision, especially after the climactic moment "on the train," when "all three of them laughed with relief . . ." (160). A possible answer to Sam's question, however, is suggested by the setting of Callie and Edgar's apartment.

Although it is a realistically described setting, as many settings are in Munro's fiction, it once again seems to associate Callie with the skating-rink moon. Both the moon's strong yellow light and its pattern of shifting shadows are repeated in the flashy color-scheme of Callie's interior decor: "[g]old brocade" with a "[g]old plushy carpet," a "ceiling sparkling with stars," and "a dull-gold mirror in which Sam sees himself crisscrossed by veins of black and silver. Lights hang from chains, in globes of amber glass" (158). And when Sam wonders about their long-ago "moment of happiness," he defines it thematically in terms of light: "Do such moments really mean . . . that we have a life of happiness with which we only occasionally, knowingly, intersect? Do they shed such light before and after that all that has happened to us in our lives—or that we've made happen—can be dismissed?" (160).[26] In an article, Munro rather reluctantly concedes that "things are symbolic," but insists "that their symbolism is infinitely complex and never completely discovered" ("The Colonel's Hash Resettled," 182). Her insistence on a symbol's complexity fits the moon's constantly changing image to suggest that the unexpected, shifting patterns of life often obscure the deeply hidden, strong yellow light of happiness; it is glimpsed, therefore, only in brief flashes. The last sentence of the story is such a flash; describing Edgar smiling with "satisfaction" in their golden apartment, Callie says, "He's happy" (159, 161). Perhaps he is happy because his present physical dependence on his wife reflects the psychological dependence he intuitively recognized and permanently established at the moment of his sudden decision to marry her. A picture of them together, taken years after their wedding, significantly shows Callie's face as "authoritative," another term for *powerful* (159).

The tone of this story, especially in the clumsy voyeur scene (which Munro could have made much uglier by narrating it from Callie's point of view), and the concluding emphasis on Edgar's happiness, even though the reasons for it remain confusing and mysterious to Sam, make this story dramatically different from the ones preceding it.[27] The humiliations of love seem to have disappeared, and the power to control things seems to be—at least from Sam's limited observation of the spunky Callie—a matter of "delight, deception and pleasure," as in the free skating evenings she finesses for the three of them (156). This tone and this emphasis are especially significant if one compares the marriage in this story to those in "At the Other Place" and "Fits."

Although written more than thirty years apart, "At the Other Place" and this story have several similarities. In both stories an observer watches a married couple from the periphery of the main situation, the marriage, in which the wife has always been the dominant partner. And in both cases one spouse is near death. But here the similarities end. In the earlier story, the relationship seems charged with a perverse sexuality, which affects the couple's many children, and in the final scene Uncle Bert takes advantage of his wife's powerlessness to avenge himself for a lifetime of humiliation. In this story, however, the childless marriage seems strangely asexual; Sam theorizes that Callie "[p]erhaps . . . was too small, or not developed in the usual way" (160). But, in spite of her "sorry female state," the stricken Edgar seems to be serenely satisfied with the life that his wife has arranged and dominated (160).

The mystified observer's point of view is common to all three of these stories, for like the child watching the adults in "At the Other Place" and like Robert observing the Weebles in "Fits," Sam remains outside the situation. But through Sam's great temporal and spatial distance from the marriage, Munro makes the mystery of this marriage a reversal of conventional assumptions about a wife who is not traditionally "feminine" but plays the dominant role. Thus, Callie's association with the moon, traditionally a symbol of changeable femininity, finally becomes ironic, for she is no more traditionally feminine than the lightbulb inside the can is a real moon. Once again, therefore, Munro seems to be reminding her readers that their assumptions are not always true, for her infinitely complex symbol reveals another contradiction. Callie has power, but she does not seem to have used it to humiliate her husband. As in "Fits," the readers are not allowed to understand exactly what has happened or why, but, although Edgar's senility remains mysterious, it is serene.

Isabel Vogelsang, the unfaithful wife in "White Dump," also acquires power, but for a different purpose: to break out of a marriage in which sex is just another wifely chore and in which she has been hoping for "freedom," or at least for a free moment in which she can relax her "constant and clever exertions" to maintain her marriage and "to make [Laurence, her husband,] a man" (303, 304). Initially Isabel, much like Rose in "The Beggar Maid," is a poor college freshman who works in the college cafeteria and wears Woolworth sweaters. When she meets Laurence and he takes her home, she sees herself as a challenge to Sophie, his professor mother. However, by her husband's fortieth birthday, Isabel has wearied of her role and longs for freedom instead. But Munro develops her character's conception of freedom with a subtly shifting irony that makes it impossible to pour her plot into a feminist mold.

The idea of freedom is emphasized by the symbolic date of the story's main action, 14 July 1969, not only Laurence's fortieth birthday but also, as Sophie remembers, Bastille Day. (The story was originally published two weeks after Bastille Day, in the 28 July 1986 issue of the *New Yorker*.) Some of the key events on this day commemorating the freeing of prisoners are narrated three times in an overlapping technique that Munro has never used before. Although she uses a triple point of view in "Labor Day Dinner," in "White Dump" she develops the possibilities of this technique much further. Dividing the story into three major, numbered sections, she develops all three of her protagonists much more fully by narrating some of the main events from the point of view of each of the three female Vogelsangs: Denise, the daughter; Isabel, the mother; and Sophie, the mother-in-law. Munro uses this technique to show why Isabel's marriage ends. What the child Denise views only from the periphery of the action and does not fully understand, even as an adult, and what Sophie experiences, first as an outrage and then as an apprehension of unwanted change, become the destructive turning-point of Isabel's marriage. This overlapping technique, which Munro has defined as "mak[ing] a mosaic," emphasizes not only the confusion of several differing points of view but also the clear-cut yet very ironic moment of Isabel's conscious choice (Slopen, 76). At this climactic moment, Munro introduces a fourth point of view, that of an ironic first-person narrator. In its fully developed manipulation of a multiple point of view, this story is therefore significantly different from Munro's earlier stories. And in its climactic, explicit development of the key elements of several earlier stories, it is also a very important and revealing story.

The first section of the story begins in the present time of Denise's adult point of view. She is visiting her father and Magda, his second wife, who has renovated the Log House, the dark and spartan cottage in the Rideau Lake area where the events of her father's birthday took place in 1969. Denise remembers watching her parents on that day. She suspected that they concealed something from her, "[s]omething between them" that she could never comprehend because "[t]hey would not let her" (PL, 282). This attitude defines her function in the story as their watcher, alert to the sexual tension she vaguely senses between her still very attractive mother and her subtly dissatisfied father, but unable to understand it. On her father's birthday Denise arranges a ride in a small plane for him, and her mother orders a birthday cake from the airplane pilot's wife, a caterer.

A year after this birthday plane ride, the pilot's wife suddenly appears at the Vogelsangs' house and asks to speak to Laurence. Denise, standing on tiptoe and spying on their conference through a window, much like the young narrator in "At the Other Place," still does not understand what is happening. But when the young voyeur hears "the terrible sound" of the woman's "crying," she remembers the plane ride and the pilot's anecdote about seeing "St. Elmo's fire" during a flight through a thunderstorm. First, he saw "blue rings of fire around the propellers," and then "flames came shooting out of [his] fingers." Hearing this story, Denise had "a picture in her mind of the pilot with cold blue fire shooting out of his fingertips," an image she associates both with a memory of touching "an electric fence" and with the painful "spurts of sounds" she hears from the closed room where the pilot's wife is still sobbing (287, 288).

The first section ends by returning to the present, with Denise hearing Magda "humming a tune from an opera. 'Home to Our Mountains'" (288). The reference is to the duet sung in *Il Trovatore*, "*Ai nostri monti ritorneremo.*" In the duet, the imprisoned Azucena and Manrico, who believes he is her son, sing about escaping from prison and returning to the old peace of their mountain home (Act IV, Scene 2). This ironic allusion to peace introduces the second and third sections of the story, flashbacks narrated from Sophie's and Isabel's point of view, respectively.

The electrical images that Denise remembers in the first section reappear briefly in the second section and climactically in the third section. At the climax, these images show that the old peace was deceptive and was suddenly split by lightning on Bastille Day. For Isabel, home itself, the dark and gloomy Log House, was the prison. But the operatic allusion that Munro deleted from the original *New Yorker* version of this story suggests the connotations of lightning much more dramatically. In the original version, Magda hums a melody from Gounod's *Faust* (31). Thus the cold blue flames that Denise imagines spurting from the pilot's fingertips associate him with Mephistopheles and his supernatural powers, which help Faust to seduce Margareta.[28] The Mephistophelian pilot is himself the seducer, and the erotic electrical metaphors suggest why Isabel finds him so exciting.

But, although Munro replaced this allusion to *Faust* with the one to *Il Trovatore* when she revised the story, the electrical metaphors still unify its three sections and connect this story with earlier ones. In the second section of the story, Sophie recalls a "ball of lightning danc[ing] across the bedroom floor . . ." (294). This ball and the St. Elmo's fire that Denise remembers in the first section are both "electrical discharges in the atmosphere" (287). These are manifestations of the same power that electrifies the narrator in "Images," that recurs in Del's sexual fantasies about Mr. Chamberlain and sexual ecstasies with Garnet, and that Frances associates with "a crazy and shattering, painful kind of lust" in "Accident" (MJ, 85). In the ironic climax of "White Dump," this electric power is specifically associated with Isabel's lustful fantasies about the pilot, fantasies kindled by an incident earlier that day.

This climactic incident is narrated partially from Sophie's and partially from Isabel's points of view. Early in the morning, while Laurence and Isabel are having intercourse, just another hurried chore for Isabel, Sophie goes swimming in the buff, as she has always done at the lake. Here her memories reveal that she has been a bravely unconventional woman who did not let the birth of Laurence, her illegitimate son, prevent her from having an academic career. But now both her age and her unconventionality make her vulnerable to humiliation. Some hippies, who "could have been watching, could have seen her take off her bathrobe and go into the water," find her discarded robe and rip it apart (PL, 292). When they imitate her and laugh at her, just as the hippies mock the elderly Mr. Lougheed in "Walking on Water," she is outraged by her humiliation. But before returning to her cottage, she sits down and carefully calms herself. Then she arrives, stark naked.

The scene of Sophie's arrival is narrated from Isabel's point of view as the watcher. She seems to be emotionally distanced and therefore in control, but the emotional distance turns out to be ironically deceptive.

The effect of distance is partially derived from the similarity of this scene to the one in which Del watches Mr. Chamberlain masturbate. Just as he is the first man that Del sees naked, so "this was the first time Isabel had ever seen an old woman naked" (300). And just as Del observes and describes Mr. Chamberlain's penis in clinical detail, so Isabel observes Sophie's "slung down" breasts, scanty pubic hair, and "slackly filled" skin (300). The effect of emotional distance is also derived from the contrast between Isabel and the horrified Laurence, who snatches up a tablecloth to cover his mother. Isabel watches his "shamed blood rising hotly up his neck" and notes his "trembling" voice (301). But because she is unaware of how Sophie achieved her carefully controlled composure, she believes that Sophie is exposing herself on purpose, much as Mr. Chamberlain exposed himself to Del. When Sophie fails to cover herself adequately with the tablecloth, Isabel thinks, "The stagy old showoff. Showing off her purity, her high-mindedness, her simplicity. Perverse old fraud" (301). This angry description imputes to Sophie the theatrical perversity of Mr. Chamberlain. But Isabel's anger becomes very ironic when she begins to fantasize about the airplane pilot.

Before the plane ride, as Isabel looks him over with avid curiosity, the irony is heightened by her resemblance, not to Del with Mr. Chamberlain, but to Rose with the "minister" in "Wild Swans." The pilot also distinctly resembles the "minister." The fake clergyman is "between fifty and sixty years old" and has "bright waves of gray hair combed straight up from his forehead" (WDY, 60). The pilot is perhaps "fifty—with waves of very blond or white hair, . . . combed straight back from his forehead" (PL, 302). "[S]harply self-possessed," the pilot, unlike Isabel's husband, does not have to be made a man (302). After the plane ride, which Isabel does not share, the pilot casually remarks that she could always go for a ride, too. When Isabel interprets this remark as a sexual invitation, she gives the word *ride* the same vulgar connotation that it has in "Thanks for the Ride." This connotation reveals that Isabel has not been emotionally distanced, after all. On the contrary, she has been projecting: she has been criticizing Sophie's fraudulent purity because her own erotic thoughts are impure. "Isabel . . . knew what it was that had unhinged her. It was Sophie's story. It was the idea of herself, not Sophie, walking naked out of the water, toward those capering boys. . . . That made her long for, and imagine, some leaping, radical invitation. She was kindled for it" (305). So, as they are leaving the airport, she imagines an exciting scene in which she and the pilot "turned at the same time, . . . looked at each other, just as in some romantic movie, operatic story, high-school fantasy. They . . . exchanged a promise that was no less real though they might never meet again.

And the promise hit her like lightning, split her like lightning, though she moved on smoothly, intact" (305).

The allusion of this climax to the instantly electrifying excitement of an operatic meeting is a self-reflexive echo of the first meeting of Del and Garnet, "like a recognition in an opera" (LGW, 211). At this critical moment, an ironically omniscient first-person narrator suddenly intrudes into Isabel's fantasy to comment:

> Oh, certainly. All of that.
> But, it isn't like lightning, it isn't a blow from outside. We only pretend that it is. (PL, 305)

The last two sentences of this deflating analysis are not in the original *New Yorker* version.[29] The addition of this passage of narratorial disparity to the revised version therefore suggests Munro's reason for deleting the allusion to *Faust* from this version: she is rejecting her own earlier use of the lightning metaphor in "Baptizing," to reemphasize that what the adolescent Del initially imagines as an irresistible external force is invariably an internal one. Much as the retrospective Del both sympathizes with and criticizes her adolescent self, so this narrator in "White Dump," by using the first-person plural pronoun, *we*, simultaneously shares Isabel's fantasy and rejects it. Therefore Isabel's yielding to her fantasy involves not dramatic helplessness but conscious choice. Paradoxically, however, this choice is to behave in an essentially childish way. Her childishness is apparent both in the meaning of the story's title and in the relationship that title creates between this story and earlier ones.

When Laurence and Sophie tell Isabel about their plane ride over the Rideau Lake area, they mention seeing a "silica quarry from the air," "[w]hite marble" shining "like a snowfield" (306). This description reminds Isabel of the white dump—an "enormous pile of white candy," of "vanilla icing and nuts and hardened marshmallow globs"—periodically swept out of the cookie factory behind Isabel's school and attracting all the schoolchildren. "It was like a kid's dream," she remembers, "the most wonderful promising thing you could ever see" (306). In another passage of commentary introduced by the omniscient narrator at the end of the story, Munro equates this shining white dream of dirty, discarded candy with Isabel's greedy dream of passionate sex. Jumping ahead in time, the narrator confides that "[i]n the years ahead" Isabel "wouldn't be so astonished at the way the skin of the moment can break open" (307–8). But Isabel confesses to the grown-up Denise that her sudden break through the controlled surface of her marriage was caused by her dream of a shining sexual opportunity: "I think the best part is always right at the beginning. . . . That's the only pure part" (308). The adjective *pure* echoes Isabel's memory of the white dump, shining "like a pure white mountain" (306).

On the day after Bastille Day, Isabel, feeling "newly, and boundlessly, resourceful," goes to the pilot's house and gives herself to him (307). At the practiced touch of those "gifted" hands that the uncomprehending Denise has imagined as almost supernaturally charged with electricity, Isabel's reaction is very much like the adolescent Rose's response to the "minister's" invading hand in "Wild Swans" (308). But this time it is the real thing, "a slowly increasing declaration, over her bare neck and shoulders, bare arms and back, lightly covered breasts and hips," followed by "scenes of . . . fusing, sundering pleasure" (309, 308). This is the relationship that the pilot's sobbing wife reveals to Laurence a year later as Denise spies on them and that finally ends the Vogelsangs' marriage. By delaying this initial love scene until the end, Munro maintains erotic tension and suspense throughout her story.

Both literally and figuratively, this love scene is also the delayed consummation of the long series of earlier, sexually equivocal scenes between various adolescent heroines and older men: Del and Mr. Chamberlain, Rose and her father, Rose and the minister, Jessie and Mr. Cryderman. It is also a restaging and rewriting of the ambiguous love scene between those two middle-aged adolescents, Rose and Clifford in the ironic epilogue of "Mischief." The culmination of this long series in the erotic electricity of "White Dump" recalls, reemphasizes, and clarifies the subliminal sexual significance of the father-daughter beating scene and its cookie-eating aftermath in "Royal Beatings." W. R. Martin criticizes the "'icing and nuts and . . . marshmallow globs'" as "the somewhat obtrusive correlative" of the secret love affair in "White Dump" (*Alice Munro: Paradox and Parallel*, 185, 186). But, as already shown above, this significant correlation between sweet food and sex has occurred in several earlier stories. After fantasizing about "the surrender to sex" in *Carmen*, Del concocts and consumes "a rich, secret, sickening mixture of cocoa, corn syrup, brown sugar, coconut and chopped walnuts . . . ." Immediately afterwards, she compares her "[g]reedy eating" to masturbation (LGW, 184). Similarly, after the masochistic pleasure of being beaten by her father, Rose eats chocolate cookies washed down by chocolate milk. Later, the undertaker in "Wild Swans" uses chocolate to seduce women in his hearse, and when Rose lets the minister seduce her, her acquiescence is described as "greedy assent" (WDY, 63). Thus, in retrospect, Isabel's greedy appetite for the sweets of forbidden sex makes the subliminal sexuality of Rose's greedy hunger for cookies unmistakably explicit. And, although Isabel—like Rose in the epilogue of "Mischief"—is an adult, her "kid's dream" of the cookie factory thus makes her relationship with her fifty-year-old lover analogous to childish adolescent fantasies about forbidden sex with an older man (PL, 306). Rose's father, therefore, far from being the "shallow . . . caricature" that George Woodcock sees, is one of the most significant male characters that Munro has created, for he is not only Rose's father but also the father of several key male characters in other stories ("The Plots of Life," 248). Casting a dark shadow both backward and forward, this immature and sadistic figure suggests the unconscious, regressive motive of many of Munro's masochistic women: they keep searching for thrilling complicity with Daddy.[30]

The relationship of "White Dump" to these earlier stories, the deletion of the original allusion to *Faust*, the addition of the omniscient narrator's ironic comments about lightning, and the dirty candy metaphor combine to work against any feminist reading of the story. It cannot be forced into the formula of a feminist story with the prescribed happy ending in which the wife triumphs over her husband by breaking free of her marriage and finding herself in a passionate affair. In an interview Munro has emphasized that her rejection of resolutions for her characters includes a rejection of the "recent" idea of "walking out on your husband, . . . living on your own [and] finding yourself" ("Interview": Hancock, 102). Thus, Isabel admits to Denise the "sordid" and "grievous" consequences that she set in motion by initiating her affair with the pilot, who wheedles money out of her after becoming her lover (PL, 308). Isabel loses not only her husband but also some of her daughter's respect. Later Isabel becomes involved with a younger lover in an "unstable" relationship, details of which her dismayed daughter feels compelled to conceal from Laurence (278). But Denise cannot side with either parent unequivocally. She rejects her own lover's "Marxist" definition of her father as "almost purely evil, . . . nothing . . . but raging defenses and greed," simply because she rejects "male definitions and airtight male arguments," but then she adds, "I'm sick of hearing myself say 'male' like that" (277). At the same time, however, although she feels that her mother "at least, has no regrets," she is repeatedly and "harshly" critical of her mother's behavior (288). Thus, by using Denise's carefully qualified point of view, as well as the omniscient narrator's comments on Isabel, Munro continues to reject oversimplified "isms," both Marxism and feminism, and continues to insist on life's lack of final resolutions and its inherent confusion and complexity.

Munro's inability to write a "woman's lib book," already mentioned above, is the direct result of her emphasis on complexity ("What Is," 15). This causal connection is demonstrated by the parallel plot structure and by the double point of view of her satirical novella, "A Queer Streak," originally published in *Granta* in 1985 and 1986 and republished in *The Progress of Love*. The novella has two third-person protagonists: Part I, subtitled "Anonymous Letters," is narrated from the point of view of Violet; Part II, "Possession," from the point of view of her nephew, Dane. From time to time, as in "White Dump," an omniscient narrator also argues about her protagonists' motives and behavior.

In Part I, the "queer streak" refers to the temporary fit of craziness experienced by Dawn Rose, Dane's mother, when she is a fourteen-year-old girl on the family farm that Violet has already left for normal school in Ottawa. Violet's absence is crucial because she has been mothering her two younger sisters ever since their mother, with whom the "queer streak" begins, was unhinged by the deaths of her first three children. When Violet is not at home to prepare Dawn for her first menstrual period, Dawn Rose, "affronted by this development," strips off her underpants and sits down in an icy creek, "resolved to get the bleeding stopped" (PL, 215). During her ensuing year of amenorrhea, she sends her father, a bewildered man who does not know how to be a farmer or a father, a series of anonymous letters threatening his life. Her sadistic fantasies about murdering him are like those of Helena in "Executioners," but lack Helena's motivation. When Violet returns home and discovers that these letters are her sister's work, she begs her fiancé, Trevor, a priggish young minister, to come and rescue her, but, fearing hereditary insanity, he breaks their engagement instead. Although he implies that he might not do so if Violet consented to her sister's institutionalization, Violet feels that she must protect her sister from such a fate. Thus, her instinctive sense of sisterhood and Dawn Rose's craziness—described as "a good trick," a hoax, or "a joke," much like Ross's in "Monsieur les Deux Chapeaux"—permanently alter the shape of Violet's life (226). But unlike Ross, Dawn Rose recovers. "No strange behavior or queerness or craziness ever surfaced in her again" (233). She grows up quite normally, marries, and has a son, Dane.

In Part II the story of the anonymous letters is pried out of Violet in her old age by her grandniece, Heather, and Gillian, Heather's friend. These two young women are college-educated transvestites, who wear boots and "army clothes" and who have been living on "the Isle of Women," "a women-ruled society" in Mexico (244, 246). Dane calls them "woman's libbers" (245). Although Munro never uses the word *sisterhood* to label the bond between Heather and Gillian, she clearly implies a contrast between Violet and Dawn Rose's natural relationship and their contrived one. When they plan to dramatize the raw material of Violet's painful old memories for their women's theater, Munro's attitude toward these characters becomes explicit. It begins to emerge in the initial parallel between the two parts of the novella, an ironic comparison between the bloodthirsty, anonymous letters that Dawn Rose writes to her father and the postcard that Heather and Gillian send to Violet after she has told them her story.

When Violet originally examines the anonymous letters to try to discover who might have written them, she notes that they are childishly "printed in pencil," but show "an understanding of sentences and capital letters" (222). When Dane, a homosexual, middle-aged architect, reads Heather's postcard to his old aunt, he makes similar observations. "It was a homemade card with childishly crayoned violets on it, and red hearts" (248). The card reads: *"You have given us a wonderful story[,] . . . a classic story of anti-patriarchal rage. Your gift to us, can we give it to others? What is called Female Craziness is nothing but centuries of Frustration and Oppression. The part about the creek is wonderful just by itself and how many women can identify!"* (248). A postscript adds: "LONGING TO SEE DOCUMENTS. PLEASE NEXT TIME. LOVE AND GRATITUDE" (249). Completely baffled by this feminist jargon, Dane asks, "Anti-patriarchal rage. . . . What do they mean by that?" and wonders "why they used capitals for Female Craziness and Frustration and Oppression" (249). This declamatory style gives the satirical impression that Dawn Rose, who never went to high school, knew more about capitalization and sentence structure than the college-educated Heather and Gillian do. In the novella's original version, the capitalized phrases in the postscript are separated only by commas (*Granta* 18 [1986]: 215). Perhaps, in her revision, Munro wished to soften her heavy-handed irony, but only to a slightly limited extent, for the satirical parallel between the two sets of characters continues.

When Violet is summoned home to cope with the crisis of the letters, she is almost immediately suspicious of her two childishly "rebellious" sisters, Dawn Rose and Bonnie Hope. "They acted as if they had some idiotic secret" (PL, 215). This secret turns out to be a double one, the story of Dawn Rose's first menstrual period and their malicious collusion in writing the letters; Bonnie Hope knew what Dawn Rose was doing. When Dane hears about Heather and Gillian, he experiences exactly the same kind of irritably "suspicious" reaction. "There was a sense he had of something concealed from him[,] . . . a tiresome, silly, malicious sort of secret" (247). By putting this suspicion into his mind rather than the aging mind of Violet, Munro shows that this reaction to Heather and Gillian is not simply a product of being old and old-fashioned. And through paralleling her two protagonists' reactions to the secrets shared by the two pairs of characters—Dawn Rose and Bonnie Hope, and Heather and Gillian—Munro makes the second pair alter egos of the first pair to satirize their common "anti-patriarchal rage" as a childishly simpleminded distortion of complicated facts.

Although Munro believes that "our society as a whole" is patriarchal, she insists that the rural society in which she was raised, a "society . . . of fairly poor people," was not "exactly . . . a patriarchal society. . . . There was no sense in that community of the women being victims of society or [of] the men" ("Interview": Hancock, 112). Thus, although Trevor is an arrogant representative of patriarchy who enters the ministry because he is "intent on power," Dawn Rose's bewildered father, the target of her letters, hardly fits the image of a patriarch (PL, 216). In the first place, he is illegitimate and therefore has *"no people"* (210). A small man, he struggles to support his family on a small and swampy farm, but he exerts no authority over this family. "It was Violet who ruled in the house . . ." (213). His nickname, King Billy, which he shares with his horse, also emphasizes his lack of paternal authority by ironically associating him with the costumed figure of King William III leading the Orange Walk, the Protestant Irish parade on the Twelfth of July. He is not only less than royal; he has not even "understood how to go about making an ordinary life . . . " (213). Thus, in a society built on "the bleak bedrock of low expectations," he lacks all the usual foundations supporting the edifice of patriarchal power—family, physical size, economic status, paternal authority, even the conventionally respectful title of father (Duchêne, 109). Like the Marxist jargon of Denise's lover in "White Dump," Heather and Gillian's feminist jargon does not apply.

The next parallel between the two parts of the novella emerges from the changed meaning of the "queer streak" in Part II and deepens the irony to suggest a thematic statement. Widowed and old, Violet is exhausted by Heather and Gillian, whose prying and probing questions revive the painful past already surfacing in her sporadic memories and distorting her imagination. Munro describes the new queer streak, Violet's "possession," through Dane's sympathetic point of view. Watching over his aunt, as she once planned to watch over his mother, Dane sees that "[n]othing in [Violet] wanted to be overtaken by a helpless and distracted, dull and stubborn old woman, with a memory or imagination out of control, bulging at random through the present scene" (244). By connoting a physical sensation of uncontrollable internal pressure, the word *bulging* suggests an analogy between Violet's mental helplessness in old age and Dawn Rose's physical helplessness in adolescence when confronted by menstruation.[31] This analogy is developed through a series of parallel images: the image of Dawn Rose's bloodstained underpants in the creek scene is linked to red images in two later scenes. In the first scene, when Violet sees Dawn Rose's arms stained by the wild strawberries she is picking and eating, she suddenly realizes that Dawn Rose wrote the anonymous letters. In the second scene, when Dane sees the elderly Violet's arms streaked with blood after she has accidentally set herself on fire, then tumbled into some rosebushes, he realizes that Violet has lost control. Through these color parallels, Munro not only emphasizes the similarity between these two periods of inevitable bodily change—the onset of puberty and of senility—but, by doing so, also suggests another important reason why "anti-patriarchal rage" is a ridiculous label for Dawn Rose's reaction to menstruation.[32]

Menstruation is a biological process. To blame the culture for it, therefore, is like blaming the culture because human beings must go through another biological process: they must grow old and die. Only limited control can be exerted over either process; uncontrollability is a physiological fact of life. Falsely blaming an outside force means refusing to accept these unpleasant facts, just as pretending that love is "a blow from outside" means refusing to accept personal responsibility for initiating an adulterous affair (PL, 305). In both stories, Munro defines such refusal as adolescent behavior.

To drive home her point, Munro shows that the uncontrollable bulges of Violet's past into her present indirectly cause her death. The circumstances of her death constitute the final parallel between the two parts of the novella, the tightly unified endings of Part I and Part II. In both of these endings, Munro uses the same symbol of tangled confusion to underline her thematic insistence on complexity, but, in dramatizing Violet's moment of crisis, her rejection by Trevor, her fiancé, Munro once again splits her protagonist in half.

In its pathological intensity and in its repetition, this split is both qualitatively and quantitatively the climax of all the splits in Munro's characters. In Part I, when Trevor breaks their engagement, Violet feels flayed. "Her whole life was being pulled away from her—her future, her love, her luck, and her hopes. All that was being pulled off like skin, and hurt as much, and left her raw and stinging" (231). This metaphor of agonizing exposure is similar to Del's vision of flesh as humiliation, with not only "the naked body but all the organs inside it . . . laid bare and helpless" (LGW, 57). And it quite naturally contains an even more intense sexual component because, deeply in love with Trevor, Violet is "convinced that if they were married, they would be having the kind of pleasures that nearly make you faint when you think about them" (PL, 216). Thus, Violet's reaction to her broken engagement is overwhelming. In her exposure, she feels so helplessly humiliated that she wants to commit suicide. As she considers various ways to do so, she feels her flayed self splitting in half to become both the audience of a play and an actress in it. The metaphor of exposure thus fuses with the theatrical metaphor: "She felt as if she was watching a play, and yet she was inside it, inside the play; she was in crazy danger" (232). In this play, she sees herself "[d]rowning" by "hugging the water, gulping it down" (231–32). "Desperate," she begins to pray to be restored to her "rightful mind," and almost like a schizophrenic experiencing auditory hallucinations, she believes she hears an answer to this prayer—instructions to abandon her ambition to teach and to devote herself instead to taking care of her family, especially Dawn Rose (232). Gratefully accepting these instructions, Violet separates herself from her "old self" with its suicidal "pain" and "humiliation" and thus keeps herself alive and purposefully functioning (232, 233). But, although this renunciation of her ambition saves Violet from drowning and gives her a temporary sense of renewed control over her life, Dawn Rose's recovery makes the sacrifice quite unnecessary. As with Rose's ironic renunciation of the dead Simon, Munro is insisting on the uncontrollability of life. Decisions that her characters reach with enormous pain and soul-searching later mock them as superfluous. At the end of Part I, Violet is so overcome by this irony that she splits in half again. Now aware that her instructions were false and have reduced her to redundancy, she hears another "voice" saying, "Her life is tragic." Like the suicidal drivers in earlier stories, she careens blindly off the road and into a tangle of hawthorn bushes, where she hides in shame "because she didn't want to be seen, if her life was tragic" (234).[33]

At the end of Part II, Violet is ashamed once again, so ashamed of the old anonymous letters that Heather insists on seeing that she tries to burn them, or old papers she mistakes for them. But, confused by her uncontrollable memory, she also believes that she is using a wood stove instead of a gas range and sets herself and her kitchen on fire. Although Dane rescues her, she then falls into some rosebushes planted by her husband, Wyck. When Dane extricates her again, she tells him how she met Wyck: he was a passing motorist who extricated her from her first thorny tangle, the hawthorn bushes, became her lover, and much later, after the death of his wife, married her. Three days later, Violet herself suddenly dies. These two sets of thorny bushes symbolize the intricately tangled complexity that Munro dramatizes in the story of Violet's long life. Even as a child, wandering among "nameless thornbushes" and wondering about the sadness of life, Violet concludes, "Confusion abounded, in the world as she knew it . . . " (208, 210).

In sharp contrast, Heather and Gillian, like Denise's Marxist lover in "White Dump," classify everything in the world in neatly explained and comfortably airtight categories. Much like the woman in "Simon's Luck" who eventually informs Rose of Simon's death—an "emaciated, bloodless, obsessed," and "mutinous-looking" feminist critic writing a paper on "the suicide of female artists"—Heather and Gillian see Violet's story simply as a stereotypical case corroborating their preconceptions (WDY, 157, 172). Munro subtly satirizes the feminist critic's obsessions by showing that, although she angrily accuses Rose of attending parties "just to meet men," she herself changes completely when she acquires a new husband (159). Abandoning her symbolic refusal to wear clothes attractive to men, the feminist critic exchanges her "fringed and soiled and stringy" outfit for the latest fashion (172).

In the novella, in addition to the ironies already discussed, Munro's historical allusions add another layer of irony to her satire of feminists. After his aunt's sudden death, Dane is at first highly indignant about the way the two feminists have behaved; but, less dogmatic than they are, he reconsiders his preconceptions and admits the possibility that "they had brought her happiness, as much as trouble" (PL, 252). But clearly he has been much more sensitively responsive to Violet's fragility than Heather and Gillian were, for, in spite of their enthusiastically professed interest in her life as a woman, their insensitive curiosity about the old documents precipitates Violet's death. During their visit they give her a Joan of Arc haircut, which symbolically links her with their transvestism in their boots and uniforms and radically alters her appearance.[34] This symbolic alteration indicates that the allusion to Joan is more than just a foreshadowing of Violet's death after the fire. It is also an ironic metaphor for the two feminists' radical reshaping and cutting of her story. For, although there are at least two earlier allusions to Joan of Arc in the novella, the final irony is that through this reshaping the feminists themselves precipitate Violet's Joan-like death. The first allusion occurs when Trevor discusses Dawn Rose's crazy letters with Violet. His arrogant attitude toward his fiancée is perhaps analogous to that of Joan's ecclesiastical judges when she dared to talk to them about God. When Violet suggests that, instead of institutionalizing her sister, they could "ask God to cure her," she realizes that Trevor considers her "insolent. It was up to him to mention God, not her" (230). The second and much more obvious allusion occurs when Violet, like Joan hearing her divine voices, imagines a voice answering her prayer. But Munro's resistance to a feminist oversimplification of these parallels is made clear by the confrontational technique of her omniscient narrator, who interrupts her narration of this scene with an argument against a feminist reading. The narrator asks: "Did she despise [Trevor], then?" The feminist reader's answer would, of course, be an angry and resounding yes. But the narrator insists, "If she did, she didn't know it. That wasn't something she could know about. If he had come after her, she would have gone back to him—gladly, gladly. . . . [S]he would have given in about Dawn Rose; she would have done anything he wanted" (231). By seeing Violet as a heroic victim of patriarchy, a feminist hero like Joan, the two feminists therefore not only oversimplify and over-dramatize her life story but also victimize her themselves. This irony, combined with Dane's carefully balanced opinion of their role, again exemplifies Munro's insistence on paradoxical complexity.

So does a similar irony in the characterization of another feminist, Rhea Streeter in "Eskimo." Although Rhea's criticism of Mary Jo's position is not "predictable . . . propaganda," as Mary Jo defensively insists, but an accurate assessment of Mary Jo's relationship with Dr. Streeter, Munro nevertheless undermines Rhea's authority as an uncompromising champion of feminine independence (PL, 192). At the age of twenty-five, Rhea is a messy, unemployed adolescent. Still her hardworking father's fat, "leisurely," and lazy dependent, she barges into his busy office to lecture his nurse and to wheedle money out of him for her motorcycle (190). She accuses her father of being "behind bombs and pollution and poverty and discrimination," but she profits from the same privileges against which she spouts her hypocritical accusations (190). This irony, set side by side with Mary Jo's unwillingness to face the truth about herself, sharpens the scalpel of Munro's continued probing into the many painful paradoxes of feminine behavior.

Such ideologically independent psychological exploration undoubtedly makes Munro's fiction unpopular with the type of feminist whom she satirizes in "Simon's Luck," "A Queer Streak," and "Eskimo." Although Munro recognizes her civic duty to support "important" feminist causes such as "homes for battered wives," she insists on total separation between such support and her fiction. If feminism is "defined . . . as an attitude to life which is imposed on me by someone else," she says, "I don't accept that. . . . In fiction I . . . don't think of feminist politics . . . or anything else; I think of what's going on *in* my story and that is all" ("Interview": Horwood, 133–34). She recognizes that the absence of such a political message "is not . . . a very popular stance" (134). But her lifelong interest in paradoxes is integral to her unflinching honesty in confronting the complexity that makes packaged messages impossible. And nowhere in her fiction is this insistence on complexity and paradox as unmistakable as in her stories of mother and daughters.

5

Controlling Memory

Mothers and Daughters, Fathers and Daughters

The attempt to control obsessive memories is the core of a group of stories that Munro has written about parents and daughters. Covering a thirty-year span, from 1956 to 1986, these stories culminate in the title stories of her last two collections, *The Moons of Jupiter* and *The Progress of Love*. Just as "The Moons of Jupiter" is a father-story and "The Progress of Love" is a mother-story, Munro has written many stories about both fathers and mothers. But the frequency with which the mother-daughter theme recurs is second only to her repeated explorations of the humiliations of love. Munro recognizes the mother-daughter theme as "an obsession" ("Interview": Hancock, 104). "[T]he whole mother-daughter relationship interests me a great deal. It probably obsesses me. . . . because I had a very intense relationship with my own mother. She became ill when I was quite young. The incurable illness of a parent makes a relationship['s] . . . stresses . . . more evident. . . . And so her illness and death and the whole tension between us . . . was very important." Therefore, she concludes, "This is just something I keep going back to over and over again" (103–4).

An early, uncollected story, "How Could I Do That?," published in

Chatelaine in March 1956, is written from the third-person point of view of a mother who in many ways resembles Mrs. Jordan in both *Dance of the Happy Shades* and *Lives of Girls and Women*. Louise, her adolescent daughter, is seen only through the mother's sad eyes when Louise humiliates her at the home of her well-to-do high school classmate, where they accidentally meet. The mother is selling stockings from door to door, and Louise, ashamed to see her in her classmate's living room and anxious to maintain a safe social distance, does not speak to her or recognize her in any way. Although the story is written from the mother's point of view, the anguished question of the title is the daughter's guilty lament over this betrayal.

In five later stories—"The Peace of Utrecht," "Winter Wind," "The Ottawa Valley," "Home," and "The Progress of Love"—the point of view is always that of the daughter. In each of these stories she is the first-person narrator struggling to achieve emotional distance from her mother through the controlled manipulation of language. This distance is difficult to achieve for several closely related reasons. The painful past to which the narrator returns in her memory is intimately involved not only with her mother but in two stories also with social humiliations directly experienced through language. Thus, as already indicated in chapter 1, the medium of control is itself suspect. The daughter's difficulties are compounded when in three stories, "The Peace of Utrecht," "Home," and "The Progress of Love," she goes home not only mentally but physically, returning to the house from which her dead mother has departed in body but not in powerfully haunting spirit. However, "The Progress of Love" is much less autobiographical than the first four stories. It begins with the mother's death, but then a story within the story goes back to the mother's childhood, narrated not from the fifty-year-old daughter's point of view but from the mother's third-person point of view as a child. The introduction of the mother's point of view reshapes and widens a key theme developed earlier in "Princess Ida," one of the important stories about Mrs. Jordan in *Lives of Girls and Women*, to show exactly what the progress of love means. Thus, a comparison of these six mother-stories—"The Peace of Utrecht," "Winter Wind," "The Ottawa Valley," "Home," "Princess Ida," and "The Progress of Love"—can demonstrate how Munro's treatment of this lifelong obsession is not repetitious. As with her treatment of the humiliations of love, she deepens and widens her themes by moving steadily away from the central, autobiographical elements and the narrowest limitations of the first-person point of view to broader, more general themes developed through increasingly complex fictional techniques.

"The Peace of Utrecht" was written in 1959, the year in which Munro's mother, Anne Chamney Laidlaw, died of Parkinson's disease after many years of illness ("Real Material," 20). In "Working for a Living," Munro has described her adolescent attitude toward her mother's disease: "Most of the time I was angry at her, for her abdication and self-absorption. We argued" (30). The haunting memory of these angry arguments is one of the painful ingredients of what Munro has repeatedly called her "most autobiographical" story ("Alice Munro," 258; "Conversation," 58). Although she has applied this label elsewhere, what she means by "most autobiographical" here is not simply her use of personal material but also her overwhelming inner compulsion to attempt to control such material. Her choice of one of her key words, *abdication,* to describe her mother reveals that there is doubly uncontrollable material here: the mother's helplessness as well as the daughter's, the powerfully combined humiliations of the mother's dying flesh and the humiliations of the writer-daughter struggling with material so compelling that *it* controls *her.* Munro has identified "The Peace Of Utrecht" as "the first story" she "absolutely had to write": "[W]hen a story takes over the way that one did with me, then . . . *I* saw that writing was about something else altogether than I had suspected it was, that it was going to be less in my control and more inescapable than I had thought" ("Real Material," 21). It was "the first time I wrote a story that tore me up . . . " ("Conversation," 58).

Originally published in the *Tamarack Review* in 1960, "The Peace of Utrecht" explores the reactions of Helen, its first-person narrator, to her mother's recent death. Evading and postponing the emotional shock of coming to terms with its meaning, the narrator divides her story into two major parts. The first section of Part I begins in the present tense with the narrator's announcement that she has been home for three weeks, visiting her older, unmarried sister, Maddy. She refers to their shared childhood in "the dim world of continuing disaster, of home," but does not define this disaster. That it was truly disastrous, however, is implied by Maddy's warning to Helen, "No exorcising here" (DHS, 191). Exorcism is clearly the psychological purpose of the narrator's activity, but once again Helen does not specify who or what must be exorcised. Instead, she describes the stories that she and Maddy tell about their childhood to Fred Powell, who may be Maddy's lover. These stories are an unrehearsed exercise in shared evasion, for the two sisters "safely" wrap their unhappy childhood memories "in a kind of mental cellophane" to entertain their listener (193).

This self-protective packaging is not split until the beginning of the second section of Part I, in which Helen explains that after an illness of many years her mother died the preceding winter but that Helen did not return home for her funeral. This explanation then leads into a brief flashback to explore a double humiliation: the terrible humiliation of the flesh, caused by the mother's bizarre, wasting disease, and her two daughters' adolescent humiliation, caused by having to cope with their invalid mother. These two humiliations, as discussed in chapter 1, are linked by the mother's loss of the controlling power of language. Interpreting for her, her daughters are forced to recognize the full horror of this involuntary abdication, but at the same time they stubbornly try to conceal both from themselves and from others what is really happening in their home. These attempts at denial and concealment prepare for the prison metaphors in the third section of Part I.

At the beginning of this section, Helen is just arriving home for her visit, three weeks before. Upon entering Maddy's empty house with her two small children, she sees herself in a mirror that reflects a face very different from the smooth-faced young girl who left that house for marriage and motherhood. Although she remembers that "panic and disorder lay behind" that deceptive surface, now she must recognize the significance of that altered surface: she has become a tensely "watchful" young mother who watches not only her children but also herself (198, 197). This recognition then precipitates an experience very close to an auditory hallucination, in which she finally dares to imagine the sound of her "mother's ruined voice call[ing] out" in a "cry for help—undisguised, oh, shamefully undisguised and raw and supplicating . . . " (198).

This experience linking the two mothers then evokes much more specific memories of her dead mother than Helen has allowed to surface in the first two sections of this part of the story; and these memories in turn introduce a series of prison metaphors describing her mother's life. In "Working for a Living," Munro refers to her mother as "walled in by increasing paralysis . . . " (37). Here Helen describes her mother as physically walled in by her "house of stone" and psychologically isolated by her daughters' coldly self-protective roles as prison guards refusing her the loving pity for which she craved and clamored. "[W]e . . . took all emotion away from our dealings with her, as you might take away meat from a prisoner to weaken him, till he died" (DHS, 199). But, although she remembers both her mother's "frenzy and frustration" and Maddy's "ten years' vigil" as her nurse, Helen begins to tell herself that perhaps their feelings about their mother were "partly imaginary," and this belief produces "the beginnings of a secret, guilty estrangement" from the situation (200, 195, 201). When she finds her old high-school notes on the Peace of Utrecht, she remembers her "old life," and in discussing her memories with Maddy, she says that sometimes she can also remember their mother before her illness (201). But she recognizes this remark as *"[c]owardly tender nostalgia, trying to get back to a gentler truth,"* especially when Maddy, also recognizing the kind of emotional distance Helen is attempting to achieve, replies, "No exorcising" (202). This remark concludes Part I of the story by bringing it back to the beginning, where Maddy's warning was quoted without any explanation of its context. This circular structure suggests that no exorcism has yet occurred.

Part II begins by echoing the beginning of Part I. Helen announces that she has been visiting her two old aunts, also sisters, and wonders if she and Maddy will resemble their aunts when they grow old. The possibility of such a resemblance is suggested by the aunts' discreet "circumlocution" in referring to something Aunt Annie wants to show Helen (204). Like Helen and Maddy, they, too, are evading something. But when Aunt Annie shows Helen her dead mother's carefully cleaned and mended clothes and offers them to her, the evasion suddenly ends. Helen's shocked refusal of "those brocades and flowered silks," those "peacock colours" in which her mother had costumed and disguised her dying body, evokes what Aunt Annie really wants to say (205).

She insists on telling Helen about her mother's frantic, dying escape from the hospital. Like a demented prisoner, wearing only a robe and slippers, she tried to run away in a snowstorm. Helen's reaction is like the narrator's unsurprised "recognition" of frightening old Joe Phippen in "Images" and also like Del's reluctance to hear anymore about her uncle's death (DHS, 38): "[S]trangely I felt no surprise, only a vague physical sense of terror, a longing not to be told—and beyond this a feeling that what I would be told I already knew, I had always known" (DHS, 207–8). Helen's terror is intensified by the transformation of the prison metaphors that she has been using to force herself to imagine her mother's condition: suddenly they are no longer metaphors. After her mother was caught and returned to the hospital, a board was nailed across her bed to prevent another escape attempt. Unable to communicate with her nurses and unable to get out of bed, Helen's mother was in a situation far worse than imprisonment. She was quite literally nailed into her coffin of silence and motionlessness before her death. What happened to her is what Del later fears, being "buried alive" (LGW, 239). Confronted by this terrible revelation of living death and by her elderly aunt's dread of a similar fate, Helen realizes what Aunt Annie has been doing: she has been summoning the ghost of Helen's mother, not exorcising it. "Is this the last function of old women," Helen wonders, "making sure the haunts we have contracted for are with us . . .?" (209). This sadistic streak in Aunt Annie's behavior resembles the "edge of betrayal, . . . greedy for your hurt," that Del feels in her mother's insistence that she "face things" by attending her uncle's funeral (LGW, 47).

But even though Helen is haunted, she attempts exorcism for Maddy in the last section of Part II. She urges her sister not to feel guilty for hospitalizing their mother but to leave and "[t]ake" her life. Just before accepting this advice, Maddy drops and breaks an old family heirloom. A slickly superficial writer would make the shattering of this bowl symbolize the breaking of all the bonds tying Maddy to her past in the disastrous family home. But Maddy's anguished question, "But why can't I, Helen? *Why can't I?*," shows Munro's rejection of this potential symbol (210). For Maddy, as for Helen, exorcising the guilty past is not so simple. The title is therefore ironic: the story's structure and metaphorical pattern both emphasize that there can be no peace. One cannot erase the past by signing a peace treaty. Memory is obsessive and uncontrollable.

This uncontrollable obsession dominates three later stories, "Winter Wind," "The Ottawa Valley," and "Home." Munro wrote the first two stories together, and all three were published in 1974 ("Real Material," 27). In these stories, she returns to the haunting theme of the dying mother, but now she raises the aesthetic and moral question of whether the use of personal material in creating fiction is a justifiable activity.

In "Winter Wind" the two old aunts of "The Peace of Utrecht" are replaced by a grandmother and a great-aunt. The retrospective first-person narrator is a schoolgirl in the time frame of the story, and the mother is still alive and capable of bursts of frenzied activity. But she is already suffering from "a slowly progressive, incurable disease" that has "partly paralyzed" her "vocal cords." The grandmother comments, "It just seems the worse her voice gets, the more she wants to talk," and when the narrator has "to act as [her mother's] interpreter," she, like Helen, is "wild with shame" (SIB, 195). This story, however, emphasizes not the mother's loss of verbal control but the grandmother's loss of emotional control, a very unusual event in the repressed Scotch-Presbyterian world of these characters. The thematic unity of the story is created by the fact that, in contrast to the narrator's mother, the other three characters carefully conceal their true feelings.

The symbolic significance of the title introduces the idea of losing control. The schoolchildren eagerly anticipate the snowstorm brought by the winter wind. Although the grandmother is "offended" by the burial of fenceposts under the deepening snow, the children, "looking forward to something disruptive," want the carefully defined boundaries of property and propriety to disappear (192). So does the narrator, for in the "crisis-charged atmosphere" of the winter storm, she nurses secret erotic fantasies about Mr. Harmon, her teacher (192). But, like the dissimulating students in earlier stories and like Rose in the later story, "Characters," she carefully conceals her feelings from a classmate by calling her teacher names and inventing wild speculations about his private life. The great-aunt also hides her feelings. Widowed after an exceptionally happy marriage, she is no longer "interested in her life," but she is "too well brought up" to reveal her depression (199). The stiffly Calvinistic grandmother, however, is the most repressed of all. She married the grandfather on the rebound from her one true love, a cousin, whom she continued to see quite regularly for the rest of their long lives. Full of "self-glorifying dangerous self-denying passion, never satisfied, never risked," she was "stubbornly, secretly, destructively romantic" (200, 201). Although everybody knew about this relationship, "in that close-mouthed place . . . . nobody ever spoke of it to her face" (201). In this repressed atmosphere, the narrator is careful to play the role of a "discreet unrevealing person . . . in [her] grandmother's house . . ." (202).

But during the crisis of the winter storm, she is astonished to discover that her grandmother can suddenly lose control. Although her grandmother has spent her whole married life encased in a rigid carapace of self-control, and although she has "ridiculed and blamed" the narrator's mother for not behaving exactly the same way, she suddenly breaks down (206). The grandmother's childhood friend, an elderly widow alone on a farm, has frozen to death during the blizzard. When the visiting narrator insists on going home during the aftermath of this storm, the surface of the grandmother's self-control is shattered. To describe this upheaval, Munro selects the same word she repeatedly uses to describe a woman's yielding power to a lover, *abdication*: "I had never heard my grandmother lose control before. I had never imagined that she could. . . . I had never heard anything like plain hurt or anger in her voice, or seen it on her face. . . . The abdication here was what amazed me. . . . She was weeping, she was furious and weeping" (204). The narrator's amazement at her grandmother's "abdication" explains the guilt motivating her earlier interruption of the grandmother's story. Breaking off her retrospective narration to return to the present, she guiltily criticizes what she has been doing. Because she has "used" her grandmother "to suit" her fictional "purposes" and implied things about her "[w]ithout any proof," she concludes, "I feel compunction. Though I am only doing in a large and public way what has always been done, what my mother did, and other people did, who mentioned to me my grandmother's story" (201). The public exposure of intensely private emotion causes this guilty compunction, for the grandmother's furious weeping over her friend's death is a humiliating exposure of physical and psychological helplessness. To inflict such humiliation in fiction is, therefore, a shameful act.

The theme of guilt and humiliation also unifies "The Ottawa Valley," a story that Munro has described as "infinitely . . . painful" ("Name,"

70). It is another story about the afflicted mother, here just beginning to suffer from what is explicitly identified as parkinsonism, the symptoms of which are introduced through the distancing device of a quotation from a medical encyclopedia. James Carscallen has described this story as "a jumble of separate memories of which the sequence hardly seems to matter" ("Alice Munro," 74). Similarly, Lorna Irvine sees it as a "loosely" linked "series of impressions of a childhood trip" ("Changing," 102). But the links are not loose at all, and the sequence, far from being jumbled, is deliberately calculated to jar the reader into experiencing the same central emotion that the narrator feels and that unifies all these memories and impressions. They are all about the humiliations of helplessness, both comic and tragic.

The first-person narrator, about twelve years old in the main time frame of the narrative, is taken to visit two aunts in the Ottawa Valley, Aunt Lena and Aunt Dodie. Watching Aunt Lena beat her children until they howl, the narrator makes the comment, already discussed in chapter 2, that, although her cousins forget their beatings a few minutes later, her reaction to such punishment would be very different. "With me, such a humiliation could last for weeks, or forever" (SIB, 232). The word *forever* is the addition of the retrospective narrator, forty-one or forty-two years old, the same age as her mother when her parkinsonism began. When this narrator looks in the mirror, she remembers her mother, just like the narrator in "The Peace of Utrecht." But here her reflection in the mirror is almost a picture of her mother. Just as The Photographer in the Epilogue to *Lives of Girls and Women* took pictures in which "[m]iddle-aged people saw in their own features the terrible, growing, inescapable likeness of their dead parents . . . ," so the thirty years that have passed since the remembered time of the story have transformed the middle-aged narrator into her mother (247). And the major humiliation that has lasted "forever" is, of course, the humiliation of the narrator's mother, as the epilogue of "The Ottawa Valley" explicitly states. But the story is full of other humiliations, too, all of which culminate in this epilogue. All of Aunt Dodie's stories—about being jilted on her wedding day, like Dickens's Miss Havisham or Katherine Anne Porter's Granny Weatherall; about sewing up a young hired hand's fly, filling him up with vinegar-spiked lemonade, and then secretly watching him expose himself to urinate; and about nursing her dying mother for five years—are stories about helplessness and nakedness, the sexual and physical humiliations of the flesh. And they correlate with the narrator's adolescent horror when, all dressed up in blue taffeta for church, she nearly loses her underpants in the churchyard. She, too, is almost exposed like the hired hand, who is in the church. The narrative links between these elements of the story become clear in Munro's conception of the structure of a short story, which, in a passage partially quoted earlier, she has compared to the structure of a house:

> Everybody knows [that] a house . . . encloses space and makes connections between one enclosed space and another and presents what is outside in a new way. This is the nearest I can come to explaining . . . what I want my stories to do for . . . people.
> So when I write a story I want to make a certain kind of structure, and I know the feeling I want to get from being inside that structure. ("What Is Real?," 5)

The feeling inside the structure of this story is a synergistic combination of the various characters' helplessness. Although Aunt Dodie gayly describes being jilted as if her tragedy were a funny story, the narrator's mother tells her that, even two years after her nonwedding day, Aunt Dodie was still crying with helpless grief, "[n]ight after night" (230). In Aunt Dodie's second funny story, about how she and the narrator's mother spied through a knothole on Allen Durrand, the hired hand, as he "ripped down his overalls altogether and let'er fly," two kinds of helplessness are combined: the image of the "clawin' and yankin'" young man, no longer able to control his overwhelming urgency, and the image of the narrator's mother, no longer able to pretend that she did not participate in arranging and enjoying this voyeuristic prank (236, 235). Watching her mother, the narrator describes "an unusual expression on her face: helplessness" (236). Then, in jarring juxtaposition, she suddenly introduces Dr. Fishbein's description of the symptoms of parkinsonism, a horrifying catalogue of physical helplessness: "[T]he patient . . . shows slowly increasing bodily rigidity, associated with tremors of the head and limbs. There may be various tics, twitches, muscle spasms, and other involuntary movements. Salivation increases and drooling is common. . . . The face begins to lose its customary expressiveness and changes slowly or not at all with passing moods. . . . No recoveries are recorded" (236–37). This abrupt shift in tone—from the coarse humor of the lemonade story, almost like a Chaucerian fabliau, to the coldly clinical definition of the medical encyclopedia—prepares not only for the churchyard scene, in which the narrator, her mother, and her aunt visit her grandparents' graves, but also for Aunt Dodie's story of her dying mother's helplessness. This story is similar to Marjory's description of nursing her dying mother in "At the Other Place," but here it is introduced by Aunt Dodie's terrifying prediction that the narrator will also have to nurse her mother: "You'll have to learn to be the mother, then" (243). When the narrator bursts into tears, Aunt Dodie "laugh[s] at" her, "threatening to let out more secrets than [she can] stand" (243). Thus the purpose of all these episodes is to link two kinds of helplessness: the twelve-year-old's horrified helplessness in the face of her mother's physically humiliating illness, and the adult narrator's humiliating helplessness and guilt in trying to control her memories of her mother by writing about them. The guilt springs from attempting to control what her mother could not.

Munro has defined the concluding paragraph of this story as "all about dissatisfaction with art." She explains this dissatisfaction as twofold: her feeling of being "*tormented* by the inadequacy and impossibility" of her story's representation of "real lives" and of being unsure about her "right to represent them at all. And I think any writer who deals with personal material comes up against this" ("Real Material," 28). Her narrator's outburst in the poignant epilogue emphasizes the first dissatisfaction:

> The problem, the only problem, is my mother. And she is the one of course that I am trying to get; it is to reach her that this whole journey has been undertaken. With what purpose? To mark her off, to describe, to illumine, to celebrate, to *get rid*, of her; and it did not work, for she looms too close, just as she always did. She is heavy as always, she weighs everything down, and yet she is indistinct, her edges melt and flow. Which means she has stuck to me as close as ever and refused to fall away, and I could go on, and on, applying what skills I have, using what tricks I know, and it would always be the same. (246)

The memory of the childhood trip, therefore, is invoked symbolically. The story is integrated into an exorcistic journey into the past, but the exorcism does not work any more permanently here than it does in "The Peace of Utrecht."

The second dissatisfaction with art receives much more explicit emphasis in "Home," an uncollected story published in *New Canadian Stories: 74*. Munro has defined this story as "sort of a final statement" on the problem of using and controlling personal material ("Real Material," 28). Here the mother has been dead for a long time, and the father and his second wife, Irlma, have modernized their farmhouse and removed most of the "[r]eminders" of the first-person narrator's mother from the house ("Home," 136). But not, of course, from the narrator's memories or from her dreams.

In the narrator's dream, her mother, painting and papering a room with feverish energy, explains that she can work only at night because she is dead. As the narrator comments, "*Mother . . . probably doesn't belong in this [story] at all but I can't come within reach of her without being invaded by her, then trying to say too much too fast to get her finished with*" (137). This italicized comment and three much longer ones like it make this story about the mother significantly different in form from "Winter Wind" and "The Ottawa Valley." The latter two stories contain passages in which the narrator abandons her persona and splits in half to comment on her own narration; in these passages Munro approaches metafiction but does not do much more than call the reader's attention to the difficulties her self-conscious narrator is experiencing with her painfully personal material. In contrast, "Home" incorporates these difficulties and this self-consciousness into a full-blown metafictional structure. Stanley Fogel defines metafiction as a scrutiny of "all facets of the literary construct—language, the conventions of plot and character, the relation of the artist to his art and to his reader" (328n3). The first-person narrator of "Home," a middle-aged writer who lives only with a typewriter, keeps a diary of her weekend visit home. But she repeatedly interrupts her entries, which do not constitute a plot, with self-scrutinizing editorial comments addressed to herself and to the reader.

These comments demonstrate that this story is metafiction because they dramatize the internal conflict of the humiliated writer, split in two by her closely related difficulties with two languages and with the characters of her two mothers. The writer's editorial persona comments on her narrator-persona, criticizing the guilty and shameful motives behind the narrator's transformation of real people, especially her stepmother, into fictional characters. The writer's dead mother was a schoolteacher whose collection of Everyman Classics is still in the house. The writer used to "rummage" through these books and read, *"Everyman, I will go with thee, in thy most need be by thy side . . . "* ("Home," 136). Her dream about her mother shows that her mother goes with her, too, and is always by her side, but her "most need" is to separate herself from this invisible but ubiquitous companion. The character of Irmla, the writer's stepmother, is a vivid contrast to this ghost. Irmla's coarsely jocular speech and grossly clinical topics of conversation, which clearly anticipate Flo's dialogue in "Characters" and *Who Do You Think You Are?*, are reproduced by the writer's narrator-persona, but with a deep sense of nagging guilt. In her editorial role, she sternly asks herself: *"Is this vengeful reporting, in spite of accuracy? Do I make it clear that she talks the way she does . . . at least partly out of anxiety . . .?"* (149). Irlma's diction is dramatically different from the dead mother's speech, which still echoes in her daughter's dream.

Her memory of the "bizarre . . . effects" of her mother's parkinsonism, "her dark and helpless . . . complaint," is indirectly linked to her editorial-persona's concern about the connotations of the story's diction, the way the characters talk (136). Although their *"misshapen language"* is distorted not by illness, but by their Huron County accent, the editor worries that the dialogue the narrator gives the characters "*sounds like parody if you take it straight,*" especially in contrast to the deliberately educated way that she talks to Irlma when her stepmother violates her cherished memories of her real mother (142). As already indicated, she self-consciously criticizes herself for speaking in "*that educated tone which in itself has the power to hurt*" (150). But, in spite of her editorial persona's objections, she needs to assume this tone not only as a form of self-defense but also as a way of reassuring herself about her own firmly defined identity, which, as shown in chapter 1, depends directly on the narrator's use of language.

This narrator is a significantly different person from the narrators in the three preceding mother-stories. Perhaps one explanation for this difference is that Munro wrote this story in 1973, when she had returned to Ontario after her divorce from James Munro in 1972, and before her marriage to Gerald Fremlin in 1976. Thus the narrator here is not the visiting young mother in "The Peace of Utrecht" who feels guilty about having left home and her sick mother. Neither is she the older narrator remembering her younger self at home in "Winter Wind" and "The Ottawa Valley." Instead, she is a panicky middle-aged writer who suddenly finds it hard to believe that she has ever left home. Her habitual retrospection turns into a trap that snaps shut: "Time and place can close in on me so fast. . . . It can easily seem to me that I have always stayed here, that all my life away was not plausible, took no hold on me, and I see myself . . . like those few half-mad, nearly useless, celibate, rusting captives there are around this country, who should have gone but didn't, couldn't, and are unfit now for any place" (151). This is the fate that the young Munro feared in "The Dimensions of a Shadow," and, when her narrator wants to "scream and run," she seems to become the lonely Miss Abelhart (151).

Thus, the title "Home" is in several senses deeply ironic. It is neither a place the narrator comes home to willingly nor a place where she feels she belongs. Paradoxically, however, it is also a place that she is afraid she has never actually left. So the "*respect*" that her editorial persona struggles to evoke for the characters' language is in sharp conflict with her own conscious decision to discard that language and with the "*value*" she insists on recognizing in her own writing (142, 152). The conflict between and within these two personae produces a confusing mixture of nervous anger, treachery, guilt, artificiality, and falseness, all the ingredients that Munro so successfully combines in her later characterization of the ambivalent, role-playing Rose, but at this point in the story all very far from either persona's conscious artistic control.

But in spite of all this complicated ambivalence, home is nevertheless still home, for even though her mother is dead, home means her father, who is old and sick and whom she anxiously accompanies to the hospital.

She feels guilty that the town in which he has lived his whole life "has faded" for her because she has "used it up" by fictionalizing it and thus escaped from it (143). In contrast to the symbolic control that this escape gives her, she is upset by her father's "abdication" when he is hospitalized and by his foreign physician's "confession of helplessness" (143, 145). As already demonstrated, these two words, *abdication* and *helplessness*, are close synonyms in Munro's lexicon; thus, the psychological similarity of patient and doctor here is "a bad omen" for the narrator's father (145). The doctor should be in control, but is not.

The continuing significance of her father and her home is focused in the story's cinematic closing image, which her editorial persona offers to the reader as an alternative closure, *"something . . . I could have worked into an ending"* (152). This offer emphasizes the story's metafictional nature by inviting the reader to participate in the narrator's creation of the story's structure. The image is a cinematic still of what home signified in the past: a memory of herself as a very small child, bundled up against the cold, sitting on a step and watching her father milk a cow by lantern light on a winter evening. The editor invites the reader to visualize *"that magic and prosaic safety"* and then, after assuring herself of its effectiveness, immediately cancels it with a double contradiction: *"I don't want any more effects, I tell you, lying. I don't know what I want. I want to do this with honour, if I possibly can"* (153). Here dissatisfaction with art has been so thoroughly explored that it has finally been worked through to achieve a moment of satisfaction. By backing off from the present and retreating into a childhood memory in which she can observe herself as a participant unaware of her future anxieties as an adult, the split writer can distance herself from these anxieties.

But not permanently. The farmhouse to which the narrator returns in "Home" seems to reappear as the central, symbolic setting of "The Progress of Love," the title story in Munro's 1986 collection. Munro has remarked, "When I look at a house, it's like looking at a person" ("Interview": Hancock, 99). Her simile suggests that the farmhouse setting contributes to the characterization of her story's narrator. Phemie Casey is a fifty-year-old real-estate agent whose occupation brings her back to the farmhouse in which she grew up and which has gone through several changes, just as Phemie herself has. The story explores her relationship to her dead mother and to her memories of the past, but it does so in a much more complicated way than the four preceding stories do. The exploration has now broadened into an analysis of how people's fictionalized memories shape and edit the narrative of their own lives and those of their family. Munro believes that "life is made into a story by the people who live it . . . " and that "[y]ou edit your life as you go along" ("Real Material," 33; "Interview": Hancock, 94).

Since she first deals with this theme in a much more limited way in "Princess Ida," the story that she has identified as the genesis of *Lives of Girls and Women*, a brief comparison of "The Progress of Love" with this earlier story can show just how her treatment of this theme has evolved ("Real Material," 24).

The two stories are alike in several ways. Both are narrated by a retrospective, first-person narrator; both develop the confusing contradictions between two adult siblings' opinions of their mothers as these contradictions are perceived by the narrator, who in each case is the granddaughter of the woman in question. In "Princess Ida," Del grows up hearing her mother, Addie, tell miserable stories about her own mother, an almost insane religious fanatic. According to Addie, Del's grandmother spent most of her life either praying on her knees or weeping helplessly in bed. When she inherited some money, she spent it all on Bibles for her supposedly heathen neighbors, even though her own children lacked warm winter clothes. Young Addie Morrison was so wretched that she tried to commit suicide. But when Del's Uncle Bill Morrison, Addie's brother, arrives for an unexpected visit, his stories of Del's grandmother recall her very differently. He remembers his mother as "some sort of a saint on earth," who saved his life when he had pneumonia and who impressed her children with the meaning of the Resurrection (LGW, 86). When a cocoon she brought into the house hatched a butterfly on Easter Sunday, she said, "'Look, at that. Never forget. That's what you saw on Easter'" (89). Dying of cancer, Uncle Bill clings to this memory of renewed life, just as he clings to Nile, his young and beautiful second wife, whose green nail polish suggests the river's resurrecting power. But hearing these stories, Del is flabbergasted by the contradiction between her uncle's lovingly recalled memories and her mother's "hard . . . certainty of having been cheated, her undiminished feelings of anger and loss" (76). As a child, she just does not know what to do with these "indigestible" contradictions, although she is keenly aware of her mother's continuing "sense of hurt" (88, 91).

In "The Progress of Love" the narrator, named Phemie after her maternal grandmother, Euphemia, is parallel to Del, and Phemie's mother, Marietta, is parallel to Addie Morrison Jordan, Del's mother. Both mothers were once schoolteachers, like Munro's mother. In "The Progress of Love" the contradictory memories are those of a sister instead of a brother, but Phemie hears them in exactly the same way as Del hears them in "Princess Ida," through a family visit when she is a child. When Phemie is twelve years old, Aunt Beryl, her mother's sister, comes for a visit and tells a story about Euphemia, the maternal grandmother, that contradicts the story that Marietta has told her daughter. Marietta has told Phemie that as a child she saw her mother about to hang herself in the barn; a rope tied to a beam was already on her neck. But Beryl says that their mother only pretended to be about to hang herself. Resentful of her handsome husband's philandering, she wanted only to frighten him. Just like Ross's "death" in "Monsieur les Deux Chapeaux" and Dawn Rose's threatening letters in "A Queer Streak," her sham suicide was "a joke" (PL, 21). Beryl saw what Marietta did not—that the rope was not actually tied to the beam, only flung over it.

What is important about Marietta's version of this story is not only its difference from Beryl's. Far more significant is its narration from Marietta's third-person point of view. "The Progress of Love" is the first major story in which the mother is fully developed from her own third-person point of view, not just perceived from the outside by a first-person narrator watching her and listening to her. For example, whereas in "Princess Ida" Del only imagines what her mother's childhood might have been like, in "The Progress of Love" Munro switches to Marietta's third-person point of view to narrate the mother's childhood story within the daughter's story. In Del's imagined reconstruction, the narrating "I" never disappears completely. Del imagines how her mother, "just a little girl then named Addie Morrison, spindly I should think, with cropped hair because her mother guarded her against vanity, would walk home from school . . . ." (LGW, 75). In contrast, in Marietta's story within Phemie's story, Phemie the narrator temporarily disappears, and the child Marietta becomes a protagonist in her own right.

In the second paragraph of the Marietta section, Phemie goes off stage: "Marietta, in my mind, was separate, not swallowed up in my mother's grownup body" (PL, 9). Then this separate Marietta, not swallowed up in the narrator's point of view either, appears as a little girl. Wandering out to the barn one spring morning, she sees a shattering sight: her mother, Euphemia, standing on a chair and "smiling in this queer, tight way," with "a shadow on her neck" of "a noose on the end of a rope that hung down from a beam overhead" (10). Like the little girl in "Walker Brothers Cowboy" and "Images," Marietta is an innocent eye here, watching incomprehensible adult behavior. She knows nothing about the sexual tension between her parents or about her mother's complicated motives in staging her joke. And, like the paralyzed child on the riverbank in "Images" and the helpless child in "The Ottawa Valley," both threatened by the possibility of a beloved parent's death, Marietta is almost paralyzed. To emphasize her permanent traumatization, Munro uses the dramatic present in this scene: "'Mama?' says Marietta . . . . 'Mama. Come down, please.' Her voice is faint because she fears that any yell or cry might jolt her mother into movement, cause her to step off the chair and throw her weight on the rope. But even if Marietta wanted to yell she couldn't. Nothing but this pitiful thread of a voice is left to her—just as in a dream when a beast or a machine is bearing down on you" (10–11). When Euphemia tells Marietta to fetch her father, Marietta, partially exposed because she is wearing only a nightgown, runs into town to find him. "With terror in her legs," she runs past loggers who laugh at her and pointedly ask, "Hadn't you better get some clothes on first?" (11). Then "howling" frantically, she runs back to the barn, where, finding no one, she thinks that her mother's corpse has "already . . . been cut down and taken away" (12). When she discovers her mother alive and sitting with Beryl in a neighbor's kitchen, Marietta faints.

Her loss of consciousness symbolically marks this experience as a permanent split in the safe surface of ordinary reality. So does her compulsive narration of this experience to her daughter. By reliving her trauma, Marietta permanently marks Phemie, too. A generation later, Marietta tells Phemie about the laughing men who still seem to be watching her running through the town in her nightgown: "A bunch of men standing out on the street . . . seemed to Marietta like a clot of poison. You tried not to hear what they were saying, but you could be sure it was vile. If they didn't say anything, they laughed and vileness spread out from them—poison—just the same" (11–12). The child Phemie, who "never asked" for a definition of "the men's poison talk" or "of the word 'vile'" associates her mother's unhappy story of that day with "a cloud, a poison, that had touched [her] mother's life. And when [Phemie] grieved her mother, [she] became part of it" (13). Phemie identifies with her mother not only out of sympathy with the terrified child who believed her mother had hanged herself but also because of her intuitive awareness of their common female bond. Like Helena in "Executioners," both mother and daughter feel themselves shamefully exposed to men's obscene remarks. Just as Helena, taunted by Howard Troy, felt "like somebody walking through a wall of flame," so Marietta in her nightgown, laughed at by the loggers, felt "scorched" (SIB, 142; PL, 12). This shared vulnerability convinces the child Phemie that her mother knows "something about [her] that [is] worse, far worse, than ordinary lies and tricks and meanness; it [is] a really sickening shame" (13). Phemie's brothers, "cheerful savages, running around free," escape this shameful vulnerability simply by being male, and so do Phemie's own sons. That is why Phemie is relieved to have no daughters: "I felt as if something could stop now—the stories, and griefs, the old puzzles you can't resist or solve" (14).

As she recalls these two different versions of the trauma in her mother's childhood, Phemie also remembers two versions of a key event in her mother's adult life, the story of how Marietta burned the money that she had inherited from her hated father. Although Phemie knew the true version of this story, she realizes that she has imagined a completely different version. The true story is that Marietta's husband, Phemie's father, knew nothing about his wife's inheritance or what she did with it. But Phemie's imagined version "seems so much the truth it is the truth; it's what [she] believe[s] about them" (30). In this imagined version, her father lovingly protects her mother's right to do what she wants with the money, even though the family is poor; in fact, he calmly watches her burn $3,000!

All these confused memories of her mother's life come flooding back when Phemie visits the old family farmhouse with a lover and they stand in the same room that she remembers helping her mother repaper for Aunt Beryl's visit so many years ago. That old wallpaper is still visible under two coats of paint and another, now torn layer of wallpaper. These layers of wallcovering are analogous to the layers of stories that have accumulated, one version on top of another, in Phemie's memory, to make her the woman that she now is in middle age. She resents and criticizes the hippies who rented the house after her parents' death, turned it into a commune, and painted a naked couple on the wall. But when her lover looks at the painted couple's "not so private parts" and remarks in a voice "thickened" by "lust," "I guess this was where they carried on their sexual shenanigans," Phemie's reply is suddenly the angry reply of Marietta's daughter, permanently affected by the cloud of poison spreading out from the men who laughed at Marietta in her nightgown two generations earlier (27). Phemie lashes out: "Just say the words 'hippie' or 'commune' and all you guys can think about is screwing! . . . I get so sick of that—it's all so stupid it just makes me sick!" (27) Although she later attempts to conciliate her lover, the links between the three generations of women complete the old puzzle: the grandmother wanted to frighten her philandering husband, the mother dreaded laughing men, and the granddaughter, reversing her own critical opinion of hippies, suddenly defends them against the male sexuality that oversimplifies and distorts their lifestyle into nothing but a symbol of "orgies and . . . non-stop screwing" (27). These links, as well as Phemie's lovingly imagined version of her father's protective role in the money-burning episode, represent the title's complicated progress of love.

In these stories one can also trace the progress of Munro's treatment of the mother-daughter theme. The guilt-stricken question in the title of "How Could I Do That?" introduces the daughter's emotional role. In "The Peace of Utrecht" the daughter becomes the first-person narrator struggling to control her guilty memories of a very recent, humiliating past. From this beginning, Munro progresses to increasingly broader questions about shaping the medium of control, her fictional techniques, the most important of which is her manipulation of point of view. In "Winter Wind" and "The Ottawa Valley," the daughter-narrator and the daughter-protagonist briefly part company in the incipiently metafictional epilogues. In the full-blown metafiction of "Home," the absence of a plot erases the protagonist's role. The daughter is a writer who repeatedly splits—not into a narrator and a protagonist—but into an editor and an author of fiction. The observing editor criticizes the narrating author for her humiliating failures in handling the language and characterization of her stepmother. These failures are at least partially the result of the daughter's emotional closeness to her real mother. The still-living father is introduced and evokes one happy childhood memory, but the real mother, though long dead, is the focus of the daughter's most central concerns. In the story within a story in "The Progress of Love," the daughter as first-person narrator temporarily disappears, and the mother finally develops into a protagonist in her own right. Although her story is still framed within the narrating daughter's story and although the umbilical cord tying them together is still twisted by guilty shame, the schoolteacher mother is now a separate character, seen through her own eyes and allowed to speak in her own undistorted voice.

The original *New Yorker* version of this story, however, did not have a first-person narrator. In the story as it was published on 7 October 1985, Phemie was a third-person protagonist. As already indicated in the discussions of "Jesse and Meribeth," "The Moon in the Orange Street Skating Rink," "White Dump," and "A Queer Streak," Munro often revises her stories between their original publication in a periodical and the republication in a collection.[1] For example, she frequently writes a story from both the third-person and first-person point of view before deciding which to use in the final version ("Real Material," 24).[2] This is obviously what she has done here, and the switch to a first-person narrator makes the collected version of this story much more like the earlier mother-stories, all of which are narrated in the first person. In the original *New Yorker* version, the fact that *both* Phemie and Marietta are third-person protagonists makes them equally important characters, even though the length of Marietta's story within Phemie's story is the same in both versions. By making Phemie the narrator in the second version, Munro emphasizes Phemie's retrospective, authorial function. Although Phemie is a real-estate agent in both versions, in the second version she is nevertheless clearly also a writer who imagines the story within the story, while in the original version the author herself is the narrator of both characters' stories. Thus, in the original version the author maintains an equal distance from both of her third-person protagonists, while in the revision she fuses once again with the narrator-daughter.

In a way, therefore, Munro's return to the first-person narrator's point of view in this story represents a narrowing of the considerably wider emotional distance of the first version. This narrowing naturally focuses much more attention on the remembering, imagining, editing process of narration, in short, on the creative activity of the writer herself. It also makes the reader who has recently read the original version conscious of a process of artistic flux that, while it certainly cannot be labelled a regression, nevertheless looks like a temporary opening-out of a new direction, followed by a cautious backing-off from a partially explored possibility. This process thus demonstrates the futility of trying to set up airtight categories in the work of a still active, prolific, and intensely self-critical writer, whose revisions of this story are much like the layers of wallcovering in the farmhouse bedroom. For the reader, these two versions correspond to each other in such a way that the revised, first-person version becomes metafiction within metafiction, a commentary not only on the Marietta-story within the story itself, but also, with even greater although more oblique self-reflexiveness, on the earlier third-person version underneath. Munro herself, of course, is highly conscious of what she is doing in these changing mother-stories. She has candidly admitted her inability to "get rid" of her mother, but she adds: "[E]ven the admission that you don't get rid of those thoughts is a great thing. The acceptance of the truth of where you are is the most releasing thing I know" ("Name," 70).

Another shift—in some ways much more significant—occurs in an earlier story, "The Moons of Jupiter," a father-story originally published in 1978, two years after the death of Munro's father during cardiac surgery, and republished as the title story of Munro's fifth book (Slopen, 77; Dahlie, "Alice Munro and Her Works," 215). Although the narrator in "The Peace of Utrecht" and Phemie in "The Progress of Love" are both mothers, the thematic emphasis in these two stories is not on their adult roles as such, but on their original roles as their mothers' daughters. In "The Moons of Jupiter," however, Janet, the first-person narrator, is seen as the daughter of her father rather than of her mother and also as the mother of adult daughters herself. The narrator thus functions in a double role, in the middle between her dying father and her independent daughters. Only as a middle-aged parent herself does Janet realize that in the past she did not really understand her father's life. Now she can see the difference between her self-perception and the way her daughters perceive her, and from this double point of view she can recognize how presumptuously she assessed both her parents when she was around her daughters' present age. Discussing her parents with a friend, she "deplored [them], . . . filed them away, defined them beyond any possibility of change" (MJ, 222). She suspects that now her

daughters are discussing *her*, "comparing notes, . . . analyzing, regret-
ting, blaming, forgiving," just as she and her friend once did (222). But
the story is not so much about what Janet gains in perspective as about
what she loses from her life.

"The Moons of Jupiter" is a quietly moving story about a simultaneous, double loss: the death of Janet's father, which seems imminent just
beyond the story's conclusion, and the departure of both her daughters.
Judith goes off to Mexico with her lover; Nichola, although in Toronto,
refuses to communicate with her mother. To assert her independent
identity, she has chosen to be "incommunicado" (221). Struggling to
cope with her nerve-wracking anxiety about her father, hospitalized for
medical tests, Janet searches for some distracting activity. First she tries
shopping, but this attempt reminds her of how she did exactly the same
thing when as a young mother she mistakenly feared that medical tests
on the baby Nichola would confirm a diagnosis of leukemia. Dreading
this devastating possibility, she touched the child on her lap "with a
difference, ... a care—not a withdrawal exactly but a care—not to feel
anything˙ much" (229–30).³ This emotional parallel between the two
shopping trips emphasizes that, although Janet did not lose Nichola
then, she has lost her now, just as she will inevitably lose her father.
And to minimize her double loss, to try to control her experience, Janet
once again repeats in the present what she did in the past. She tries
to withdraw, to back off, in order to reduce the pain of what she feels.
Abandoning her pointless shopping, she visits the Planetarium.

The show that she sees in the Planetarium is both implicitly and
explicitly linked to an earlier scene in this tightly unified story, a visit
to her hospitalized father who has chosen to have cardiac surgery in
an attempt to prolong his life. In this earlier scene, her father quotes
the opening stanza of Joaquin Miller's poem "Columbus":

Behind him lay the gray Azores,
Behind the gate of Hercules;
Before him not the ghost of shores,
Before him only shoreless seas. (MJ, 225)

After quoting it, he comments on his "great temptation to believe in—
You know," and "feeling an appalling rush of love and recognition,"
Janet immediately supplies the words he wants, "the 'soul'" (226). He
has been reading about the out-of-body experiences of patients resusci-
tated after cardiac arrests: "They'd float up to the ceiling and look down
on themselves and see the doctors working on them, on their bodies."
Then, after they had been revived, "they found themselves back in the
body and feeling all the mortal pain . . . " (226). This experience of

withdrawal, in which the medically dead patient splits into two personae, his body and his "soul," and his floating soul watches his body below, is very much like Munro's definition of the writer's split into the observer and the participant. Therefore, it is analogous to the experience of many of her key characters, for example, to Del's in "Baptizing," and, most particularly, to the experience Eugene, the writer-figure, hopes to achieve by "walking on water."

Visiting the Planetarium, Janet is consciously seeking such an out-of-body experience. Like her father thinking about the "shoreless seas" that he must face when he dies, she sees the ceiling of the Planetarium fill up with "billions of galaxies. Innumerable repetitions, innumerable variations," "unknowns and horrible immensities" (231). In an explicit thematic summary at the end of the story, once more like those in *Dance of the Happy Shades*, Janet feels that seeing the Planetarium show has fulfilled its purpose, "done what [she] wanted it to after all—calmed [her] down, drained [her]." It has produced this effect by giving her an experience analogous to that of the cardiac patients described in the articles: "I felt like one of those people who have floated up to the ceiling, enjoying a brief death. A relief, while it lasts" (233). The Planetarium ceiling and the ceiling where the patients' disembodied souls hover and watch the suffering below have fused the actual and the imaginary experience in Janet's mind. In this mood she is able to tell herself that if she accidentally happens to see Nichola, whom she has been hoping to glimpse somewhere in Toronto, she "might just sit and watch," detached from her maternal participation in her child's life, transformed, although with deeply painful reluctance, into a passive observer (233).[4]

Thus, the experience of withdrawal that Janet's father reads about and that Janet actively seeks unifies the story both thematically and psychologically by shaping the characterization of the narrator whose experience embodies the theme. Her split into two personae, the observer and the participant, defines her double role as her father's daughter and as her daughters' mother. In participating in her own life, Janet has been only the observer on the periphery of both her father's life and her daughters' lives, and they have been the observers of hers. When her father once remarked that his memory of her childhood years was "all just a kind of blur," she, able to remember those years "with pain and clarity," was hurt. But now, trying to remember the childhood years of her own daughters, she is forced to acknowledge, "yes, blur is the word for it" (222). However, she fully realizes these facts only when, instead of holding her baby daughter on her lap but fearing to lose her, she is pushed to the periphery of the adult Nichola's life, where all she can do is pretend to "sit and watch" the daughter whom she has lost (233). She has become Nichola's satellite. Hence, as Geoff Hancock has recognized, Janet's pre-operative conversation with her father about the moons of Jupiter suggests that the story's title is symbolic ("Interview": Hancock, 91). Just as Jupiter is the center around which its moons revolve, so each member of a family finally perceives that he or she is both the center around which the others revolve and a moon in all the other members' orbits. Thus the generations revolve around each other, daughters and mothers and fathers, and mothers and daughters again. In the inevitable flux of human life, these concentric circles also define the progress of love.

6

Conclusion

Point of View, Metaphor, and Paradox

Janet's double point of view as both observer and participant in "The Moons of Jupiter" is especially appropriate, for, like many other Munro narrators and protagonists, Janet is a writer.[1] Like "Connection," "The Moons of Jupiter," first published in the *New Yorker* on 27 May 1978, was originally to be collected in *Who Do You Think You Are?*, which in its "first version . . . contained a group of stories about Rose and a group of stories about Janet" ("Real Material," 29). In the second half of the book, Janet was to be the author who had written the first half, the stories about Rose. However, although Munro originally "liked the idea," she "eventually rejected it" ("Interview": Hancock, 88).[2]

But her rejection is misleading. For whichever point of view Munro uses, first or third, she follows a pattern very similar to this rejected arrangement. Her original idea of having Janet write the Rose stories in the third person and narrate the Janet stories in the first person suggests the split point of view that appears not only in "The Moons of Jupiter" but also in Munro's other retrospective first-person stories, especially "Baptizing" and "Epilogue: The Photographer." In the latter story, as L. M. Eldredge says, we see Del, the narrator, eerily "overtak[ing] her own story and becom[ing] the author of it" (112). Although the retrospective first-person narrators are much fewer in *The Progress of Love* than in earlier works, the most striking illustration of Munro's rejected Rose-Janet arrangement is the revised version of this collection's title story. Here the first-person narrator temporarily disappears from the story of her mother, and the mother becomes a third-person protagonist. A later story, "Meneseteung" (1988), repeats the same device: a first-person narrator in the present imagines the life of a third-person protagonist, a nineteenth-century woman writer; the narrator's comments frame and interpret her character's story.

The rejected arrangement is also reflected in the split point of view in Munro's third-person stories, where, instead of a split within the observing and participating first-person narrator, there is a split between the participating third-person protagonist(s) and the omniscient author. Such a split is especially significant in "White Dump" and "A Queer Streak." But, like the first-person narrators, these omniscient authors are also much fewer in *The Progress of Love*. However, the third-person protagonists in stories like "Fits" and "The Moon in the Orange Street Skating Rink" are detached observers who function in much the same way as the omniscient authors in other stories, temporally or spatially outside the action experienced by the participants in the center.

The position of this detached observer, whether in the first person or the third, is one that Munro, like many other writers, deliberately adopted. Her definition of the author as a watcher, as a person who changes "from a participant into an observer," makes this clear ("Author's Commentary," 125). But now it is also clear that this position was one of which she was naturally aware, long before she ever began to write. In "An Open Letter" to *Jubilee*, a Wingham, Ontario, journal named after her fictional town, she has remarked, "When I was quite young I got a feeling about Wingham . . . which is only possible, I think, for a child and an outsider. I was an outsider; I came into town everyday to go to school, but I didn't belong there. So everything seemed a bit foreign, and particularly clear and important to me" (6).

But living outside the town, "outside the whole social structure," was not the only reason that made Munro feel this way ("What Is," 18). As I have shown, her initial sense of being an outsider developed into a compound of many painful elements. She was physically clumsy, female, and poor. She spoke grammatically at home and ungrammatically away from home. Most important, just as her own powers were beginning to develop, she had to watch her mother's helpless loss of power. The emotional impact of all these factors was intensified by her enormously retentive memory, her penetrating intelligence, and her vividly visual imagination. Just as her house-metaphor for a story, a "structure" that "encloses space and makes connections between one enclosed space and another," illuminates the unifying purpose of the thematic parallels *in* many of her stories—"Executioners," "The Ottawa Valley," "Royal Beatings," "The Moons of Jupiter," "Fits," "Miles City, Montana," "Circle of Prayer," and "A Queer Streak"—so the combination of all these causal factors results in unifying parallels *between* her stories ("What Is Real?," 5).

One of the most obvious parallels between her stories is that many of her major and minor characters are outsiders, people who, like her, do not belong. Her first published story and similar later stories about teachers repeatedly emphasize her fear that intelligence and imagination are the outsider's stigmata. Miss Abelhart, Mr. Torrance, and Mr. Cleaver are all despised by the community. In the ironic epilogue of "Characters," the adult Rose discovers that Mr. Cleaver's former students regretfully recall him as "brilliant" and "unappreciated" (82). Two other teachers, Miss Farris and Arthur Comber, achieve some recognition while they are still teaching, but it is mixed with mockery. And Miss Marsalles, the music teacher of retarded children in "Dance of the Happy Shades," lives in an "other country" (DHS, 224).

So do the poor characters who leave their rural poverty and move into town. Many of Munro's outsiders, both female and male, come into town and confront the same painful fact: that as bright students they are doubly stigmatized by their "publicly proclaimed braininess and poverty" (WDY, 71). Alva, the country high-school girl in "Sunday Afternoon," feels mute and invisible on the edge of her wealthy employers' lives. Jessie, in "Jesse and Meribeth," is in a similarly peripheral position at the Crydermans' home; but, in spite of her marginal life of "narrowness and proud caution and threadbare decency," she is determined to "snip one little hole" in Mr. Cryderman's "contempt" for her small "town and everybody in it" (PL, 168, 175). Rose in "The Beggar Maid" and Isabel in "White Dump" are also both outsiders, not only at the university but at the home of their future in-laws, too. Like Violet in "A Queer Streak," who fears the label of "hillbilly" and has only "one good dress" in normal school, both students are badly dressed, and Isabel is acutely self-conscious about "being the brightest pupil from a working-class high school" (PL, 223, 216, 303). Sam and Edgar, the two badly dressed country students in "The Moon in the Orange Street Skating Rink," are obviously outsiders, too. Their position as such is dramatized by the fact that getting *into* the skating rink, the center of the small town's winter social life, is an event of such exciting magnitude that after fifty years Sam still remembers it vividly.

Some of Munro's other characters are outsiders in several other senses. Ted Makkavala in "Accident" and Robert Kuiper in "Fits" are newcomers in the community in which the action is set and by which its events are shaped. The childless Roy Fowler in "Wood" is an outsider in the community of his wife's huge clan. Mary Jo, the small-town nurse in "Eskimo," lives her life inside Dr. Streeter's dual-purpose building, but paradoxically this isolation makes her an outsider watching his real life from the edge. The "secret weight" of Colin's self-appointed duty in "Monsieur les Deux Chapeaux" is even more paradoxical, for being his brother's keeper marks him as an outsider like Cain (PL, 66). Munro's "overwhelming interest in the process of aging" can also be ascribed to her identification with outsiders ("Writing's," E1). Her many elderly characters, Dorothy in "Marrakesh," the dislocated Mr. Lougheed in "Walking on Water," and the hallucinating Violet in Part II of "A Queer Streak," are all outsiders. They are out of place because, having lived too long, they are now living in the wrong time. So is the elderly Sophie in "White Dump," who, after her experience with the hippies, ascends in the plane with her son and grandchildren and, looking down from the air, feels both disconnected and diminished, "as if it was she, not the things on earth, that had shrunk, was still shrinking—or [as if] they were all shrinking together" (PL, 296).

But the most significant outsiders are the writer-narrator of "The Office," Del, Rose, and the many other characters who, like Munro herself, experience exclusion in several combined senses. By virtue of their temperament and their talent, they are constitutionally incapable of ever being insiders at home or in their original community. Although both warmed and sheltered at home and deeply rooted in their region, at the same time they always know that they do not fully belong in either place. This paradox of belonging but not belonging is one of the major reasons for their intense ambivalence. They are also outsiders because, like their creator, who has moved back to within twenty miles of her birthplace, they left their community but then returned to it. Therefore, they are doubly outsiders, both in the place to which they went and in the changed but still hostile place to which they have returned.

Munro has remarked, "I always felt when I lived in Vancouver and Victoria that I had to go home to die, because life on the west coast wasn't real in the same way" ("Interview": Horwood, 135). Therefore, even though she lived in British Columbia for twenty years, she is "not at all sure" that she ever acquired an authentic feel for its "texture" ("Conversation," 56). This uncertainty suggests that she would concur with George Woodcock's assessment that she has written "all her best work about the seedy town edges of southern Ontario, where she grew up . . ." ("Introduction," 3). And reflecting the circular pattern of her own life-experience, she brings many of her characters back to the place where they once possessed their original *Fingerspitzengefühl*. In her retrospective imagination, Del goes back to Jubilee; Rose returns to Hanratty as an actress; Frances, Bonnie, and several other characters return to their hometowns for funerals; Sam Grazier revisits Ontario after fifty years on the West Coast; Denise returns to her childhood summer home; and, most importantly, the narrators of "The Peace of Utrecht," "Home," and "The Progress of Love" also go home.

But it is no longer home. All these characters record, remember, watch, and wonder about unsolved and unsolvable mysteries, unsolvable partly because the persistently hostile community confronts each of these outsiders with the same question: "Who do you think you are?"[3] In the title story of Munro's second novel, Rose notes: "This was not the first time in her life [she] had been asked who she thought she was; in fact the question had often struck her like a monotonous gong . . ." (WDY, 196). In chapter 1, I suggested that the answer to this question had to be a double one because Munro recognizes herself as "two rather different people" ("Interview": Hancock, 103). A corollary to that initial answer is a second one: "I am the outsider." That is the first and the most fruitful paradox of Munro's persistently peripheral point of view as the ambivalent but compulsive watcher, for the person to whom "everything seem[s] a bit foreign, [but] particularly clear and important" is by definition the artist ("An Open Letter," 6).

But Munro's definition of the artist also stresses another recurring paradox: that the artist *herself* must be a double person, both a voyeur and an actress, both a member of the audience and an imperilled performer of dramatic tricks—in short, a person who exposes not only others but also herself. This paradoxical definition is another parallel that connects many of her stories. Munro explicitly defines "a fiction writer" as a member of a theatrical audience, fascinated by "the way people live in the eyes of others. Every life is a drama, everybody is on stage" ("An Open Letter," 6). One of these "others" is the sharp-eyed voyeur who not only watches the stage, sporadically illumined, but also penetrates the "hidden rooms" and secrets concealed by the protective surfaces of walls or clothes ("An Open Letter," 5). Watching in the darkness or peering through doors and windows and knotholes, she sees other people's sexuality and nakedness. But by taking the stage, she also repeatedly exposes *herself* to the possible shame of public ridicule. She attempts miracles. She splits herself in half and tries, like Miss Farris and Eugene, to walk on water. In "Simon's Luck," the feminist critic's long list of female artists who committed suicide includes Virginia Woolf, who drowned herself (WDY, 157). Thus, if the artist-actress fails in the performance of her double role, she might break through another concealing surface and drown, like Edna Pontellier, the failed artist in *The Awakening*.

This possibility suggests the dangers inherent in what is concealed. These hidden dangers are another parallel between many Munro stories. Under clothes, there is the hungry, sexual body; under the bedclothes, there is the pregnant mother; underwater, there is death. In "Miles City, Montana," sex inevitably leads to parenthood, but life just as inevitably leads to death: "our fears are based on nothing but the truth. . . " (DHS, 43). What the remembered child dimly senses about death and pregnancy in "Images" and what Del discovers about sex in "Baptizing" are what the narrators know in "Jesse and Meribeth" and "Miles City, Montana." Munro has not only described "Images" as the story "closest" to her in her first collection, but has also acknowledged her narrator's definition of the real basis of "our fears" as her own credo: "Yes, . . . that's what I believe" ("Conversation," 58; "Alice Munro," 255). These secret, hidden fears are still intrinsically connected in the imagination of her most recent narrators in *The Progress of Love* and beyond, whose stories about sex, pregnancy, and drowning are retrospective not only within the narrative framework but also self-reflexively beyond it.

This connection is at the root of the shared significance of the metaphorical parallels between her stories, of the forces that repeatedly threaten to split the concealing and protective safety of surfaces: the bursting boil and the blazing house; the underground stream, the earthquake, or the erupting volcano that breaks through the earth's crust; the lightning that splits the sky; the flash of light that illumines the darkness; the sudden shot that splits a boy's life; the waves of pain that rend a woman in labor; and, most often, the water that literally or metaphorically drowns—or threatens to drown—many characters. Janet's dying father, like Columbus, sees himself menaced by "shoreless seas" (MJ, 225). Miss Farris, Marion Sherriff, Caroline in Del's unwritten novel, Sandy Desmond, Frank McArter, and Steve Gauley actually drown. Many other characters—Miss Abelhart, the passengers on the Irish emigrant ship, Char Desmond, Jeanette, Blair King, Eugene, Mr. Lougheed, Rose, the narrator of "Bardon Bus," little Meg, and Violet— are all threatened by actual or metaphorical drowning. And in the dramatic climax of "Baptizing," Del must fight against both types of drowning at once.

But why do drowned characters appear so often, and why is drowning such an obsessive metaphor in Munro's fiction? In *Lives of Girls and Women*, there are several references to the spring flooding of the Wawanash River; the actual source of these fictional events is identified in an article, "Everything Here is Touchable and Mysterious," in which Munro describes the Maitland River and "the Flood" that "came upon [the people of Wingham, Ontario] with a Biblical inevitability" every spring and evoked both their "respect" and their "amazed" contemplation (33). Another possible source of Munro's repeated references to drowning is that the "near-drowning" of the writer-narrator's daughter in "Miles City, Montana" is based on an event that "actually happened" to her own daughter (Kolson, 4C). However, neither Munro's early familiarity with seasonal flooding nor the narrowly averted drowning of one of her daughters necessarily explains why she uses drowning as a metaphor for the helplessness and loss of control that constitute the predominant dangers in her stories.

But her criticism of the different kinds of helplessness that she calls "abdication" reveals a crucial connection between actual drowning and metaphors of helplessness. Her horror of helplessness pervades both her nonfictional and fictional criticism of her mother's disintegration. In "Working for a Living," Munro admits her adolescent anger at her stricken mother's "abdication" to her disease (30). Her anger is also reflected in her narrator's irrational conviction in "The Ottawa Valley" that her mother "gave her consent" to her affliction: "As long as she lived, and through all the changes that happened to her, and after I had received the medical explanations of what was happening, I still felt secretly that she had given her consent" (SIB, 244). In the same way, Munro also criticizes the many female characters who abdicate in love affairs, who hand over their power to their lovers, for they, much more than her mother, consent to their own helplessness by yielding to the humiliations of the flesh. For example, Et criticizes Char, entangled with Blaikie in the summer grass and helpless as a drowned corpse. Et knows "what Char looked like when she lost her powers, abdicated. Sandy drowned, with green stuff clogging his nostrils, couldn't look more lost than that" (SIB, 11).

These recurrent images and metaphors of drowning and Munro's repeated criticism of helplessly drowning characters suggest a close causal link between what seems to be her own fear of abdication, that is, her fear that she might give up or lose her own artistic powers, and her deeply paradoxical thematic obsession with control. In story after story, she reiterates her underlying theme: although helplessness is inevitable, it must nevertheless be controlled. This theme is most fully dramatized in the character closest to her. Fearing drowning in both the literal and the metaphorical sense, Del dreads being buried alive in the water and not being free to write. Both of these fears seem to reflect Munro's own apprehension about controlling her writing. For example, explaining why she writes short stories instead of conventionally structured novels, she has admitted, "[Y]es, yes, . . . I may indeed fear loss of control" ("Real Material," 15).

This fear began with her "training" as a girl who grew up in a rigidly self-controlled community ("Real Material," 15). In early adolescence, when her mother's fatal illness began, she discovered that the world is a perilous place in which surfaces can never be trusted to remain intact or firm. In such a frightening world, the control so sternly prescribed by her community became even more demandingly difficult. As she began her writing career, her fears developed into those of the woman who had to struggle for many years not to abdicate, not to yield either to her frustration about her lack of recognition, or, paradoxically, to her typically feminine fear of that recognition. Her "frustration" was the result of the "grindingly slow process" of "establishing [her] credentials as a writer of fiction in Canada in the 1950s." In his introduction to *The Oxford Book of Canadian Short Stories in English*, Robert Weaver points out that no contemporary young writer of Munro's caliber has been forced to wait fifteen long years, as she did, for the recognition of her first collection of short stories (xviii). And she herself has commented, "It is very hard for any artist to get through the first 15 years," especially in defiance of the *Zeitgeist's* prescription of childlessness for women writers. "You do feel rather doubtful that you can disprove it all, and you have enough to cope with" ("Writing's," E1). But at the same time, her fear of success, which sprang from her dread of being considered "unappealing" and "unwomanly," fed her often-confessed ambivalence about fulfilling her ambition (Kolson, 4C). Therefore, the powers of this woman struggling to maintain control were those of a split person struggling to survive in a split world.

The repeatedly relived tragedy of her mother is also intrinsically connected with Munro's own dual nature. Just as the narrator of "The Peace of Utrecht" sees her dying mother imprisoned by her paralyzing disease, so Munro defines the "abdicat[ing]" woman writer as a prisoner fettered by the "shackles" of her marriage ("Conversation," 59). And in a later interview, she wonders "whether in choosing freedom you have to deliberately put" the "happiness [of erotic love] behind you . . ." ("Who," 5). These prison metaphors show that erotic love is inherently dangerous. Fascinated by characters who succumb to this danger, Munro stresses her "fear" of "how easily it can happen" ("Writing's,"). And driven by this fear, she makes Del and Rose, her two major artist-figures, choose freedom for analogous reasons. If Del had chosen to abdicate her powers, her fate would have been that of the wordless and walled-in mother, a living death. Similarly, Munro insists that the divorced Rose, though not "a kind of modern everywoman," is a woman who "wants . . . to keep herself whole . . . " ("Who," 5–6).

But to keep herself whole in this dangerous world, the artist must, paradoxically, split herself in half. She must become both the voyeur who cautiously backs off to watch from the edge of the deep, entombing water and the trickster or miracle-performer who crazily tries to walk on it. These are both images of Munro's peripheral point of view, for only by *deliberately* splitting in half can the artist try to control the frightening revelations of a world and a self that are both always liable to split. This deliberate split is the second creative paradox of Munro's fiction.

And this split is the reason that metaphors suggesting spatial relationships—inside, outside, on top of, at the edge of, at the bottom of, underneath—are central to Munro's conception of the artist. Just before her shattering vision of humiliation at the funeral, Del ruefully recognizes her position as "a *borderline case*" (LGW, 57).[4] From this border, the artist perceives dangers invisible to others. Joan Fordyce, the protagonist of "Oh, What Avails" (1987), has a similarly shattering vision. Once an art student, she revisits Logan, her hometown. "[S]uddenly, without warning," she sees that "underneath" the solid, "connected," and "necessary" world of its streets lies a world of "[r]ubble." Threatened by this "new danger," she "wants to keep this idea of rubble at bay, . . . " and to do so, she "pays attention . . . to all the ways in which people seem to do that." The connotations of *seem* emphasize her consciousness of the "gaps" in their illusory attempts at control (59).

But to effect her own control, the artist deliberately exposes herself to these gaps, submits herself to the dangerously split surface that separates the world of appearances from the world below. Such submission is doubly dangerous. Because the artist herself is split, the two worlds separated by the surface are just as much within her ambivalent self as they are outside her. The potential danger of the artist's submission is emphasized not only by Del's self-conscious pun on "borderline case" and Eugene's delusive experiment but also by the ironic fate of Almeda, the protagonist of the uncollected *New Yorker* story symbolically entitled "Meneseteung," the Indian name of the Maitland River ("Everything," 33).

In this story the artist is doubly split. First, there are two artists, the first-person narrator and Almeda, a nineteenth-century amateur poet whose life the narrator imagines. Second, Almeda herself is also split. Her house on the edge of town, between the community's respectable and disreputable sections, symbolizes her social position as an outsider and her psychological position as a borderline case. Although she yearns to marry Jarvis, her cautious suitor, and fantasizes about submitting to him, her yearning is ambivalent. Like many masochistic Munro heroines, she sees the man in her life as a father-figure: she "shiver[s]" with erotic excitement because Jarvis smells like her father ("Meneseteung," 31). But, unlike earlier heroines, she does not yield to her masochism. However, although the voyeur-scene in which she is scorched by a sexual "ball of fire" resolves her ambivalence about Jarvis, the resolution is once again ironic (33).

After overhearing the violent, drunken quarrel and nearly murderous copulation of a "self-abandon[ing]" couple from the disreputable part of town, she summons Jarvis's help (34). When he sees the bloody, half-naked woman, still sprawled on the ground the next morning, and hears her masochistic "yowl" of "anguished pleasure," he is "stirred" by the same "aphrodisiac prickles of disgust" that Munro criticizes in "Privilege" (35, 36; WDY, 26). Rejecting marriage to such a man, whom she now imagines as a tombstone, Almeda chooses the pursuit of artistic mastery. Like Munro, she wants to effect control through language. She wants to shape words to "catch" and "understand" the electric moment when everything "explode[s]" (36). To do so, she "looks deep, deep into the river of her mind," and beginning to menstruate, she feels her creative juices also start to "flow" (37). But this equation of menstruation and artistic creation is deeply ironic. Almeda tells herself "she knows that she is sane," but because menstruation signals the absence of conception—the lack of new creation—her certainty that her imagination does not compromise her rationality is a delusion (37). Absorbed in her thoughts, she has forgotten two symbolically related things: that she has been making grape jelly and that she should have put on a sanitary towel. The forgotten grape juice running all over the floor and "her escaping blood" both symbolize waste (37).

Almeda's wasted artistic potentiality is ironically emphasized by the mode of her death. She does not drown in love, but she slowly drowns in the river of her mind. Cautiously distanced from her character, the first-person narrator recounts what she has read about her in an old newspaper: her "mind . . . somewhat clouded," Almeda died after becoming "thoroughly wet from a ramble" in swampy water (37, 38). Although she may have been chased into the water by some persecuting children, her death is foreshadowed by one of her own poems, in which she describes herself underwater, sitting *"at the bottom of sleep,/As on the floor of the sea"* (36). Both the children and the allusion to figurative drowning echo Miss Abelhart's situation in "The Dimensions of a Shadow," Munro's first story: ridiculed by school children, she was left "alone in bottomless silence" (10).

The reason for the lifelong persistence of these submarine images in Munro's fiction is suggested by her description of what *she* does when she writes. Like Almeda, Munro dives underwater: "I go into this peculiar limbo and this kind of shady area to look for the story . . . "

("Interview": Hancock, 86). The "story is a spell, rather than a narrative" (Slopen, 77). And in this dark and enchanted place, the depths in herself and in the water are always there, "deep holes, ominous beckoning places" ("Everything," 33). But there is a significant difference: by submitting herself to the destructive element, the successful artist does *not* drown. With her unwavering honesty about the painfully complex and permanently mysterious human condition, Alice Munro makes the deep, deep sea keep her up.[5] She walks on water.

Notes

Chapter 1

1. For a good review of Pfaus's very bad book, see Lorraine M. York, "Joyless in Jubilee?" *Essays on Canadian Writing* 34 (1987): 157–61.

2. When listed, the dates given in parentheses after the titles of stories are always the original dates of publication, not the dates of republication in Munro's six books. Some stories, however, were published for the first time in a collection. In the primary sources, I list all the stories in chronological order of their original publication and also all the stories included in each collection. My list includes material from Robert Thacker's annotated bibliography of Alice Munro in *The Annotated Bibliography of Canada's Major Authors*, V, 358–60, and also material that Munro has published since 1982, the cut-off date of Thacker's bibliography. For uncollected stories, all page references in the text are to the periodicals or anthologies in which they were published. (Nine of Munro's uncollected stories were published between 1950 and 1957; twelve of her recent stories, from 1974 to March 1989, are uncollected, the last seven of these published since her most recent collection, *The Progress of Love* [1986].) For all collected stories, the page references in the text are to the collections in which they appear. I use the following abbreviations for these collections: *Dance of the Happy Shades*, DHS; *Lives of Girls and Women*, LGW; *Something I've Been Meaning To Tell You*, SIB; *Who Do You Think You Are?*, WDY; *The Moons of Jupiter*, MJ; and *The Progress of Love*, PL. Between their original appearance and later publication in a collection, Munro often revises her stories and sometimes retitles them, too. I use the revised version and the revised title of all her collected stories. In the few cases in which I compare the original version with the revised version, I refer to both the periodical publication and the book publication.

3. In "Clear Jelly," Robert Thacker discusses the development of Munro's retrospective point of view in her early uncollected stories, in *Dance of the Happy Shades*, and briefly beyond.

4. In "'The Other Side of Dailiness,'" Lorraine M. York shows how Susan Sontag's *On Photography* can help to answer the question of "why paradox is so congenial to" Munro's fiction (49).

5. Susan J. Warwick discusses some of the "stage metaphors" in the two novels as instrumental in the maturation of the two heroines who think in these metaphors (211–25). In "Three Jokers: The Shape of Alice Munro's Stories," James Carscallen defines some of Munro's characters as "spectator[s]" watching "from a distance." He sees them not as theatrical spectators, however, but often as photographers taking pictures of what the actors in "the centre" are doing (143).

6. It is interesting to speculate on whether this key word in Munro's lexicon entered her vocabulary at the time of King Edward VIII's abdication in 1936. Although she was only five years old at the time, she would have heard her parents and other adults discussing the event and would also have learned about it at school. I base this assumption on the fact that as a schoolchild in Ontario at the same time, I, too, learned this word under these circumstances.

7. See SIB, 124, 201, 246; "The Colonel's Hash Resettled," 182; and "The Real Material," 6.

8. In addition to the key words discussed above, see another list of "Munro's words" in Lorraine M. York's "'Gulfs' and 'Connections': The Fiction of Alice Munro."

9. Not all critics share Moss's opinion about the absence of allusions from Munro's work. J. R. Struthers ("Reality and Ordering"), W. R. Martin ("Alice Munro and James Joyce"), and Barbara Godard have all explored her allusions to James Joyce. Carscallen discusses Munro's Egyptian allusions in both "Three Jokers" and "The Shining House." Lorraine M. York ("The Rival Bards") has analyzed her allusions to Tennyson and Browning. See also W. R. Martin, *Alice Munro: Paradox and Parallel*, 189–90.

10. Munro's father owned a turkey barn where her brother and sister both worked. She did not work there, for she was away at college ("Visit," 13).

11. These stories about old people include two others, "The Widower" (1951) and "The Idyllic Summer" (1954), the latter also about a teacher of the classics. In "Clear Jelly" Thacker discusses the second story (38–39).

12. Rowena Fowler compares the endings of the two novels as if Rose were a writer, too.

Chapter 2

1. The sources for Munro's documentary script were Susanna Moodie and an Irish couple's diary and letters (Adachi D3).

2. In "The Fiction of Alice Munro," Hallvard Dahlie compares Munro to Flannery O'Connor in their shared "vision" of "worlds . . . suddenly violated by . . . some unexpected force or event" (58). See also Andrew Stubbs (56) and Catherine Sheldrick Ross (112).

3. Although Miss Abelhart, the protagonist of "The Dimensions of a Shadow," is not a narrator, she is actually Munro's first split character, for her imaginary other self, the male student, is in many ways a younger persona. (See chapter 1.)

4. Eileen Dombrowski defines Munro's first three books as illustrations of her "vision" of "life as slipping away in a relentless movement toward death" (21). See also the conclusion of John Orange's essay: "At the centre of the maze is death . . ." (97).

5. The second phrase is not Munro's own, but when Ken Murch interviewed her for *Chatelaine* in August 1975 and remarked, "Many of your stories seem to involve the tremendous guilt over the death of someone," she agreed: "Yes . . . you're very perceptive . . . . That's probably the thing with my mother. . . yes" ("Name," 70).

6. Critics disagree on the meaning of the parallels between the beatings in this story and even on the question of whether there are any parallels. They also have somewhat different interpretations of the theatrical metaphors. See Lawrence Mathews, 185–87; Warwick, 211; Barry Cameron, viii; Hallvard Dahlie, "Alice Munro and Her Works," 248–9; J. R. (Tim) Struthers, "Alice Munro's Fictive Imagination," 109–10; and Martin, *Alice Munro: Paradox and Parallel*, 104–6.

7. In "'The Other Side of Dailiness,'" York quotes this passage about the linoleum as an illustration of the paradox that "even familiar objects are not man's familiars" (51). In "'Gulfs' and 'Connections,'" she sees the father in this scene as "a hate-filled child beater" (141).

8. Compare "A Trip to the Coast" where the child May thinks: "If her grandmother capitulated [to the hypnotist] it would be as unsettling an event as an earthquake . . ." (DHS, 188).

9. The phrase "with a self-conscious brutality" occurs in the original version of "Fits" in *Grand Street* 5 (1986): 58, but Munro deleted it from the revised version in *The Progress of Love*. Compare the fight and the violent copulation in "Meneseteung," *New Yorker*, 11 Jan. 1988: 33–34.

10. Lorna Irvine emphasizes "the opposition between" the two sisters and ignores the story's ironic conclusion ("Changing," 104–5). Although Margaret Anne Fitzpatrick recognizes that the "vice [Eileen] accuses her sister of turns out to be her own," Fitzpatrick does not discuss the shifts in point of view that reveal this "projection" (19).

11. Although Dorrit Cohn's discussion in this passage is about a first-person point of view, her comment is applicable to sudden shifts from a limited third-person point of view.

12. W. R. Martin, who criticizes this story as one about "naked, unrefined sexual desire," does not recognize the triple point of view Munro uses in its narration (*Alice Munro: Paradox and Parallel*, 138).

13. James Carscallen includes an analysis of "Wood" in "The Shining House," 93–94, 97–100. W. R. Martin also discusses this story in *Alice Munro: Paradox and Parallel*, 168–70.

14. Accidents continue to play a key role in two later, uncollected *New Yorker* stories. In "Oh, What Avails" (1987), Morris Fordyce is blinded in one eye as the result of a childhood accident. Scorned as "Deadeye Dick" and rejected by the woman he loves, he remains a bachelor all his life. In "Five Points" (1988), Cornelius Zendt is so badly injured in a salt-mine accident that he can no longer work at the mine and often has to "lie on the livingroom floor, coping with the pain" (34). His wife copes by taking a lover.

Chapter 3

1. Compare MJ, 22.

2. Margaret Gail Osachoff discusses the "child's logic" in the comment, but she does not point out what the child does not know: why Mary has come (66).

3. In "Alice in the Looking Glass," John Moss recognizes Del's reaction as disgust at the grotesqueness of "[t]he birth process" (61). In "Reality and Ordering: The Growth of a Young Artist in *Lives of Girls and Women*," J. R. (Tim) Struthers interprets Del's reaction as completely aesthetic (35).

4. In "Alice in the Looking Glass," Moss has pointed out that "[d]eath, typically at this age, holds a dark fascination for Del which she connects naturally with her knowledge of the processes of life, the dark areas of sexuality" (62). But Moss does not define the precise nature of this connection between death and sex or recognize it as a characteristic component of much of Munro's fiction. Christl Verduyn, on the other hand, limits Del's comment on flesh as humiliation to female sexuality: "When the boys at school whisper vague obscenities, Del feels that 'to be made of flesh was humiliation'" (451). Such a limitation wrenches the passage out of its funeral context to give it a completely erroneous feminist interpretation.

5. Compare Linda Lamont-Stewart who defines *Lives of Girls and Women* as an illustration of "the development of the writer's art as a defensive, organizing response to the humiliating absurdity of life" (115).

6. In "Alice in the Looking Glass," Moss incorrectly states that Del "never gets around to telling Naomi of this adventure . . ." (63).

7. In *Living Stories, Telling Lives*, Joanne S. Frye defines one of the key functions of a first-person narrator as "narrative interpretation" and "reinterpretation" of the past, and she emphasizes this function as one of the characteristics of Del's narration in the novel (57, 59). But when Frye later quotes the passage about Del's adolescent reaction to the article, she ignores the adult narrator's later, ironic comment (93). Frye's thesis is that *Lives* is a consciously feminist novel, the function of which is to fulfill the woman reader's "need," not to "personalize" art, as the article in *Lives* suggests, but "to escape the confines of the purely personal: to find, in the acknowledgment of shared experiences, a confirmation or clarification of what has been culturally denied or trivialized" (191, 192). But the adult Del's ironic recognition that the article described exactly what she was doing weakens the validity of Frye's thesis.

8. McMullen, 150, 158–59; Howells, 84.

9. Lorraine McMullen sees only that Munro is "anti-romantic" (159). Helen Hoy sees that she is anti-romantic but "she does not strip sex of its power and wonder" (111). Martin also emphasizes Del's double feelings in *Alice Munro: Paradox and Parallel*, 62.

10. See "Real Material," 26–27 and 34, where Munro discusses working on "The Ferguson Girls Must Never Marry."

11. Martin confuses the two stories that Bonnie wrote. He refers to "the novel that Bonnie wrote as a child of nine, . . . which 'was supposed to be something like the story of the Braddock family' . . ." (*Alice Munro: Paradox and Parallel*, 172). But the "story Bonnie had written when she was nine years old

[was] about some children in Mexico, and an idol with a curse on it" (*Grand Street* 1.3 [1982]: 36).

12. Martin, who reads this story as a religious allegory, says that Bonnie's "soul is born" because the last scene of the story "is the admission of Bonnie to the Catholic Church" (*Alice Munro: Paradox and Parallel*, 171, 174). This reading overlooks Bonnie's opinion of Ted's treatment of his wife.

Chapter 4

1. The original version of "Jesse and Meribeth," entitled "Secrets Between Friends," appeared in *Mademoiselle* in November 1985. A few of Munro's revisions of the original story are discussed later in this chapter.

2. In contrast to Osachoff, who argues that both the lover's death and the other woman are the narrator's inventions (77–79), many critics believe that the narrator's lover is really dead and that Patricia, the other woman, exists. See Brandon Conron (120–21), Gerald Noonan (176), B. Pfaus (33) and Lorraine M. York ("'Distant Parts of Myself,'" 35).

3. Critical opinion is divided on how Char dies. Orange believes that Et poisons her sister (91); W. H. New discerns "possible poisons" (42); Sandra Djwa (187), W. R. Martin (*Alice Munro: Paradox and Parallel*, 80) and Hallvard Dahlie ("Alice Munro and Her Works," 242) believe that Char commits suicide.

4. W. R. Martin compares Eugene's disappearance from his room at the end of the story to the resurrected Christ's disappearance from His tomb ("Hanging Pictures Together," 26; *Alice Munro: Paradox and Parallel*, 84).

5. Lawrence Mathews finds this "passage's function in 'Privilege' . . . unclear" because "we hear nothing more on the subject of male illusions about women" (181).

6. The phrase *funeral-play* occurs not in "Privilege" but in an uncollected earlier story, "The Dangerous One," published in *Chatelaine* in July 1957, in which the ten-year-old who is the "corpse" frightens the other little girls playing the game because she pretends to be really dead (50).

7. Compare Lorna Irvine's definition of one of the key questions of *The Moons of Jupiter*: "If women give in to sexual desire, do they becomes powerless characters?" (*Sub/Version*, 98).

8. Barbara Godard and Joseph Gold both recognize allusions to Yeats in this story, but neither critic develops them. Godard refers to "erotic overtones . . . through allusions to Yeats" (46), while Gold mentions that the minister's comment on the "cool" weather "inevitably reminds one of 'The Wild Swans at Coole'" (10).

9. The character of the lecherous minister who really is not a minister but is perceived as one, who excites an adolescent girl, and who is confused with God first appears in "Story for Sunday," published in *Folio* in December 1950. Its protagonist, the fifteen-year-old Evelyn, has a crush on Mr. Willens, the Sunday-school superintendent, who has excited her by kissing her in the vestry. Although he is not a minister, she sees him as "a slender young priest in a black robe" (7). In an early example of Munro's characteristic voyeur scenes, Evelyn, "noiselessly" peeking through a door, discovers that he kisses a different female

parishioner every Sunday. She consoles herself, however, by deliberately confusing his face with the "face of the immaculate Christ" Who loves everyone (8).

10. Compare "Secrets Between Friends," *Mademoiselle* Nov. 1985: 228.

11. In an interview, Munro describes this scene as "tremendously comic" ("Who," 5).

12. In "Real Material," Munro discusses her revision of "Simon's Luck" for *Who Do You Think You Are?*. It was originally "a long three-part story" about the "three women in Simon's life." Because Emily was the first of these women, "Emily" was the original title of the previously published version in the August 1978 issue of *Viva* (31).

13. Susan Sontag discusses the same paradox (167).

14. Marcia Allentuck very briefly discusses "The Office" as an example of Munro's "subliminal conviction that whatever efforts" the characters in her first three books "expend," their "emotional dependence" on men makes it impossible for them to achieve independence (341–42, 340).

15. For example, one feminist argues that "the general superiority of power of men over women has meant that women have been more anxious to please men than men have been to please women: to capture and keep their men women do all they can in the cause of beauty, while 'Man demands in his arrogance to be loved as he is,' as Germaine Greer said" (Richards, 196).

16. In *Sub/Version* Irvine applies this statement to the "silence" of the narrator's old aunts, "dessicated women" about whom the narrator is unable to write because they lack all desire (98). But in the sentence directly preceding the statement about "people's secrets," the narrator clearly refers to the hermit's silence: "I would have made a horrible, plausible connection between that silence of his, and the manner of his death [from cancer of the tongue]" (MJ, 35).

17. On the use of the triple point of view in another story in *The Moons of Jupiter*, see the discussion of "Accident" in chapter 2.

18. Willa Cather built Whale Cove Cottage on Grand Manan Island, New Brunswick (Woodress 197–98).

19. In 1981 Munro visited Sian, or Xian, as a member of a group of seven Canadian writers, guests of the Chinese Writers' Association. Her comments on her Chinese trip are in "Through the Jade Curtain," excerpts from an interview with Geoff Hancock. She became familiar with Australia because, "as the first Canadian winner of the Canada-Australia Literary Prize," she "spent a term at Queensland University in Brisbane" (Dahlie, "Alice Munro and Her Works," 217).

20. By arguing that Dennis introduces the "concept" of "renewal," but finally fails because his "train of thought leads to 'renunciation' and life-denying 'deprivation,'" Martin does not recognize the sadism in Dennis's sexist comments (*Alice Munro: Paradox and Parallel*, 143).

21. Irvine diminishes the pain of the narrator's personal memory by reducing the woman in this scene to a "female character" in a "fantasy" (*Sub/Version*, 104).

22. In discussing this story, Irvine asks, "Is it possible for women writers to release themselves from their bodies?" (*Sub/Version*, 100). To demonstrate that such a release is possible, she emphasizes the female narrator's "objectif[ying]" distance from her character, Roberta, but she ignores Munro's use of George's

point of view to achieve similar distance (99).

23. By mistakenly describing Roberta and George as a married couple, Martin diminishes Roberta's sense of helpless vulnerability in her relationship (*Alice Munro: Paradox and Parallel*, 146, 148).

24. Two of the main characters in "Oh, What Avails," an uncollected 1987 *New Yorker* story, are alter egos, alike in several important ways. Morris and Matilda both have names beginning with *M*; both are physically "marked," Morris by being blind in one eye and Matilda by being exceptionally beautiful; both take care of an elderly mother; and both nurse a hopeless love (46). Morris is "stern[ly]" in love with Matilda, but she is "stubbornly" in love with her ex-husband, a bigamist, to whom her marriage has been annulled. Thus, these alter egos are "terribly, perfectly balanced, each with stubbornly preserved, and wholeheartedly accepted, flaws. Flaws they could quite easily disregard or repair. But they could never do that" (56).

25. See Irvine, "Changing," 102 and Joanne S. Frye, 56. Frye argues that a woman writer who creates a first-person female narrator does so specifically to affirm the culturally denied ability of a woman to be a controlling agent, shaping and interpreting the narrative of her own experience. If this generalization applies to Munro, as Frye says that it does in *Lives of Girls and Women*, then Munro's creation of a male narrator in "Thanks for the Ride" and also of an increasing number of male protagonists suggests that she endows her male characters with at least some of the same powers, especially in stories like "Fits" and "The Moon in the Orange Street Skating Rink," where the protagonists function as observers, commenting upon and interpreting the narrative.

26. Compare WDY, 95, where Rose makes a similar statement about "the possibility of happiness."

27. The details that Munro added to the voyeur-scene in her revision of the original *New Yorker* version make the second version more explicit and therefore uglier than the first. Compare *New Yorker* 31 Mar. 1986: 33 and PL, 145–46. But by making these details something that Sam simply observes rather than something that Callie actually feels, Munro keeps the reader distanced from Callie's sexual experience in both versions.

28. In the original *New Yorker* version, the "tune from an opera" is *Avant de quitter ces lieux*, which Valentine, Margareta's brother, sings just before his initial encounter with Mephistopheles. In this encounter, the devil makes a fiery liquor flow from a tavern sign; then, when Valentine attacks him, Mephistopheles snaps the sword in his attacker's hand and draws a fiery magic circle around himself. In most productions, electric sparks flash from Mephistopheles' fingertips as he performs these tricks.

29. Compare *New Yorker* 28 July 1986: 39. For an earlier example of narratorial disparity, see pages 57–59.

30. In "'Distant Parts of Myself,'" York contrasts Hallvard Dahlie's suggestion of "fantasy in Rose's sexual experience" in "Wild Swans" ("Alice Munro and Her Works") and W. R. Martin's assumption that "the experience has happened" (*Alice Munro: Paradox and Parallel*). She then concludes that "the issue of fictionalizing which Dahlie has raised is crucial to a reading of the story, and that the sexual encounter which Rose claims to experience lies in no ambiguous

territory—it is ficton, pure and simple, about fiction" (37). But York's metafictional reading does not consider the obsessive repetition of similar sexual scenes in Munro's fiction.

31. Compare Del's description of menstruation. She refers to "that little extra gush of blood . . . that no Kotex is going to hold, that will trickle horrifyingly down the inside of the thighs" (LGW, 179).

32. Compare WDY, 185, where Rose thinks that Flo, her stepmother, "felt her death moving in her like a child," ready to be born, "getting ready to tear her." Although Rose is mistaken because Flo does not die quickly, here again Munro is comparing a woman's physical helplessness at widely separate moments of her life cycle, childbirth and death.

33. This "voice" that talks to Violet is reminiscent of the imaginary boy in "The Dimensions of a Shadow" because he, too, voices what Miss Abelhart knows about herself and her tragic life. Both characters are hallucinating.

34. Joan of Arc's haircut was a crucial part of her controversial transvestism. See Warren, 143, 145–46.

Chapter 5

1. For some other examples of revisions, see Thacker's comparison of "Goodby, Myra" (1965) and its retitled second version, "Day of the Butterfly" (1968), in "Clear Jelly" (43–49); "Real Material," 31; notes 27–29 in chapter 4; and notes 1–2 in chapter 6.

2. The original New Yorker version of "Dulse," for example, was in the first person (21 July 1980).

3. Martin misreads this passage as a generalization about Janet's customary behavior and therefore an indication of her "partiality to Nichola," "detected and resented" by Judith (Alice Munro: Paradox and Parallel, 158).

4. Irvine defines the loss of children as a goal to be consciously sought. She describes Janet as a mother who is "attempting separation from her children" because "[w]ithout such separation, she fears that she will be unable to write, will be . . . drained of creativity . . ." (Sub/Version, 109).

Chapter 6

1. In the original manuscript, Janet was a writer. In the New Yorker version she became a painter. "But," Munro told an interviewer, "I don't think I know very much about painters and so I changed her back" ("Interview": Hancock, 85).

2. For Munro's discussions of the complicated publishing history of Who Do You Think You Are?, see "Who," 2–3 and "The Real Material," 29–32. Martin summarizes her discussions in Alice Munro: Paradox and Parallel, 100–101.

3. See Munro's discussion of the present hostility of Wingham. She has received "sad, black," angry, "almost illiterate" hate letters, and The Wingham Advance Times has attacked her in an editorial ("Writing's," E1).

4. On this point, see also Stubbs, 61, and Ross, 121.

5. The allusion is to Stein's advice to Jim in chapter 19 of Joseph Conrad's Lord Jim: "to the destructive element submit yourself, and with the exertions of your hands and feet in the water make the deep, deep sea keep you up."

Bibliography

In each category, entries are listed chronologically by date of publication.

Primary Sources
Stories

Laidlaw, Alice. "The Dimensions of a Shadow." *Folio* Apr. 1950: [4–10].
———. "Story for Sunday." *Folio* Dec. 1950: [4–8].
———. "The Widower." *Folio* Apr. 1951: [7-11].
Munro, Alice. "A Basket of Strawberries." *Mayfair* Nov. 1953: 32-33, 78–80, 82.
Munro, Alice Laidlaw. "The Idyllic Summer." *Canadian Forum* Aug. 1954: 106–7, 109–10.
Laidlaw, Alice. "At the Other Place." *Canadian Forum* Sept. 1955: 131–33.
Munroe [*sic*], Alice. "The Edge of Town." *Queen's Quarterly* 62 (1955): 368–80.
Munro, Alice Laidlaw. "How Could I Do That?" *Chatelaine* Mar. 1956: 16–17, 65–70.
Laidlaw, Alice. "The Time of Death." *Canadian Forum* June 1956: 63–66.
Munro, Alice. "Good-By, Myra." *Chatelaine* July 1956: 16–17, 55–58.
———. "Thanks for the Ride." *Tamarack Review* 2 (1957): 25–37.
———. "The Dangerous One." *Chatelaine* July 1957: 48–51.
———. "Sunday Afternoon." *Canadian Forum* Sept. 1957: 127–30.
———. "The Peace of Utrecht." *Tamarack Review* 15 (1960): 5–21.
———. "The Trip to the Coast." *Ten for Wednesday Night*. Ed. Robert Weaver. Toronto: McClelland and Stewart, 1961. 74–92.
———. "Dance of the Happy Shades." *Montrealer* Feb. 1961: 22–26.
———. "An Ounce of Cure." *Montrealer* May 1961: 26–30.
———. "The Office." *Montrealer* Sept. 1962: 18–23.
———. "Boys and Girls." *Montrealer* Dec. 1964: 25–34.

——. "Red Dress—1946." *Montrealer* May 1965: 28–34.

——. "Postcard." *Tamarack Review* 47 (1968): 22–31, 33–39.

——. *Dance of the Happy Shades*. New York: McGraw-Hill, 1968. Includes "Walker Brothers Cowboy," "The Shining Houses," "Images," "Thanks for the Ride," "The Office" (revised), "An Ounce of Cure," "The Time of Death" (revised), "Day of the Butterfly" ("Good-By, Myra" revised), "Boys and Girls," "Postcard," "Red Dress—1946," "Sunday Afternoon," "A Trip to the Coast" (revised), "The Peace of Utrecht" (revised), and "Dance of the Happy Shades."

——. *Lives of Girls and Women*. Toronto: McGraw-Hill Ryerson, 1971. Includes "The Flats Road, "Heirs of the Living Body," "Princess Ida," "Age of Faith," "Changes and Ceremonies," "Lives of Girls and Women," "Baptizing," and "Epilogue: The Photographer."

——. "Material." *Tamarack Review* 61 (Nov. 1973): 7–25.

——. "Home." *New Canadian Stories: 74*. Ed. and introd. David Helwig and Joan Harcourt. Ottawa: Oberon, 1974. 133–53.

——. "How I Met My Husband." *McCall's* Feb. 1974: 84–85, 123–27.

——. "Tell Me Yes or No." *Chatelaine* Mar. 1974: 34–35, 54, 56–60, 62.

——. "Forgiveness in Families." *McCall's* Apr. 1974: 92–93, 138, 140, 142, 144, 146.

——. *Something I've Been Meaning To Tell You*. Toronto: McGraw-Hill Ryerson, 1974. Includes "Something I've Been Meaning To Tell You," "Material," "How I Met My Husband" (revised), "Walking on Water," "Forgiveness in Families," "Tell Me Yes or No," "The Found Boat," "Executioners," "Marrakesh," "The Spanish Lady," "Winter Wind," "Memorial," and "The Ottawa Valley."

——. "Privilege." *Tamarack Review* 70 (1977): 14–28.

——. "Royal Beatings." *New Yorker* 14 Mar. 1977: 36–44.

——. "The Beggar Maid." *New Yorker* 27 June 1977: 31, 35–41, 44–47.

——. "Providence." *Redbook* Aug. 1977: 98–99, 158–63.

——. "Accident." *Toronto Life* Nov. 1977: 61, 87–90, 92–95, 149– 50, 153–56, 159–60, 162–65, 167, 169–73.

——. "Mischief." *Viva* Apr. 1978: 99–109.

——. "Wild Swans." *Toronto Life* Apr. 1978: 52–53, 124–25.

——. "Half a Grapefruit." *Redbook* May 1978: 132–33, 176, 178, 180, 182, 183.

——. "The Moons of Jupiter." *New Yorker* 22 May 1978: 32–39.

——. "Spelling" [excerpt]. *Weekend Magazine* 17 June 1978: 24, 26–27.

——. "Characters." *Ploughshares* 4.3 (1978): 72–82.

——. "Emily." *Viva* Aug. 1978: 99–105.

——. "Honeyman's Granddaughter" ("Privilege" revised). *Ms.* Oct. 1978: 56–57, 75–76, 79.

——. "Connection." *Chatelaine* Nov. 1978: 66–67, 97–98, 101, 104, 106.

——. *Who Do You Think You Are?* Toronto: Macmillan, 1978 [*The Beggar Maid: Stories of Flo and Rose* in the United States]. Includes "Royal Beatings" (revised), "Privilege" (revised), "Half a Grapefruit" (revised), "Wild Swans," "The Beggar Maid" (revised), "Mischief" (revised), "Providence" (revised), "Simon's Luck" ("Emily" revised), "Spelling" (revised and expanded), and "Who Do You Think You Are?"

——. "A Better Place Than Home." *The Newcomers: Inhabiting a New Land*. Ed.

Charles E. Israel. Toronto. McClelland and Stewart, 1979. 113–24.

———. "The Stone in the Field." *Saturday Night* Apr. 1979: 40–45.

———. "Dulse." *New Yorker* 21 July 1980: 30–39.

———. "Wood." *New Yorker* 24 Nov. 1980: 46–54.

———. "The Turkey Season." *New Yorker* 29 Dec. 1980: 36–44.

———. "Prue." *New Yorker* 30 Mar. 1981: 34–35.

———. "Labor Day Dinner." *New Yorker* 28 Sept. 1981: 47–56, 59–60, 65–66, 70, 75–76.

———. "Mrs. Cross and Mrs. Kidd." *Tamarack Review* 83–84 (1982): 5–24.

———. "The Ferguson Girls Must Never Marry." *Grand Street* 1.3 (1982): 27–64.

———. "Visitors." *Atlantic Monthly* Apr. 1982: 90, 91–96.

———. *The Moons of Jupiter.* Toronto: Macmillan, 1982. Includes "Chaddeleys and Flemings: I *Connection* (revised) and II *The Stone in the Field*" (revised), "Dulse" (revised), "The Turkey Season" (revised), "Accident," "Bardon Bus," "Prue," "Labor Day Dinner," "Mrs. Cross and Mrs. Kidd," "Hard-Luck Stories," "Visitors," and "The Moons of Jupiter" (revised).

———. "Miles City, Montana." *New Yorker* 14 Jan. 1985: 30–40.

———. "Monsieur les Deux Chapeaux." *Grand Street* 4.3 (1985): 7–33.

———. "Lichen." *New Yorker* 15 July 1985: 26–36.

———. "The Progress of Love." *New Yorker* 7 Oct. 1985: 35–46, 49–50, 53–54, 57–58.

———. "Secrets Between Friends." *Mademoiselle* Nov. 1985: 116, 118, 120, 122, 124, 126, 128, 130, 228, 230.

———. "A Queer Streak. Part One: Anonymous Letters." *Granta* 17 (1985): 187–212.

———. "Eskimo." *Gentlemen's Quarterly* Dec. 1985: 262–66, 301–2, 304.

———. "Fits." *Grand Street* 5.2 (1986): 36–61.

———. "The Moon in the Orange Street Skating Rink." *New Yorker* 31 Mar. 1986: 26–36, 38–41, 44.

———. "A Queer Streak. Part Two: Possession." *Granta* 18 (1986): 201–19.

———. "White Dump." *New Yorker* 28 July 1986: 25–39, 42–43.

———. "Circle of Prayer." *Paris Review* 100 (1986): 31–51.

———. *The Progress of Love.* Toronto: McClelland and Stewart, 1986. Includes "The Progress of Love" (revised), "Lichen," "Monsieur les Deux Chapeaux," "Miles City, Montana" (revised), "Fits" (revised), "The Moon in the Orange Street Skating Rink" (revised), "Jesse and Meribeth" ("Secrets Between Friends," revised), "Eskimo," "A Queer Streak" (revised), "Circle of Prayer," and "White Dump" (revised).

———. "Oh, What Avails." *New Yorker* 16 Nov. 1987: 42–52, 55–56, 58–59, 62, 64–65, 67.

———. "Meneseteung." *New Yorker* 11 Jan. 1988: 28–38.

———. "Five Points." *New Yorker* 14 Mar. 1988: 34–43.

———. "Oranges and Apples." *New Yorker* 24 Oct. 1988: 36–48, 52, 54.

———. "Hold Me Fast, Don't Let Me Pass." *Atlantic Monthly* Dec. 1988: 58–66, 68–70.

———. "Differently." *New Yorker* 2 Jan. 1989: 23–36.

———. "Goodness and Mercy." *New Yorker* 20 Mar. 1989: 38–48.

Articles and Letters

Munro, Alice. "Author's Commentary." *Sixteen by Twelve: Short Stories by Canadian Writers*. Ed. John Metcalf. Toronto: Ryerson, 1970. 125–26.

———. "The Colonel's Hash Resettled." *The Narrative Voice: Short Stories and Reflections by Canadian Authors*. Ed. John Metcalf. Toronto: McGraw-Hill Ryerson, 1972. 181–83.

———. "Everything Here Is Touchable and Mysterious." *Weekend Magazine* 11 May 1974: 33.

———. "An Open Letter." *Jubilee* 1 (1974): 5–7.

———. "On Writing 'The Office.'" *Transitions II: Short Fiction. A Source Book of Canadian Literature*. Ed. Edward Peck. Vancouver: Commcept, 1978. 259–62.

———. "Working for a Living." *Grand Street* 1.1 (1981): 9–37.

———. "What is Real?" *Canadian Forum* Sept. 1982: 5, 36. (Republished in *Making It New: Contemporary Canadian Stories*. Ed. John Metcalf. Toronto: Methuen, 1982. 223–26)

Interviews

Munro, Alice. "Alice Munro Talks with Mari Stainsby." *British Columbia Library Quarterly* July 1971: 27-30. [cited in text as "Talks"]

———. "A Conversation with Alice Munro." *Journal of Canadian Fiction*. With John Metcalf. 1.4 (1972): 54-62. ["Conversation"]

———. "Alice Munro." *Eleven Canadian Novelists Interviewed by Graeme Gibson*. Toronto: House of Anansi, 1973. 237–64. ["Alice Munro"]

———. "Great Dames." *MacLean's*. By Barbara Frum. Apr. 1973: 32, 38. ["Great Dames"]

———. Untitled Interview with Alice Munro. Appendix. "The Early Short Stories of Alice Munro." Jill M. Gardiner. M.A. Thesis, New Brunswick U, 1973. 169–82. [Untitled]

———. "Name: Alice Munro. Occupation: Writer." *Chatelaine*. By Ken Murch. Aug. 1975: 42–3, 69–72. ["Name"]

———. "Who Do You Think You Are? Review-Interview with Alice Munro." *Room of One's Own*. By Carole Gerson. 4.4 (1979): 2–7. ["Who"]

———. "What Is: Alice Munro." *For Openers: Conversation with Twenty-four Canadian Writers*. With Alan Twigg. Madeira Park, B. C.: Harbour, 1981. 13–20. ["What Is"]

———. "An Interview with Alice Munro." *Canadian Fiction Magazine*. By Geoff Hancock. 43 (1982): 75–114. ["Interview": Hancock]

———. "Through the Jade Curtain." *Chinada: Memoirs of the Gang of Seven*. With Geoff Hancock. Dunvegan, Ont.: Quadrant Editions, 1982. 51–55.

———. "A Visit with Alice Munro." *Monday Magazine* [Victoria]. By Stephen Scobie. 19–25 Nov. 1982: 12–13. ["Visit"]

"Writing's Something I Did, Like the Ironing." *Toronto Globe and Mail* 11 Dec. 1982, sec. 4: E1 ["Writing's"]

Munro, Alice. "The Real Material: An Interview with Alice Munro." By J. R. (Tim)Struthers. *Probable Fictions: Alice Munro's Narrative Acts*. Ed. Louis K. MacKendrick. Downsview, Ont.: ECW, 1983. 5–36. ["Real Material"]

———. "Interview with Alice Munro." By Harold Horwood. *The Art of Alice*

Munro: Saying the Unsayable. Ed. Judith Miller. Waterloo: U of Waterloo P, 1984. 123–35. ["Interview": Horwood]

Secondary Sources

Adachi, Ken. "Alice Munro Puts Her Pen to Script for CBC-TV Drama." *Toronto Star* 6 Jan. 1978: D3.

Allentuck, Marcia. "Resolution and Independence in the Work of Alice Munro." *World Literature Written in English* 16 (1977): 340–43.

Atwood, Margaret. "Writing the Male Character." *This Magazine* Sept. 1982: 4–10. Republished in *Second Words: Selected Critical Prose*. Boston: Beacon, 1984. 412–30.

Blodgett, E. D. *Alice Munro*. Boston: Twayne, 1988.

Cameron, Barry. Introduction. *Making It New: Contemporary Canadian Stories*. Ed. John Metcalf. Toronto: Methuen, 1982. vii–x.

Carscallen, James. "Alice Munro." *Profiles in Canadian Literature* 2. Ed. Jeffrey M. Heath. Toronto and Charlottetown: Dundurn, 1980. 73–80.

———. "Three Jokers: The Shape of Alice Munro's Stories." *Centre and Labyrinth: Essays in Honour of Northrop Frye*. Ed. Eleanor Cook et al. Toronto: U of Toronto P, 1983. 128–46.

———. "The Shining House: A Group of Stories." Miller 85–101.

Cohn, Dorrit. *Transparent Minds: Narrative Modes for Presenting Consciousness in Fiction*. Princeton: Princeton UP, 1978.

Conron, Brandon. "Munro's Wonderland." *Canadian Literature* 78 (1978): 109–12, 114–18, 120–23.

Coward, Rosalind. *Female Desires: How They Are Sought, Bought and Packaged*. New York: Grove, 1985.

Dahlie, Hallvard. "The Fiction of Alice Munro." *Ploughshares* 4.3 (1978): 56–71.

———. "Alice Munro and Her Works." *Canadian Writers and Their Works*. Ed. Robert Lecker, Jack David, and Ellen Quigley. Fiction Series 7. Toronto: ECW, 1985. 215–56.

Djwa, Sandra. "Deep Caves and Kitchen Linoleum: Psychological Violence in the Fiction of Alice Munro." *Violence in the Canadian Novel Since 1960/dans le roman Canadien depuis 1960*. Ed. Virginia Harger-Grinling and Terry Goldie. St. John's: Memorial University of Newfoundland. 1981. 177–90.

Dombrowski, Eileen. "'Down to Death': Alice Munro and Transcience." *University of Windsor Review* 14.1 (1978): 21–29.

Duchêne, Anne. "Respect for the Facts." Rev. of *The Progress of Love*, by Alice Munro. *Times Literary Supplement* 30 Jan. 1987: 109.

Eldredge, L. M. "A Sense of Ending in *Lives of Girls and Women*." *Studies in Canadian Literature* 9 (1984): 110–15.

Fitzpatrick, Margaret Anne. "'Projection' in Alice Munro's *Something I've Been Meaning To Tell You*." Miller 15–20.

Fogel, Stanley. "'And All the Little Typtopies': Notes on Language Theory in the Contemporary Experimental Novel." *Modern Fiction Studies* 20 (1974): 328–36.

Fowler, Rowena. "The Art of Alice Munro: *The Beggar Maid* and *Lives of Girls and*

Women." Critique: Studies in Modern Fiction 25.4 (1984): 189–98.

Freud, Sigmund. "A Child Is Being Beaten." Collected Papers. Ed. Ernest Jones. Trans. Alix and James Strachey. New York: Basic Books, 1959. II, 172–201.

Frye, Joanne S. Living Stories, Telling Lives: Women and the Novel in Contemporary Experience. Ann Arbor: U of Michigan P, 1986.

Godard, Barbara. "'Heirs of the Living Body': Alice Munro and the Question of a Female Aesthetic." Miller 43–71.

Gold, Joseph. "Our Feeling Exactly: The Writing of Alice Munro." Miller 1–13.

Horney, Karen. Neurosis and Human Growth: The Struggle Toward Self-Realization. New York: Norton, 1950.

Howells, Coral Ann. "Alice Munro: Lives of Girls and Women, The Beggar Maid." Private and Fictional Words: Canadian Women Novelists of the 1970s and 1980s. London and New York: Methuen, 1987. 71–88.

Hoy, Helen. "'Dull, Simple, Amazing and Unfathomable': Paradox and Double Vision in Alice Munro's Fiction." Studies in Canadian Literature 5 (1980): 100–15.

Irvine, Lorna. "Changing Is the Word I Want." MacKendrick 99– 111.

———. "Women's Desire/Women's Power: The Moons of Jupiter." Sub/Version: Canadian Fictions by Women. Toronto: ECW, 1986. 91–110.

Jespersen, Otto. Essentials of English Grammar. New York: Holt, 1933.

Kolodny, Annette. "Some Notes on Defining a 'Feminist Literary Criticism.'" Critical Inquiry 2 (1975): 75–92.

Kolson, Ann. "Writing Was Her Secret." The Philadelphia Inquirer 7 Nov. 1986: 1C, 4C.

Lamont-Stewart, Linda. "Order from Chaos: Writing as Self-Defense in the Fiction of Alice Munro and Clark Blaise." Miller 113–21.

MacKendrick, Louis K. ed. Probable Fictions: Alice Munro's Narrative Acts. Downsview, Ont.: ECW, 1983.

McMullen, Lorraine. "'Shameless, Marvellous, Shattering Absurdity': The Humour of Paradox in Alice Munro." MacKendrick 144–62.

Mallet, Gina. "A Good Time to be a Canadian Writer." Toronto Star 20 Oct. 1981: F1, F3.

Martin, W. R. "Alice Munro and James Joyce." Journal of Canadian Fiction 24 (1979): 120–26.

———. "The Strange and the Familiar in Alice Munro." Studies in Canadian Literature 7 (1982): 214–26.

———. "Hanging Pictures Together: Something I've Been Meaning To Tell You." Miller 21–34.

———. Alice Munro: Paradox and Parallel. Edmonton: U of Alberta P, 1987.

Mathews, Lawrence. "Who Do You Think You Are?: Alice Munro's Art of Disarrangement." MacKendrick 181–93.

Miller, Judith, ed. The Art of Alice Munro: Saying the Unsayable. Waterloo: U of Waterloo P, 1984.

Moss, John. "Alice in the Looking Glass: Munro's Lives of Girls and Women." Sex and Violence in the Canadian Novel: The Ancestral Present. Toronto: McClelland and Stewart, 1977. 54–68.

———. Introduction. The Canadian Novel: Here and Now. Ed. John Moss. Toronto: NC, 1978. 7–15.

New, W. H. "Pronouns and Propositions: Alice Munro's Stories." *Open Letter* 3rd ser., 5 (1976): 40–49. (Republished in *Dreams of Speech and Violence.* Toronto: U of Toronto P, 1987. 201–10)

Noonan, Gerald. "The Structure of Style in Alice Munro's Fiction." MacKendrick 163–80.

Orange, John. "Alice Munro and A Maze of Time." MacKendrick 83–98.

Osachoff, Margaret Gail. "'Treacheries of the Heart': Memoir, Confession, and Meditation in the Stories of Alice Munro." MacKendrick 61–82.

Pfaus, B. *Alice Munro.* Ottawa: The Golden Dog, 1984.

Richards, Janet Radcliffe. *The Sceptical Feminist: A Philosophical Inquiry.* London: Routledge and Kegan Paul, 1980.

Ross, Catherine Sheldrick. "'At least part legend': The Fiction of Alice Munro." MacKendrick 112–26.

Slopen, Beverley. "PW Interviews Alice Munro." *Publisher's Weekly* 22 Aug. 1986: 76–77.

Sontag, Susan. *On Photography.* New York: Farrar, Straus, and Giroux, 1977.

Stouck, David. "Alice Munro." *Major Canadian Authors: A Critical Introduction.* Lincoln: U of Nebraska P, 1984. 257–72.

Struthers, J. R. (Tim). "Reality and Ordering: The Growth of a Young Artist in *Lives of Girls and Women.*" *Essays on Canadian Writing* 3 (1975): 32–46.

———. "Alice Munro and the American South." *The Canadian Novel: Here and Now.* Ed. John Moss. Toronto: NC, 1978. 121–33.

———. "Alice Munro's Fictive Imagination." Miller 103–12.

Stubbs, Andrew. "Fictional Landscape: Mythology and Dialectic in the Fiction of Alice Munro." *World Literature Written in English* 23 (1984): 53–62.

Taylor, Michael. "The Unimaginable Vancouvers: Alice Munro's Words." MacKendrick 127–43.

Thacker, Robert. "Alice Munro: An Annotated Bibliography." *The Annotated Bibliography of Canada's Major Authors.* Ed. Robert Lecker and Jack David. Downsview, Ont.: ECW, 1984. V, 354–414.

———. "'Clear Jelly': Alice Munro's Narrative Dialectics." MacKendrick 37–60.

Verduyn, Christl. "From 'The Word on Flesh' to 'The Flesh Made Word': Women's Fiction in Canada." *The American Review of Canadian Studies* 15:4 (1985): 449–64.

Wallace, Bronwen. "Women's Lives: Alice Munro." *The Human Elements: Critical Essays.* Ed. David Helwig. Ottawa: Oberon, 1978. 52–67.

Warren, Marina. *Joan of Arc: The Image of Female Heroism.* New York: Knopf, 1981.

Warwick, Susan J. "Growing Up: The Novels of Alice Munroe." *Essays on Canadian Writing* 29 (1984): 204–25.

Weaver, Robert. Introduction II. *The Oxford Book of Canadian Short Stories in English.* Toronto: Oxford UP, 1986. xvii–xix.

Woodcock, George. Introduction. *Canadian Writers and Their Works.* Ed. Robert Lecker, Jack David, and Ellen Quigley. Fiction Series 7. Toronto: ECW, 1985. 1–17.

———."The Plots of Life: The Realism of Alice Munro." *Queen's Quarterly* 93.2 (1986): 235–50. (Republished in *Northern Spring: The Flowering of Canadian Literature.* Vancouver/Toronto: Douglas & McIntyre, 1987. 132–46).

Woodress, James. *Willa Cather: Her Life and Art.* Lincoln: U of Nebraska P, 1970.

Yeats, William Butler. *The Collected Poems of W. B. Yeats*. New York: Macmillan, 1959.

York, Lorraine M. "'The Other Side of Dailiness': The Paradox of Photography in Alice Munro's Fiction." *Studies in Canadian Literature* 8 (1983): 49–60.

———."Joyless in Jubilee?" *Essays on Canadian Writing* 34 (1987): 157–61.

———."The Rival Bards: Alice Munro's *Lives of Girls and Women* and Victorian Poetry." *Canadian Literature* 112 (1987): 211–16.

———."'Gulfs' and 'Connections': The Fiction of Alice Munro." *Essays on Canadian Writing* 35 (1987): 135–46.

———."'Distant Parts of Myself': The Topography of Alice Munro's Fiction." *The American Review of Canadian Studies* 18:1 (1988): 33–8.

General Index

Opera, allusions to. *See* Allusions:
operatic
Orange, John, 115, 219n.4, 221n.3
Osachoff, Margaret Gail, 29, 110,
220n.2, 221n.2

Paradox: of ambivalence, 90–91, 143,
146; of causality, 67–68, 143; of death
and sex, 11–12, 68–70; and photography, 140, 218n.4, 222n.13;
psychological, 21–22, 29–30, 40–41,
130, 137, 138, 144, 147, 153, 174, 176,
183, 213; self-reflexive, 5; of self-
watching voyeur, 152; social, 21, 22–
30; in style and structure, 4, 78, 110,
112, 138, 141, 144. *See also* Art:
paradox of; Artist: paradox of;
Paradoxical: theme
Paradoxical: disguise, 125–28, 137;
freedom, 77, 93; theme, 5, 39, 212–
13, 214. *See also* Uncontrollable, The
Paris Review, The, 15
Pfaus, B., 4, 217n.1, 221n.2
Point of view, 5
—argumentative narrator, 159, 182–83
—compared, 125–27, 131, 134, 155
—first-person narrator, 6–8, 14–15,
16, 30, 35–38, 40, 43, 48–49, 68–70,
71–94, 102, 103, 104, 105–12, 120,
126, 128–31, 140–41, 144, 148–55,
185–98, 199–205, 207, 214–15,
224n.2(ch.5); double, 145, 153–55; in
feminist novel, 220n.7, 223n.25
—innocent eye, 7, 36–38, 72–76, 198
—male narrator, 103, 107–9
—male protagonists, 52–55, 159, 165–
70, 177, 178, 179–80, 182, 223n.25
—multiple, 6, 8, 103, 145, 159; alternating, 60–63, 101, 162–65; double,
176–83; triple, 60, 155, 170–76,
219n.12, 222n.17
—observer, 6, 7, 31–32, 52–55, 57–59,
89–90, 94, 95, 104, 105, 106, 107–8,
109, 112–13, 119, 131, 133–34, 169–70,
204, 207, 223n.25
—omniscient author, 6, 7, 8, 10, 13, 45,
56, 58–59, 60, 61, 62, 63, 64, 100, 122,

123, 126–27, 128, 131, 132–33, 145,
155, 174, 207
—participant, 31–32, 94, 95, 102, 104,
106, 107, 109, 112–13, 119, 131, 133–
34, 148, 204, 207
—retrospective, 6–7, 8, 15, 51–52, 74,
79, 87–88, 101, 119, 128, 130–31, 207,
217n.3
—revisions of, 201–2, 224n.2(ch.5)
—shifts in, 152, 156–57, 219n.10–11
(*see also* Narratorial disparity)
—split, 4, 6–8, 31, 36, 39, 43, 45, 59,
64, 72–76, 93, 102–3, 106, 119–20,
121–22, 131, 132–34, 137, 140, 148,
155, 164, 167, 174, 194–96, 201, 203–5,
206–7, 210, 214, 215 (*see also* Characters: alter egos; Characters:
ambivalent; Characters: split)
—third-person, 6, 7–8, 18, 19, 38,
102–5, 113–17, 126, 131, 159–60,
165–67, 168, 169–70, 177, 185, 198–
99, 201–2, 207

Queensland University (Australia),
222n.19

Realism, documentary, 4, 118
Richards, Janet Radcliffe, 222n.15
Ross, Catherine Sheldrick, 37, 218n.2,
224n.4(ch.6)

Satire, 12, 28, 57, 101, 154–55, 158, 176,
177–80, 181–83. *See also* Feminism,
Munro's attitude toward
Scobie, Stephen. *See* "Visit" (Title
Index, interviews)
Self-reflexivity, 14–15, 30, 120–22, 144,
154, 174, 190, 193, 202. *See also*
Narrative time, epilogues; Lan-
guage: ambivalent attitude toward;
Metafiction
Slopen, Beverly, 3, 5, 34, 39, 171, 202,
216
Sontag, Susan, 8, 10, 164, 218n.4,
222n.13
Stainsby, Mari. *See* "Talks" (Title Index,
interviews)

Title Index

Stories

Articles and Letters